PROS

AND

CONS

THE CRIMINALS WHO PLAY IN THE NFL

JEFF BENEDICT & DON YAEGER

WARNER BOOKS

A Time Warner Company

WARNER BOOKS EDITION

Cover art and design by Mike Stromberg

Warner Books, Inc.
1271 Avenue of the Americas
New York, NY 10020

Visit our Web site at
www.warnerbooks.com

 A Time Warner Company

Printed in the United States of America

Originally published in hardcover by Warner Books.
First Paperback Printing: October 1999

10 9 8 7 6 5 4 3 2 1

Contents

Authors' Note

From day one, we never doubted that this book would hold people's attention. But one moment stands out in our minds as the point when we knew how deep the problem of criminals in the NFL actually ran.

It was near the end of March in 1998. Both of us were on the road doing research in separate states. One of us went to a maximum security prison to interview an inmate who is an ex-NFL player doing forty-one years for ordering the murders of a judge and a witness who testified against the player in a federal drug trial. (That story is detailed later in the book.)

The other one of us was in a city where an NFL team is located. There an attractive woman, her hair tucked underneath a baseball cap, arrived for a prearranged private meeting. She wore an oversized coat and looked nervously over her shoulder out of fear that someone may have followed her there.

In a private location, the woman pulled from her purse a handheld tape recorder and a handful of minicassette tapes containing messages recorded off her home answering machine. With her permission, the author used his own tape recorder to record what she played back on hers.

The voice on the tape was that of her ex-husband, a player in the NFL today. The author felt the hair raising on his arms as he listened to death threats left by the player on the woman's answering machine. He dared her to call the cops. He promised he would take her life. His abuse drove her to finally leave him.

After playing the tape for the author, the woman reached forward, her hand shaking terribly, and shut off the recorder. She was embarrassed, and so was the author.

"You can't use my name or tell my story in your book," the woman explained in a hushed tone. "If you do, he *will* kill me. I have no doubt of that. So I know I've taken a big risk in letting you hear these tapes, but I wanted you to understand how real this problem is. And I'm not the only woman. There are many others like me who go through this with these players."

The particulars of this woman's experience are not detailed in this book. Her name is not revealed either, nor is her ex-husband's. But her disclosure to us and the wealth of other information she provided reinforced something we already had come to know all too well in the course of writing this book—there are an untold number of NFL players whose off-field character is in sharp contrast to the heroic persona projected on television.

There are a number of victims whose true names and identifying characteristics have been changed. (Pseudonyms are indicated by asterisks.) But in order to get you, the reader, beyond the made-for-TV image of these criminal players, there is little else that we have held back in our reporting. Thus this warning: the material contained on these pages is extremely graphic. Names are named and violent, sometimes heinous crimes are detailed. The final product, we confess, is not something we are putting on our mothers' reading lists. Put simply, this is no book for the faint of heart.

We've written this way for a reason. You see, those responsible for the mayhem chronicled on these pages are no ordinary criminals. They are perceived as heroes. Rather than being stigmatized like most cons, these pros are cheered, idolized, and highly paid because they bring us thrills.

And we are not talking about just a few bad apples, here. Our research shows that 21 percent—one of every five—of the players in the NFL have been charged with a serious crime. How did we get that number?

The authors began in 1997 compiling a computerized list which identified the names of the approximately 1,590 players who played in the NFL during the 1996–97 season, then added the names of players from the 1997 draft. We then set out to identify how many of those players had a criminal record, a study never before undertaken. Three primary methods were used for checking players' criminal histories.

First, we solicited records from state criminal repositories on players who resided in states where public information laws allow access to individuals' criminal histories. For example, Florida, which has the most unrestricted public access laws in the nation, will make available upon written request and the payment of a nominal fee the complete criminal history of any individual who has been charged with a crime by any state or local police agency in the state.

After determining that a total of 480 NFL players from the 1996–97 season and 1997 draft class had resided in Florida at one time or another, we submitted all 480 names with attached birth dates to the Florida Department of Law

Enforcement in Tallahassee. In return, we received approximately 100 pages of computer printouts identifying the names and crimes of every player among the 480 who had a record in the state of Florida. (We then contacted individual law enforcement agencies throughout Florida to obtain the actual police reports and court files on many of those cases.) A similar process was repeated in other states which allow public access, albeit more limited in scope than Florida, to an individual's criminal history.

Second: in states which allow little or no access to criminal history information, we, where possible, performed county-by-county searches of the criminal court docket sheets in those states. This required, in some cases, going to a state and running players' names and birth dates through public access computer terminals at municipal and district courthouses. In Seattle, for example, we ran approximately fifty names of players who had resided in Washington through a statewide computer database maintained at the King County District Court. In other instances, such as in Texas—home at one time or another to nearly 500 players who played during 1996–97—we relied on computer software which permits access to the criminal court docket listings in three of the state's biggest counties: Dallas, Travis, and Bexar. The names and birth dates of all players were run through those databases. This method of identifying players who had been charged with a crime was used in Texas, Ohio, Minnesota, Michigan, Washington, and Georgia, as well as in California's Los Angeles County.

Third: we contacted by telephone and written correspondence over forty-five police departments around the country seeking to obtain information on player arrests. Of the departments whose policies permit the release of such information, we then sent individual names and birth dates of players to the records' clerks and in return received reports documenting players who had been charged with crimes in those jurisdictions.

Ultimately, of the approximately 1,590 NFL players from the 1996–97 season, there were 509 players (over a third of the entire league) whose criminal histories were sufficiently researched to form the sample base for this study. Relying on the methods explained above, any NFL player whose criminal history was either 1) checked by the authors in two states or more, or 2) checked in one state where the player resided for five years or longer made it into the sample. These criteria qualify our sampling as being random because the players in the survey group were chosen purely on the basis of record availability, a factor determined by state law.

"This selection criterion should be independent of whether any individual had an arrest history," said Carnegie Mellon University Professor Alfred Blumstein, the nation's leading expert on crime statistics, "and so the sample can be seen as reasonably representative of the players in the NFL." (At our request, Professor Blumstein reviewed the research and provided a written review of our work. More of his analysis can be found in Appendix II.)

Of the 509 players in our study, an eye-popping 109 (21 percent) were found to have been formally charged (arrested or indicted) with a serious crime.* That's right—one in five. (A complete break-down of the statistics is provided in Chapter 1.)

---

*Serious crimes include: homicide, rape, kidnapping, robbery, assault, battery, domestic violence, reckless endangerment, fraud, larceny, burglary, theft, property destruction, drug-related offenses, illegal use or possession of a weapon, DUI, disorderly conduct, and resisting arrest.

While the statistics generated from the authors' 509-player index provide the foundation for this book, they do not begin to tell the story. In fact, the numbers may actually be the bright side of the story.

In all, the authors reviewed over 400 reports of NFL players being formally charged with a crime. Over 625 interviews, many of which were tape-recorded, were conducted with individuals from the NFL (both players and coaches, past and present), law enforcement officials, judges, attorneys, crime victims, witnesses, physicians, jurors, sports agents, and scholars, among others, in order to better understand the cases and topics reported in this book. Additionally, the authors reviewed over 120 criminal case files containing police reports, witness statements, affidavits, crime scene photographs, and medical evidence.

At no time, however, were private investigators used in the collection of data for this book—all research was done by the authors themselves or by paid legal researchers. Nor were any records or criminal history documents obtained that are not lawfully available through the proper filing of a public records request. In all, the authors filed over 100 such requests with law enforcement agencies and courts.

In the end, one conclusion rang true: NFL teams are recruiting a new breed of criminal players, the likes of which should disturb all NFL fans. Gone are the good old days of NFL recruits having rap sheets detailing merely drunken brawls and vandalism. In are the days of lethal violence, rape, armed robbery, home invasion, kidnapping, and drug dealing.

Although much of what is reported in this book will be news to readers, the same cannot be said for the league. All of the players whose crimes are chronicled in these pages had been deemed fit to play after undergoing intense investigation conducted by private investigators employed by the NFL and by individual teams' scouts.

How do we know how good these investigators are? Consider: while collecting data for this book, the authors hired Northeastern University student J.R. Mastroianni to aid us in filing public records requests.

Several weeks into his work, Mastroianni had an unexpected visitor. A man showed up at Mastroianni's fraternity house, a copy of the college student's cable television bill in hand. When one of Mastroianni's roommates told the man that the young research assistant was not there, the man identified himself as Larry Frisoli, left his phone number, and left instructions for Mastroianni to call him. When Mastroianni arrived at his fraternity house, his roommate told him that "a man from the cable company" had stopped by and left his number.

Frisoli, however, was not from the cable company. He is the president of Special Agent Systems Consultants, a Boston-based private investigation firm. When Mastroianni returned the call, Frisoli began peppering him with questions about a police report Mastroianni had requested from a police department in another state. "Are you working for those guys writing the book on the NFL?" Frisoli asked, indicating how much investigative work he already had done. Frisoli did not volunteer how he obtained a copy of Mastroianni's cable bill, though it appeared the bill may have been used by Frisoli to find Mastroianni's home address. Unlike the police records requests Mastroianni was filing, cable bills are not public record.

Frisoli, it turns out, works on contract for the NFL. His team of private investigators is one of twenty-nine such firms the NFL employs to keep track of players—and those who may do damage to player reputations—in NFL cities from Buffalo to San Diego. Repeated messages left at Frisoli's firm by the authors went unanswered. The NFL, too, refused to discuss how—and why—one of its hired hands was taking time to track down college researchers, instead of, say, tracking down the same criminals that Mastroianni was.

Questions surrounding Frisoli's actions weren't the only ones the authors didn't get to ask. In March 1998, when the research for this book was concluded and statistics and police reports compiled, the authors wrote to NFL Commissioner Paul Tagliabue asking for the opportunity to share the information with him and ask questions about league policy. Through his top press aide, Greg Aiello, Tagliabue declined to answer the questions. "We'll read the book, I'm sure," Aiello said. "When it comes out, if anyone wants us to respond, then we'll respond at that time. But we're not interested in being part of the book. I appreciate the opportunity.

"We think we have a pretty good handle on what our players are involved in—the good and the bad," Aiello continued. "This book is going to portray half of our players as a group of criminals and I don't think there is any way that we are going to be able to change that."

Half of our players? Our research suggested it was closer to a quarter of the players. Maybe he knows something the authors don't.

PROS
AND
CONS

1

Crime Pays

"I s your son an organ donor?"

That was the question a medical assistant asked Sara Boyd at 1:30 A.M. on May 11, 1996, as she stood over her twenty-one-year-old son, Bryan, while he lay unconscious on a gurney in the trauma center at John Peter Smith Hospital in Fort Worth, Texas. Thirty minutes earlier, Sara and her husband, Doug, were awakened by the middle-of-the-night telephone call that every parent dreads. "Mrs. Boyd," a friend of Bryan's said as he choked back tears, "I just want you to know that Bryan has been jumped. It's serious. I prayed with him before the EMTs put him on a stretcher. He moved his lips. I know he heard me." Other than saying that Bryan was being taken to a nearby hospital, little more by way of detail was provided.

According to the incident report filled out by police officers who responded to a reported "gang fight" outside Bobby McGee's, a Fort Worth, Texas, bar, "Bryan Boyd was beaten by several white male TCU football players." Unbeknownst to officers who discovered Boyd lying in a puddle of his own blood that night, Boyd had previously sued TCU football player J.W. Wilson after Wilson assaulted him the previous year. One week before the incident at Bobby McGee's, Wilson had reached an out-of-court settlement to pay Boyd $6,000 compensation for medical injuries sustained as a result of Wilson's attack. When Boyd and Wilson crossed paths inside Bobby McGee's on May 10, Wilson's teammates asked, "Isn't that [Boyd] the guy you beat up last Thanksgiving?"

Later, as the 180-pound Boyd left the bar, Wilson's teammates Ryan Tucker, J.P. McFarland, Jay Davern, and Billy Thompson—three of whom weighed over 250 pounds—followed him outside. It was payback time. First, words were exchanged. Then, fists started flying in a four-on-one attack. After fracturing Boyd's skull by ramming him head-first into a brick wall, Wilson's four teammates nearly kicked Boyd to death while he lay unconscious and hemorrhaging, facedown in the parking lot. Six witnesses, including a bouncer for the bar, told police that the players repeatedly kicked Boyd in the head. The players were then seen running away from the motionless Boyd and speeding off in two vehicles, a blue Blazer and a red Jeep Cherokee. The police report described Boyd as "bleeding from the nose, the ear, around the eyes, possible broken shoulder, busted upper lip, bleeding from back of head."

When Sara Boyd arrived at the hospital, a doctor and nurse were waiting for her outside the trauma center. "Mrs. Boyd, we're doing all we can," said the physician, as he escorted her inside. "But we've seen patients with less serious head injuries and lost them." The nurse suddenly stopped Mrs. Boyd as the group was about to proceed through the double doors into the trauma unit's emergency treatment area. "Mrs. Boyd, I don't think you're prepared for what you're about to see," the nurse cautioned. "I've never seen a worse assault."

Hooked up to an IV, Bryan had oxygen tubes running into his nose. A shiny metal pan was positioned under his ear to catch the blood and fluid that was still draining from his head. Much of his upper body was covered in bandages. His face was swollen beyond twice its normal size. Seeing black tread marks resembling the imprint of a car tire across her son's torso and back, Sara thought that her son had been run over by a car. He had not. The doctor explained that those were imprints from the soles of the shoes worn by the football players.

The doctor left Sara alone, encouraging her to talk softly to her unconscious son. Unable to find a big enough portion of unmolested skin on which to place her hand, Sara gently clutched her son's garment and prayed. Suddenly, a flash of light interrupted her whispers. A police photographer had entered the room and started taking pictures of Bryan from the foot of the bed.

"Why are you taking pictures?" Sara pleaded with the officer. "This kid is dying."

"I'm sorry, ma'am," the officer responded respectfully, having just come from the crime scene. "But I have to take these. I'm working this as a potential homicide."

Ultimately, Bryan Boyd survived, but not without paralysis, memory loss, and permanent brain damage. On June 17, 1996, all four football players were indicted for assault with a deadly weapon capable of causing death or serious bodily injury. None of the players, however, were suspended from the TCU football team. Head coach Pat Sullivan saw no reason to suspend the players "until the criminal justice process has run its course." It was a convenient stance, given the indicted players' importance to the team. More particularly, Sullivan's decision saved the career of Ryan Tucker, TCU's

All-Conference center, who was able to play through the 1996 season, catching the attention of NFL scouts looking for mean and nasty linemen.

Tucker didn't need to worry that his criminal act would cost him a shot at the NFL. He had every reason to believe he would be welcomed into the league with open arms—at least with the arms that aren't bound together by handcuffs. But why should Ryan Tucker worry? Although the Boyd family may find it hard to imagine, Ryan Tucker was by no means the worst character in the National Football League.

In April of 1997, while awaiting trial for the violent felony, Tucker was selected in the fourth round by the St. Louis Rams. Reporters, aware of the Rams' recent problems with criminally deviant players, asked the coaching staff about the decision. "He can finish a fight, that's a positive," head coach Dick Vermeil quipped in downplaying to reporters the seriousness of Tucker's case. Vermeil's portrayal of the four-on-one beating as a "fight" went unchallenged. Ironically, with the team under scrutiny for the off-field woes of running back Lawrence Phillips, reporters asked little more about the Rams' willingness to sign a guy who could very well go to prison for his part in nearly killing a man.

Phillips and other high-profile, criminally convicted players such as Michael Irvin not only receive an inordinate amount of attention for their behavior, they also deflect attention from countless other lesser known players with far more disturbing criminal histories. Ryan Tucker, whose past includes two additional allegations of violent assaults, is a classic example. In researching this book, the authors were repeatedly asked, tongue-in-cheek, "How many chapters do you have on the Dallas Cowboys?" The answer to this question was always the same: "None." Although Michael Irvin is briefly mentioned in the book, the Cowboys are not the focus of a single chapter. The reasons are simple: 1) their problems have already been overreported, and 2) few of the crimes which Cowboys players have been convicted for in recent years compare in seriousness to the crimes detailed in this book.

It's no secret that NFL teams draft players who have had run-ins with the law, even players who have served time. (As long as they are "players," of course.) And why not, the logic goes. These guys are not being drafted into the Boy Scouts of America. This is pro football. Besides, if you listen to coaches and NFL team spokespersons, these past "indiscretions of youth" are not serious crimes. Consider Dick Vermeil's comments after drafting Ryan Tucker. "First off," Vermeil explained to the press, "character guys get in fights from time to time, especially when they didn't start it. I like the guys that don't start it but finish it. I like those kind of guys. This is a physical contact game. . . . But we've got a ton of guys in the National Football League that have some true character problems. I don't believe this guy does." Of course not. What coach wouldn't try to minimize the negative public exposure that his team may face when drafting a violent criminal?

Another popular excuse used by team and league officials to justify the drafting of criminally convicted players goes something like this: as long as these players have served their jail time, it would be unfair to deny them an opportunity to earn a living and become productive members of society. After all, what adult wants to be judged on the basis of the follies of adolescence?

Sounds fair enough. But with mottos like "Just Win Baby," how far will NFL teams go to rationalize giving players with checkered pasts a new lease on life? Will they forgive a habitual criminal offender if he can run a 4.3 forty? Or draft a violent felon because he can bench-press over 500 pounds? How about a drug dealer? A convicted sex offender? A member of a violent street gang? An accused killer?

The evidence suggests the answer is yes to all of the above.

In researching this book, the authors identified 509 players whose criminal records could be checked in two states or more (see Authors' Note). Of these 509 players, an amazing 109 had been formally charged with a serious crime.

With NFL Commissioner Paul Tagliabue's recent strong public stance against players' off-field deviance, one might wonder how many of the players in the authors' survey were kicked out of the league.

Answer: zero.

The closest Tagliabue has come to taking a stand against a criminal player was in 1990. Four years earlier, backup offensive lineman Kevin Allen was cut from the Philadelphia Eagles due to poor performance. Days later, he raped a woman and was arrested. After serving thirty-three months in jail following his conviction, he petitioned the league for the opportunity to play again. Tagliabue denied the petition, saying, "The public perception of [Allen's] being released from prison and then being allowed to return to football is very negative, and there's validity in the perception. There is a negative public reaction to NFL players who engage in criminal conduct and then are allowed to re-enter the league."

The commissioner's stand against a journeyman lineman rings hollow considering the number of other players *in the league today* who have served time in jail or prison for serious crimes. And his statement in the Allen case flies in the face of the league's more commonly stated approach toward criminal conduct. "We're not the criminal justice system,"

NFL spokesperson Greg Aiello told the *Washington Post* in 1994. "We can't cure every ill in society. You know, we're putting on football games. And unless it impacts on the business, we have to be very careful [from a legal standpoint] about disciplinary action we take. A player has rights too."

Unless, of course, he gambles. This misdemeanor offense will get a player banned right quick, and there will be little clamoring from the NFL about due process. Why? Because gambling, like steroids, gives the image of an artificial on-field product, which has a direct correlation to, as Aiello said, the "business" of the NFL. Violent crime, on the other hand, apparently does not.

Together, the 109 players who showed up in the authors' survey with a criminal history had been arrested a combined 264 times. That's an average of 2.42 arrests per player.

Keep in mind that the 264 arrests involve only the most serious offenses. Although the authors discovered a substantial number of players who had been charged with minor misdemeanors (credit card theft, shoplifting, urinating in public, disturbing the peace, etc.) and traffic offenses (speeding and driving with a suspended license), none of these offenses are included in the authors' statistics. The intent was to deal strictly with the more serious criminals in the NFL and the very serious crimes they commit.

A breakdown of the 264 arrests shows:

- 2 for homicide
- 7 for rape
- 4 for kidnapping
- 45 for domestic violence
- 42 for aggravated assault/assault and battery (nondomestic violence cases)

25 for other crimes against persons, including robbery and armed robbery

15 for drug crimes, including intent to distribute cocaine, possession of cocaine, and possession of marijuana

32 for crimes against property, including fraud, larceny, burglary, theft, and property destruction

35 for driving under the influence of alcohol or drugs

17 for resisting arrest

40 for other public safety crimes, including illegal use or possession of a weapon and trespassing. (Note: Trespassing was included only when connected to a domestic violence complaint or an incident involving multiple defendants where someone was charged with a more serious offense.)

As astonishing as these numbers are, it may well be only the tip of the iceberg, albeit an iceberg of *Titanic* proportions. Challenges posed by restrictive public access laws, a near-complete block-out of juvenile criminal records, and the transient nature of NFL players made it impossible to have a complete accounting of all NFL players' criminal histories.

For example, Oakland Raiders running back Derrick Fenner, who is among the 509 players whose history was checked by the authors, was charged with murder in 1987 in Washington, D.C. (He was ultimately exonerated.) This arrest does not show up in the authors' statistics because the District of Columbia is not among the jurisdictions that provided criminal history records to the authors.

In all, the authors discovered over fifty additional players whose criminal histories *as adults* included serious crimes. But these players were *not* included in the authors' statistics because their crimes were discovered by methods that failed to meet the strict standard set for inclusion in the database, as explained in the Authors' Note. (In other words, records checks were done in only one state or in a state where the players resided for less than five years.)

Put simply, the number of crimes (264) and criminals (109) recorded here are conservative.

"Have you done a study asking how many serious crimes are committed by a group of 1,700 lawyers or 1,700 plumbers?" asked Aiello, when contacted by the authors for this book. "How are you supposed to know if this [21 percent of the players formally charged with serious crimes] is unusual?"

Yes, all this data begs the question: Are professional athletes in general or NFL players in particular more prone to criminal behavior than the general population? The answer depends on who you compare them to. If you compare them to their ethnic, demographic, and economic "peers"—adult males under thirty-two who have completed college and earn at least six-figure salaries (of the 509 players in the survey, all earn over $150,000 per year—the minimum salary in the NFL—and most earn considerably more, and virtually all attended four years of college)—NFL players would clearly be overrepresented. Typically, college-educated, high-income earners do not commit violent crime.

However, it is somewhat misleading to compare professional football players to others who complete college and earn salaries comparable to those of NFL players. Why? First, unlike NFL players, individuals earning six- and seven-figure salaries are generally not employed to engage in violence for a living. Second, very few people who obtain college degrees and earn NFL-like salaries come from backgrounds similar to those of many NFL players. For starters, 78 percent of the 509 players in the authors' survey are black. (This figure is consistent with the overall percentage of blacks in the NFL, which was 67 percent during the 1996–97 season.) The research revealed that a fair number of these players come from disadvantaged backgrounds (For a more comprehensive discussion on race, see Chapter 11).

Yet, some point out that it is inappropriate to compare NFL players to men from disadvantaged backgrounds. Most people who grow up in "disadvantaged" circumstances are not given the opportunity to receive a free college education, earn millions of dollars, and become celebrated citizens. Given that NFL players have extraordinary earning opportunities, conventional wisdom suggests they would be less inclined to turn to crime in college for fear of risking all those potential millions as pros. Further, logic dictates that once they enter the NFL, pros would be even less likely to commit crimes because they have so much at stake were they to be convicted.

Neither of these theories were supported by the authors' findings. Of the 109 players who had been charged with a serious crime, thirty-two were arrested *before* entering the NFL, sixty-one were arrested *after* entering the NFL, and sixteen had been arrested both *before and after* joining the NFL.

The reason, it seems, for this break from conventional wisdom is simple. Virtually every other profession that pays employees NFL-like salaries would hardly recruit criminals. Even fewer would retain workers who commit serious crimes after being hired. And those who earn six- and seven-figure salaries are, at least in part, discouraged from participating in serious crime by the knowledge that to act in that manner would jeopardize the wealth and freedom they enjoy.

But nothing in the data suggests that criminal activity puts an NFL player's career in jeopardy. Why worry about breaking the law if there is no real risk of losing your millions? The old saying "Crime doesn't pay" reads a little differently for NFL players. "If you can *play,* you don't have to pay."

The NFL may continue to argue that there is no scientific study proving that its players are disproportionately involved in crime. This posture, however, is slouching under the weight of recurring arrests of players. And this fact remains: at least 21 percent of the men from the most visible class of role models in America have been charged with a serious crime—an average of nearly two and a half times per arrested player. To ask for statistical proof that they are worse than the other criminals in society as a prerequisite for doing something about it is to ask the wrong question.

"That should not be the context or basis by which you make your policy," explained former U.S. Education Secretary and Drug Czar William Bennett in an interview for this book. "You make your policy based on the laws of the land, on the expectation you have for your athletes, on the recognition that they are role models for young people—whether we like it or not. It's natural for boys, in particular, to look up to these big, fast, strong men. They have a larger place in a child's imagination and aspirations than the posse of heroes from other categories. They dominate the stage. They are who kids are looking at most. So what they do is critical. They have the possibility for encouraging or discouraging responsible behavior.

"As a result, the expectation of standards ought to be higher for professional athletes," Bennett continued, "because of the public nature of their profession—the high salaries, public exposure, and adulation. With all the benefits comes responsibility. The fact that some of these criminals are getting a waiver because they are athletes not only corrupts sports, it corrupts the legal system. So, ask the right questions and look in the right places."

Besides, focusing on whether athletes are any worse than other criminals really misses the more noteworthy point— that professional football players are rarely held accountable for their crimes or stigmatized for their actions due to their athleticism. Simply put, the NFL's criminal players are treated differently than virtually every other criminal who commits similar crimes.

In March of 1998, after playing through the entire 1997–98 season while under indictment for assault with a deadly weapon, Ryan Tucker walked into a Fort Worth courtroom with his high-priced lawyer beside him. Tucker pleaded no contest to aggravated assault in connection with his role in the beating of Bryan Boyd.* Tucker was sentenced to 180 days in jail. A Fort Worth judge, however, agreed to suspend the jail sentence on the condition that Tucker successfully complete his community service obligation. He was also put on probation for five years and fined $5,000. As a result, his career with the Rams went uninterrupted and he is free to compete for a starting position in 1998.

---

*Co-defendants J.P. McFarland and Jay Davern transferred to Stephen F. Austin State University, where they continued to play college football. In March of 1998, shortly after Tucker pleaded no contest, they each pleaded no contest to aggravated assault as well. They too were spared jail time. Each was sentenced to five years' probation, 400 hours of community service, and ordered to undergo counseling and pay restitution to Bryan Boyd. Davern was hoping to sign as a free agent with an NFL team at the time this book went to press. Billy Thompson, the fourth co-defendant, stood trial for aggravated assault in March of 1998. A jury acquitted him.

2

Crimes and Punishments

At 10:00 A.M. on Thursday February 26, 1998, Atlanta Falcons head coach Dan Reeves left his office to drive to the Atlanta airport. On the way, Reeves spoke via car phone to the authors about how he handles players who commit crimes. Coincidentally, as the interview began, Falcons starting linebacker Cornelius Bennett stood in a Buffalo, New York, courtroom being sentenced to two months in jail for sexually assaulting a woman in May of 1997.

Before taking over in Atlanta, Reeves coached the New York Giants from 1993 through 1996. In his last draft as coach of the Giants, Reeves objected to picking Nebraska's star defensive lineman Christian Peter on account of his storied history of criminal allegations involving women. "My philosophy is that you don't need to bring someone in who already has a problem," Reeves told the authors. "That's the reason I was against drafting Peter. Now, I believe in giving people a second chance, don't get me wrong. But unless it's an unusual circumstance, I don't see why you would want to start out with a problem."

For a guy who doesn't like starting out with problems, Reeves's first couple of months on the job in Atlanta could not have been worse. Hired on January 27, 1997, he barely got used to his new desk before police reports were on top of it detailing crimes far worse than anything for which Christian Peter was ever convicted. On March 19, Fulton County police arrested Falcons defensive back Patrick Bates and charged him with simple battery. Reeves soon discovered, however, that the battery wasn't so simple. The victim, Bates's girlfriend, Sophia Billan, was nine months pregnant at the time of the alleged assault. According to the police report, "Mr. Bates pulled her out of bed by her hair and dragged her around the apartment." The police also documented that Billan was bruised and claimed to have been beaten by Bates previously.

Although not at all pleased with the news, Reeves decided to give Bates one more chance. Not drafting criminal players is one thing, but cutting loose criminally accused players who are under contract is another. Don't they count against the salary cap? "Once you have someone who becomes part of your organization, to me they are just like family," Reeves told the authors. "If they've got a problem, you have to, just like you would your own children, try to get them help. You have to work with them. I talked to Patrick after his arrest and told him that we could not have those situations."

Coach to player like parent to child? Maybe in the Lombardi era. But not today. Not with players whose pasts are a tangled web of crime, violence, family breakdown, and, in some cases, poverty. Patrick Bates allegedly was a combination of all these things. A source close to Bates told the authors that as one of three children, Bates grew up amidst poverty in Galveston, Texas. His father abandoned him. Bates, the authors were told, later witnessed the killing of his only brother. The authors confirmed that at age nineteen Bates entered the criminal justice system. According to records obtained from the Galveston County Courthouse, he was charged with assault causing bodily injury and criminal trespass in 1989. Both charges were later dropped by prosecutors. He went on to play football at Texas A&M. In 1993, after his junior season, he left school and became the Raiders' first-round pick (twelfth overall). In his rookie year in Los Angeles, he met Billan and got her pregnant. Bates declined through his agent to be interviewed for this book.

Bates and other players whose tough upbringing has hardened them are hardly prime candidates for the fatherly approach from coaches. Reeves himself admitted that the league and the players are different today. "Some of the problems we face today with our young people are things that we never thought about years ago," said Reeves. "I think the game has changed because young people's lives have changed."

By the end of March, Billan had given birth to a baby boy, Jarius Bates. Patrick, at that point, had moved into his own apartment. On April 16, three weeks after coming home from the hospital, Billan was nursing her baby at 12:30 A.M. when Bates showed up unannounced. According to police reports obtained by the authors, Bates used a keypad to enter the apartment through the garage. Once inside the garage, he kicked in the door separating the garage from the apartment. Bates then yanked three-week-old Jarius from Billan's arms before pulling out a handgun. Threatening to kill her, the baby, and himself, Bates proceeded to beat Billan about the head with the gun. "He also advised that if she called the police then he would get in a shoot-out with police and kill them too," the report states.

Bates did not break into Billan's apartment alone, but brought with him another female, Amanda Marr. He called Marr into the bedroom and instructed her to pack the baby's things and then take the baby to the car. Meanwhile, he continued to hit Billan over the head with the gun, "saying he was going to soften her head so that she would suffer brain damage." The police report noted officers' observations that Billan had bruises and lacerations to her head, hands, legs, and feet.

Before forcing Billan out of the apartment and into the back seat of the Mitsubishi Montero that he and Marr had driven, Bates pushed Billan into the shower at gunpoint and ordered her to rinse the blood off herself. Once inside the vehicle, Marr drove while Bates sat in the back seat with Billan and their baby son. According to the police report, he held the gun alternately to the head of Billan and the baby, threatening to shoot. Billan later told police that as Marr drove toward Bates's apartment in nearby Duluth, Patrick smashed a glass object over Billan's head. Officers later recovered glass fragments from a broken drinking glass in the rear seat.

After arriving at Bates's apartment, Bates, according to the report, "advised Amanda she could leave, that she didn't have to be a party to this." But Marr said she wanted to stay with Bates. And she ignored Billan's pleas for her to call the police.

Bates then tied Billan's hands and feet with shoelaces and ordered her to lie on his bed. Billan told authorities that at that point, Bates took a knife, cut the laces, and threatened to stab her. But their crying baby, who was being held by

Marr, distracted him momentarily. Bates took the baby from Marr, told the infant that he loved him, and then ordered Billan to lie down on the bed. "He told the victim he was going to have to kill the baby, the victim, and himself," the report indicates.

In the confusion, Billan asked for permission to first wash the blood from her hands. Though Bates gave his permission, he threatened to harm the child if she tried to escape. But when Billan spotted the keys to the Mitsubishi sitting on the kitchen counter when she was rinsing her hands off in the sink, she grabbed them and dashed out the door. Before she could start the vehicle, Marr came running from the apartment in an attempt to stop her. Quickly locking the doors, Billan started the car and sped off toward her apartment to get help.

When Billan reached her apartment complex, she went directly to a neighbor's apartment. "I gave her a towel to clean up the blood," her neighbor said in an interview for this book. "Then I called the police. When they showed up at my house, the officers referred to Patrick as 'the Falcons person.' One of the officers had responded to a domestic violence call at their home before."

After Billan went to the hospital for medical treatment, the police went to Bates's apartment and arrested him for aggravated assault, kidnapping and endangerment to a child. Marr was also arrested and charged with being an accessory to kidnapping.

This time Reeves took a different approach. One week after Bates's arrest, on April 24, the Falcons quietly placed his name on the waiver wire. At the time, there were no press releases, formal statements, or explanations from the Falcons' brass. Nearly ten months later Reeves explained the move in an interview for this book. "We just had to let the players and our fans know that we just weren't going to put up with that kind of person on our football team," Reeves said.

For Reeves, it was the first time that he could recall outright releasing someone over a criminal matter. In fact, cutting a player who had yet to be convicted of anything was virtually unheard of in the NFL. In the more than 500 arrest reports reviewed during the research for this book, the authors were able to document only one other player, Tampa Bay's Lamar Thomas, who was released after only an arrest, and he was signed by another team weeks later (see Chapter 8). In numerous interviews with representatives from teams around the league, the biggest explanation for not releasing players solely on the basis of an arrest was a respect for the player's due process rights. In other words, it is only fair to let the courts determine guilt or innocence before firing a guy.

Reeves, however, did not take the due process factor into consideration. "I wasn't worried about that," Reeves said. "I talked to Patrick and Patrick understood what my stance was. He and I were on the same page. He felt that a change of scenery might be good for him too."

Through his agent, Steve Zucker, Bates declined a request from the authors to be interviewed about his dismissal from Atlanta. However, Ian Greengross, an attorney in Zucker's office, confirmed that Bates met with Reeves following the incident and left the team on good terms. However, his explanation for why the Falcons cut Bates loose was considerably different. "They released him a few weeks after the draft," Greengross explained. "They drafted a couple guys who play his position in the draft. When we talked to the Falcons, our entire conversations with them were based not really on the off-the-field thing, although that was a contributing factor. But it was more of how they saw him in their plans than anything else."

And there's the rub. Bates was a second-string player, not even able to maintain a starting position on the Falcons, who went 3-13 in 1996. His absence from the roster would not be missed. "If he had started sixteen games, he wouldn't have been cut for this incident," confirmed Greengross. "If you're a strong starter and a valuable contributor to the team, they're not going to exercise the full option of cutting you as they can under these nonguaranteed contracts."

So, what would Reeves and the Falcons do if a key starter got charged with a violent felony? Not three weeks passed from the time Bates was cut before the Falcons got their chance to decide. On May 19, a Buffalo, New York, woman filed a police complaint after being treated at an area hospital for injuries sustained in a rape the previous night. Her alleged attacker? Falcons starting linebacker Cornelius Bennett, a ten-year veteran who was an All-Pro and who had played in four Super Bowls. A key free agent acquisition in 1996, Bennett was earning $13.6 million over four years.

The report filled out by an investigator from the Buffalo Police Department Sex Crimes Unit identified Bennett's crimes as "rape, sodomy, sexual abuse and unlawful imprisonment." Facing serious felony charges in New York, Bennett soon met privately with Reeves in Atlanta. "I sat down and talked to Cornelius," Reeves confirmed. "He explained to me what his side of the story was. And it was one of those deals where you have to let the law take its course."

Unlike his position in the Bates case, Reeves chose the "wait and see" approach while prosecutors built their case against Bennett. As it turned out, Bennett pleaded guilty to a reduced charge of sexual misconduct on September 9, 1997. Under New York law, "A person is guilty of sexual misconduct when: 1. Being a male, he engages in sexual intercourse with a female without her consent; or 2. He engages in deviate sexual intercourse with another person without the latter's consent."

When Bennett entered his plea of guilty, Bates still had not even been indicted. By legal standards, he was still innocent. That could no longer be said for Bennett. Nonetheless, Reeves opted not to suspend or fine him, much less release him. "I think pleading guilty certainly isn't what you would like for him to do," Reeves admitted, speaking from a coach's perspective. "But sometimes there are circumstances where that is the best way to go. The lawyers make that call. All I did was listen to what Cornelius's story was and why he did what he did. And I was satisfied with it and didn't take any action."

Hours after Bennett's plea, the press asked Reeves what action, if any, he would take. "We'll have to wait and see what the judge does," Reeves said back in September of 1997. "When he makes a decision, then we'll decide what to do."

Reeves insisted that the difference in his handling of Bates and Bennett had nothing to do with their importance to the team as players. Instead, he pointed to two more practical factors that influenced his actions: 1) the lack of information available to him in the Bennett case and 2) league policy.

"One big difference in these two situations is that I had

access to Patrick's police reports, but not to Cornelius's because his happened in Buffalo," Reeves said in an interview for this book. "I've seen police reports and gone through them with the police in other cases. Normally you do that. But since Cornelius's case was in Buffalo, I didn't have access to them. So I didn't pursue it. But I was satisfied with what took place and what Cornelius had told me."

Of course, the Falcons, like any citizen willing to file a public records request, could have obtained those reports had they wanted to. But beyond that, Reeves said he was told that the league would handle the investigation into Bennett to determine whether punishment was warranted. "A lot of the things that individual teams were able to do in the past we are no longer able to do," said Reeves, referring to new league policy that places investigative powers for off-the-field matters in the hands of the commissioner's office. "Now the league takes charge. The league said that they were going to take care of the investigation into Bennett's arrest, and that they would alert us about anything that they don't agree with. And they never did that."

Reeves and the Falcons weren't the only ones told by the league that they would handle the investigation into the Bennett incident. The public heard the same thing. When Bennett pleaded guilty, NFL spokesperson Greg Aiello told the Associated Press that the league was "in the process of obtaining court documents and looking into it." When asked if Bennett would face possible sanctions from the league, Aiello said, "I wouldn't rule it out at this point. In a general sense, any person in the league who's involved in a violation of the law is subject to possible disciplinary action by the commissioner."

Emphasis on the word "possible." In theory, it is possible

for any player to be punished by the league for committing a criminal offense. In reality, it doesn't happen unless the crime involves gambling or substance abuse. When pressed to explain why he didn't as much as fine Bennett in light of having fired Bates, Reeves told the authors: "The league didn't see that there was any disciplinary action that should be taken as far as Cornelius's incident was concerned."

This leads to the question: Did the league really investigate the crime or did they just placate the press by saying they were *going* to conduct an investigation?

After months of letter writing and telephone calls, the authors obtained the police reports, the police investigation log, the criminal complaint, and the victim's sworn deposition in the Bennett matter. Due to the sexual nature of the crime, the victim's name had to be expunged from all the documents before the authors could obtain them. The following account is based on those documents, as well as numerous interviews conducted with law enforcement officials and Judge Robert T. Russell, who presided over the case. The authors also spoke with the victim's mother on numerous occasions by telephone.

On May 18, 1997, Cornelius Bennett was in Buffalo to attend a social event honoring ex-Bills quarterback Jim Kelly. While in town, Bennett stayed at the Hyatt Hotel located at 2 Fountain Plaza. At 5:30 on the afternoon of the eighteenth, Bennett asked twenty-six-year-old Clarisse Messner* to come to room 1611, which the Hyatt's hotel register listed as being occupied by Cornelius Bennett. His pregnant wife did not accompany him to Buffalo, choosing instead to remain behind in Atlanta.

Messner was well acquainted with Bennett from his days with the Bills. She first met him when she was sixteen years old. Having known him for ten years, she went willingly to his room. "While there, he asked me to remove my clothes, which I did," Messner said in her deposition. She was willing to go along with Bennett until what began as another garden-variety case of an athlete cheating on his wife turned painfully violent. "During the course of kissing, Cornelius Bennett did . . . insert his penis into my rectum," Messner's deposition continued. "At no point did I give consent to this type of sexual intercourse."

The report filed by the police on May 19 charged Bennett with sodomy, a first-degree felony. In New York, sodomy is the technical term for anal rape. The statute defines sodomy as forcing a person to "engage in deviate sexual intercourse," which New York courts have defined as " 'contact' between the penis and the anus, [or] the mouth and the penis. . . ."

Bennett was also charged with unlawful imprisonment. According to the police report, Messner "was not permitted to leave when she asked to do so."

The prosecutor's complaint filed on September 4, 1997, indicated that "the defendant . . . did subject the victim to deviate sexual intercourse without her consent by inserting his penis into her rectum, causing pain and lacerations." After Bennett's lawyer reached a plea agreement with prosecutors, the words "by inserting his penis into her rectum causing pain and lacerations" in the complaint had a line drawn through them. The words may have changed, but that did not erase the fact that Messner had actually suffered injuries from sexual assault that required medical treatment. According to the Sex Crimes Unit's case log, officers noted on May 19 that the "victim was treated at [name deleted] hospital, following the attack." On May 21, the log notes that a rape kit was performed, but the details are blotted out in order to protect the victim's privacy. Finally, when Judge Russell accepted Bennett's guilty plea, he had to postpone sentencing because all the medical costs—which Bennett was required to pay—had not been assessed yet.

When Bennett was finally sentenced on February 26, he told the press, "This is the first time in my life I've ever had to go through anything like this. I just wish I could take back that night altogether." No doubt the victim had never been through anything like that either. And she probably wouldn't mind taking back that night as well.

Reading from a letter written by Messner, Judge Russell quoted her belief in Bennett's "need for a wake-up call." The judge agreed, giving Bennett sixty days in jail. He also sentenced him to three years' probation, fined him $500, ordered him to pay restitution to the victim for medical bills, and ordered him to perform 100 hours of community service.

"That sentence is excessive and unduly harsh," said Bennett's defense attorney, James M. Shaw, whose brother Joe is Bennett's agent. "There were over 30 letters of reference and testimonials from religious, sports and community leaders who recommended that Mr. Bennett be put on probation for the exemplary life he had led not only in Western New York but in Atlanta."

Shaw's response didn't exactly qualify as a news bulletin. His job as a defense lawyer is to make excuses for his clients.

The NFL, on the other hand, has no such excuse. Yet the commissioner's office chose not to so much as fine Bennett.

When the authors contacted the Buffalo Police Department in the winter of 1997 to request copies of the police reports in the Bennett case, no other request had been made for the documents up to that point in time. Lieutenant David Mann of the Sex Crimes Unit, who approves the release of any reports pertaining to sex-related offenses, informed the authors that it would take weeks for the department to go through the reports and expunge protected information such as the victim's name and address. This suggests that seven months after the police reports were filed, the NFL had not obtained copies of them from the police department. It remains a mystery what Aiello meant when he told the AP back on September 9, 1997, that the league was "obtaining court documents and looking into it."

Dan Reeves, who initially told reporters he would reserve making any disciplinary decisions until after the judge imposed a sentence, followed the NFL's lead. This despite Judge Russell's determination that Bennett's crime was sufficiently serious to send him to jail. "The sentence was fair, reasonable, and justified based on the facts of the case," Judge Russell said in an interview for this book. "He had admitted his culpability and responsibility for the offense by entering a plea of guilty. Having evaluated the medical records and the impact it had upon the victim and the victim's family life, the sentence was justified. If someone else committed the same offense, whether it was him or some other citizen who engaged in the same or similar conduct, I would have imposed the same sentence."

Contrary to popular opinion, judges do not routinely give professional athletes preferential treatment. The same cannot be said for coaches and general managers. "Our hands are tied on these things," Reeves said several times. "That is up to the league."

Strangely, Reeves admitted that he didn't wait to get a green light from the league before taking action in the Bates case. "I never talked to the league," he said. "I came in and saw the things that went on and just felt like we needed to release him."

Bennett was scheduled to begin serving his sixty-day jail term on April 13, 1998. Instead, he filed an appeal. A New York Appeals Court judge delayed the start of the jail term, allowing Bennett to remain free while the State Supreme Court determined whether his case deserved a review. The appeal was ultimately denied and on April 30, 1998, Bennett surrendered to New York authorities and began serving his sixty-day sentence. He showed up at jail with his wife and two-month-old daughter.

And whatever became of Patrick Bates?

On March 23, 1998, just weeks before Bennett's jail sentence was announced, Bates pleaded guilty to a felony charge of criminal damage to property and second degree battery. He was sentenced to five years' probation, fined $5,000, required to complete a violence class and continue psychotherapy, pay $711 to Billan for medical bills, and make child support payments. He did not get any jail time.

On May 5, 1998, he signed a free agent contract with the Oakland Raiders.

Both Bennett and Bates will be in uniform for the 1998 season.

3

Risky Business

The Falcons' experience leaves the lasting impression that the more talented the player, the higher the threshold for tolerating crime. And the Raiders' decision to sign Bates suggests even reserve players who are violent criminals can get picked up by another team as long as there is a need for their talent. These cases illustrate the dilemma of every NFL coach and general manager: What do you do when a player, particularly a starter or key role player, is convicted of a violent crime? Keep playing him, hoping it never happens again? Or punish him and risk losses?

As the authors discovered, teams have paid a high price for taking the risk of playing a star convicted of violent crimes. But the risk is irresistible—and will be taken over and over again—if the talent is there.

On March 22, 1992, Kansas City Chiefs wide receiver Tim Barnett was arrested for battery against his wife. Barnett appeared before Johnson County District Judge John Anderson III on June 25 and pleaded guilty to the lesser charge of disorderly conduct. Anderson sentenced Barnett to thirty days in jail, but agreed to suspend the sentence if Barnett completed counseling and refrained from further violation of the law for a full year.

Then on June 5, 1993, three weeks shy of completing his one-year probation term, Barnett was again arrested. This time Barnett had assaulted his wife and threatened her with a Colt Python handgun. He was charged with making a terroristic threat and aggravated assault, both felonies, as well as one count of misdemeanor assault. In another plea-bargained deal, Barnett pleaded guilty to misdemeanor assault and battery. Judge Anderson, on October 27, then revoked the suspension on Barnett's previous thirty-day jail sentence and ordered the wide receiver to jail. But the Chiefs were in mid-season and Anderson agreed to delay the imposition of the sentence until no later than January 4, 1994. Presumably, the Chiefs' season would be over by then and Barnett's incarceration would not interfere with his career.

There was one small problem. The Chiefs made the playoffs. And by the time January 4 arrived—the day Barnett was supposed to surrender himself into custody—the Chiefs were four days away from hosting the Pittsburgh Steelers in a second-round playoff game. Barnett was one of quarterback Joe Montana's primary receivers and his presence in the lineup was crucial for the Chiefs to win the game.

On the morning of January 4, Barnett's attorney, William Grimshaw, petitioned Judge Anderson to further delay the imposition of Barnett's jail sentence until after the playoffs were concluded. "Barnett's job with the Chiefs would be in jeopardy if he had to miss the playoffs Saturday," insisted Grimshaw.

Anderson, whose patience was exhausted, rejected the request and ordered Barnett to jail effective immediately. "I can't really justify treating you a whole lot different than I would treat anybody else just because you're a Kansas City Chiefs player," said Judge Anderson from the bench. "Now, am I supposed to just cross my fingers and hope this time it's going to stick, and next time we're not going to have to have you in here for hurting somebody real bad? I don't feel comfortable with that."

Hours after announcing the sentence, Judge Anderson suddenly took ill and left the courthouse. Meanwhile, Grimshaw filed a notice of appeal and moved for Barnett to be released on bond. Assistant District Attorney Melinda Whitman argued that the appeal should be denied, saying the two sides had previously agreed to sentencing terms and that the appeal would probably be withdrawn as soon as the season concluded.

District Judge Pro-Tem Robert Morse, sitting in Judge Anderson's place, said he was required to set the bond, which he did at $1,500. Grimshaw secured the bond and Barnett was released.

"That's not right," Johnson County District Attorney Paul Morrison told the *Kansas City Star* shortly after Barnett's release. "Mr. Barnett needs to be in doing his time, not because he's a Chief but because he keeps breaking the law."

Yet the Chiefs were glad to have their criminally convicted receiver available for Saturday's game. "Our understanding is that he's available to us for the rest of the season," Chiefs director of public relations Bob Moore told the *Kansas City Star.*

Having Barnett in a football uniform rather than a jail uniform proved crucial to the Chiefs' success. With less than two minutes remaining in regulation and Kansas City trailing the Steelers by seven points, Joe Montana was orchestrating one of his trademark come-from-behind drives.

Ultimately, Barnett was on the receiving end of Montana's game-tying touchdown pass, sending the game into over-time, where the Chiefs went on to win. Barnett's spectacular reception sent sold-out Arrowhead Stadium into a frenzy.

The following day, the *Kansas City Star* dubbed Barnett "the toast of the town." His clutch performance caused fans and sportswriters to quickly forget that Barnett was a twice-convicted criminal who should have been in jail. The following week Kansas City was eliminated from the playoffs. Barnett, meanwhile, remained free as he and his attorney continued his appeal.

On June 24, 1994, with Barnett still free, Judge Anderson's expressed apprehension about Barnett "hurting somebody real bad" became a reality. That morning, Barnett, along with two friends, was staying at a hotel in Milwaukee, Wisconsin. He was in town to attend a friend's wedding. At approximately 11 A.M., Tanisha Warren,* a fourteen-year-old housekeeper who was working in her first part-time job, knocked on the door to room 215. Although Barnett and his two friends were inside, they did not respond. Noticing the door was partly ajar, Warren called out, "Housekeeping." Still hearing no response, she repeated, "Housekeeping."

Convinced that the room was vacant, Warren did as she had been trained and entered the room to clean it. To her surprise, she discovered the three men when she entered. "Do you want any service?" Warren asked nervously.

"Yeah," responded one of the men.

Walking between the men, who were positioned on their respective beds, Warren restocked the room with clean towels and drinking glasses before going in to clean the bathroom. Exiting the room after completing her duties, Warren was stopped by Barnett.

"Can I ask you a question?" he asked.

"Yeah," she responded.

"What is your phone number?" Barnett asked.

Scared and not wanting to divulge her home phone number, Warren handed Barnett a Manchester Suites courtesy card, purposely misspelled her name on it, and wrote down an erroneous phone number. "I didn't want to give him the right one," she would later testify in court.

Barnett took the card from Warren. "Can I ask you a question?" he said again.

"Yes," Warren said as Barnett took her hands and pulled her down toward the bed.

"Ain't nobody been in this?" Barnett asked as he put his hands up Warren's housekeeping dress.

Thinking that he was asking whether she had ever had sex before, Warren responded, "No."

Without warning, Barnett suddenly turned Warren's shoulders and forced her onto her back. "He pulled up my dress . . . and then he started rubbing on my breasts," Warren later testified. "He was asking me if it felt good. And then he started to rub on my vagina. I kept telling him stop. I had took my leg off the bed to get up and he put my leg back up. Then he put the covers over me. . . . He started licking my ear. He asked me a couple times, 'Did it feel good?' Then he unbuttoned his pants and pulled it down . . . to his knees and started rubbing his penis against my vagina. He said he was going to put it in. Then he started rubbing on my breast again and . . . rubbing his penis against my vagina real fast, and then some of me started hurting. . . ."

Warren made a futile attempt to push against Barnett's chest as she pleaded with him to stop. But she was no match for his strength. Finally, Barnett climbed off her and scurried into the bathroom. Warren noticed that her thighs were wet and her panties had semen on them. While Barnett was in the bathroom, she pulled down her dress, grabbed her caddieful of hotel supplies, and ran out of the room to find her older sister, who also worked at the hotel.

After reporting what happened, Warren was brought to the Women's Assessment Center where she was treated and samples of blood, pubic hairs, head hairs, and smears and swabs were taken. Her clothes were placed in plastic bags for evidence. And after confiding in her parents, Warren reported the incident to the Milwaukee police.

In July, Milwaukee authorities charged Barnett with sexually assaulting a child under the age of sixteen, a felony carrying a possible ten-year state prison sentence. The following day the Chiefs, who were involved in training camp, released Barnett. "As with every decision we make, we thought it was in the best interest of our football team at this time," head coach Marty Schottenheimer told the press. Although it was quite obvious, Schottenheimer refused to confirm whether Barnett's release was a result of his arrest for sexually assaulting a minor.

On June 12, 1995, a Milwaukee jury convicted Barnett and he was later sentenced to serve three years in prison. On January 10, 1997, after being paroled from a Wisconsin state prison, Barnett returned to Kansas to serve the thirty-day jail sentence for the first assault on his wife back in 1992. By this point, his high-powered attorney had withdrawn from representing him and the Chiefs and NFL teams were no longer interested in him. Attempts to reach Barnett were unsuccessful.

*   *   *

One player, one teenage girl, one rape. It would seem enough to teach a team a lesson. It wasn't.

In October of 1997, only two years after the Barnett debacle, the Chiefs again made a decision to employ a player with a formidable criminal history. In the quest for the best record in the AFC, the Chiefs made a blockbuster mid-season trade for Wayne Simmons, starting linebacker from the Green Bay Packers. Unbeknownst to fans in Kansas City, Simmons was at that moment being investigated for the alleged rape of a teenage girl.

State of Georgia v. Wayne Simmons

HILTON HEAD, SOUTH CAROLINA, MAY 30, 1997

It was 7:00 P.M. when graduation ceremonies got underway at Hilton Head High School. Twenty-seven-year old Wayne Simmons, a 1988 graduate of Hilton Head, had been invited back to his alma mater to deliver a commencement address and have his football jersey retired. Few high school graduations have a reigning Super Bowl champion deliver a message to the grads. Following a post-graduation run-in with Simmons, graduating senior Susan Jensen* was hardly feeling privileged to be among the few who did.

When the ceremonies ended, Jensen and her friend Cyndy Johnson* joined a small group of graduates who drove to nearby Savannah, Georgia, to celebrate. After arriving in Savannah, Jensen and Johnson split off from the rest of the group, which went to get something to eat. Instead, Jensen met up with a girlfriend, Emily Scott,* who lived in Savannah, and Johnson linked up with her boyfriend Paul Benson.* The four of them then went to The Zoo, an eighteen-and-over club. Scott knew the bouncer, who ushered the four of them in for free after stamping the word "ZOO" across the back of their hands.

Once inside, Johnson and her boyfriend went off on their own. The bouncer, a cousin to the club's owner, George Murphy, proudly invited Jensen and Scott down to a private lounge below the dance floor to meet Murphy and a famous NFL player who was the club's most prestigious patron. Not much of a football fan, Jensen didn't suspect that Wayne Simmons was the guy the bouncer was referring to. Besides, she hardly expected to find Simmons, who had just spoken at her graduation, hanging out in a club for eighteen- and nineteen-year-olds. However, according to the statement Jensen would later give police, she recognized Simmons once she was introduced to him.

"Oh, yeah, you were at my graduation," said Jensen.

"Where?" said Simmons.

"On Hilton Head," replied Jensen.

"Oh yeah."

"Like they retired your jersey, right?"

"Yeah they did. Well, congratulations on your graduation."

"Thanks."

After addressing the grads, Simmons, whose driver's license had been revoked in South Carolina on account of a drunk driving conviction, asked his longtime friend Elliot Mitchell to drive him to Savannah. A divorced father of four, Mitchell was not interested in hanging out with the young crowd at The Zoo. A friend since Simmons's childhood, however, Mitchell went along with Simmons's wishes and ultimately agreed to drive him to Savannah.

In tight with The Zoo's owner, George Murphy, Simmons

got himself and Mitchell in without paying the cover charge. Mitchell later told authorities that he and Simmons were ushered to a private downstairs lounge to join Murphy. According to Mitchell, Murphy repeatedly paraded women over to meet Simmons, lifted up some of the women's skirts and grabbed their butts. "I didn't know what the hell was going on," Mitchell told authorities.

Mitchell also told authorities that he recalled two young girls (Jensen and Scott) coming over to meet Simmons. Minutes after the bouncer introduced the girls to Murphy and Simmons, the bouncer brought Jensen and Scott back upstairs to the dance floor. He then asked the girls if they were interested in accompanying him to another nearby dance club called The Rave. In her police statement, Jensen said that while en route to The Rave, she and Scott discovered that Simmons, Murphy, and Mitchell were in a car following the bouncer's vehicle.

According to Jensen, she and Scott did not like the crowd and the music at The Rave and asked to be taken back to The Zoo. When they attempted to get in the bouncer's vehicle, however, Jensen said they were told the car was full and that they would have to ride back in Mitchell's car. Jensen and Scott told the authorities that they protested, having only met the men an hour earlier. Nonetheless, they ultimately climbed in the back seat together and rode without incident back to The Zoo.

When Murphy dropped them off at The Zoo parking lot, the club was closed. The bouncer and Benson insisted that the girls come inside and play pool before heading back to Hilton Head. According to Scott, she and Jensen sat at opposite ends of the room watching Johnson and her boyfriend shoot pool. Scott also indicated that Simmons and some other guys were in the room as well. At one point, Scott saw Simmons approach Jensen and engage in conversation. Scott then went to the bathroom. When she returned, both Simmons and Jensen were gone.

Jensen told police that while she waited in the lounge for Scott to come out of the bathroom, Simmons took her into a stairwell and raped her.

The following account is based on Jensen's formal statements to the police and her subsequent statement to prosecutors.

Simmons approached Jensen and persuaded her to walk with him toward a stairwell off to the side of the room. "George asked Wayne if he needed the key," Jensen told authorities. "And Wayne said, 'Yes, I need the keys.' He started draggin' me. I kept telling them [Simmons and George] 'I have to go talk to Emily and tell her where I'm at.' I was trying anything to get out of it and I told them, I said, 'I have to talk to Emily. I can't leave without telling Emily where I'm going first.' "

Jensen described the stairwell that Simmons brought her into as poorly lit and littered with cardboard boxes and debris. The walls were covered in spray-painted graffiti, and vomit was visible on the floor in places. Police photographs taken of the stairwell confirmed Jensen's description.

"He started kissin' on me and I told him to stop and I was tryin' my best to push him away and he kinda had me," said Jensen. "He had his arms wrapped around where I couldn't move my arms out and I told him to stop. 'I don't want to do this. This is wrong. You can't do this.' He said, 'Why?' "

Jensen told him that she was raised in a churchgoing family, that she was still a virgin, and that although she had boyfriends, she had never had sex with any of them.

"Well, I'm not every other guy you've ever had," Simmons said, according to Jensen. "And he just kept on. So I started squirmin' away from him on the floor."

Jensen said that Simmons had her positioned on the third step of the cement staircase. "He was kind of like laying his upper part of his body on my shoulders and my back was going to the stairs and he pulled my underwear off and he unzipped his pants," she told police. "I guess he pulled his penis out and he was still kissing on me and I was telling him to stop."

In her interview with the police, Jensen stuttered as she described what happened next. "I was telling him how important it was . . . I, I've always been raised to . . . I couldn't. I was saving it for a marriage. I didn't want to." The following excerpt is taken from a transcript of the detective's interview with Jensen:

DETECTIVE: How do you know he pulled his penis out with his hand?

JENSEN: I saw him unzip his pants and pull it out and then he laid right back up on top of me.

DETECTIVE: Okay. And then what happened after he got his penis out?

JENSEN: He laid back on top of me and started kissing on me, telling me how important his career was and that I couldn't tell anyone.

DETECTIVE: And was he touching you at this time?

JENSEN: Uh huh.

DETECTIVE: Where?

JENSEN: Um, he had lifted his . . . bird finger or maybe it was his index finger and he uh, lifted and rubbed me on my vagina and I squirmed away from him 'cause it hurt 'cause he was pressing down into me. I told him to stop. I think he tried to penetrate me there and he noticed that he couldn't and that's why he wanted to move up the steps.

DETECTIVE: How do you know he tried to penetrate you there?

JENSEN: I felt it on the side of my leg. He was pushing my leg out and I felt what I assume would be the head of his penis pressing into me.

In her supplemental interview with prosecutors, Jensen detailed the difficulty Simmons was having trying to have intercourse with her. "He started lickin' his fingers. . . . All I remember from then on is just feeling something. It was like he was pushing down on me and then he was trying to get inside of me, my vagina and it just, I was trying my best to squirm, but you have 300 pounds on top of you. I guess he realized that the position he had me in wasn't working for him. He asked me to move . . . so I said, 'Let me up and I'll move.' "

Jensen said that when Simmons let her up she grabbed her underwear and tried to dart for the door. " 'Unt, unt,' " she recalled him saying. " 'I already pulled those off for a reason.' I said, 'No, I'm going back downstairs to find Emily.' And he said, 'No you're not.' And he grabbed me and walked me back up the stairs and laid me down. That's when he moved the brick. I guess it was in his way. He laid me down on the cement. He laid on top of me and went back inside. He, I guess, ejaculated before, when we were on the steps cause it was all over on the back of my dress. Cause I remember when I stood up and put my underwear back on it felt wet."

When Jensen recalled this part of the incident to the detective, he asked for clarification. The following excerpt is from the transcript:

DETECTIVE: Was his penis still out?

JENSEN: Yes.

DETECTIVE: And . . .

JENSEN: At that time it was.

DETECTIVE: And was it still erect?

JENSEN: Uh huh.

DETECTIVE: Okay. Had you felt the wet spot on your dress yet?

JENSEN: Yeah. I felt it the minute I stood up after he had, when he turned me around and I stood up to try and . . . walk off.

DETECTIVE: Okay. Then what happened.

JENSEN: . . . [H]e laid me down. That's when I started telling him to stop. . . . And he said, "No. I only need a few more minutes."

DETECTIVE: Uh huh.

JENSEN: And he pulled my dress up. He pulled my underwear down to my ankles and he kind of like I guess bent my legs up and spread 'em out.

DETECTIVE: Uh huh.

JENSEN: And that's when he I guess penetrated me, started moving a lot.

When it was over, according to Jensen, "He got up, zipped his pants and told me his phone number and said he would call me and we'll talk about it."

Near the end of her interview with the detective, Jensen was asked if Simmons hit or slapped her during the incident. "He not so much threatened me," Jensen explained. "But just pretty much kept saying you know, my status against your status, you're nothing."

"Were there any other sexual acts?" asked the detective. "Did you have to touch his private part?"

"He tried to put it in my face one time and I told him no," Jensen answered. "When he had my shoulders, it was right there in my face. And I moved my head away. I don't know if he was making . . . that that's what he wanted me to do or not."

Jensen's friends drove her to Candler Hospital after the incident. Jensen was examined by a Dr. Pohl, to whom she recounted the incident. She then told him that she was a virgin at the time of the attack. According to police reports, Dr. Pohl found "redness in the vaginal area and that she had a tear in the six o'clock position in the vaginal opening." A diagram was drawn describing the exact location of the injury, and then placed in the case file. Bruising was also detected in the mid-back area and on her neck, injuries which were photographed by a police photographer. According to a report filled out at the hospital, "Dr. Pohl advised . . . that these injuries are consistent with the Victim's story."

Following the exam, Jensen was given a prescription for a morning-after pill, advised to have a pregnancy test performed two weeks from the date of the incident, introduced to a rape crisis counselor, and interviewed by a police investigator. All of Jensen's clothing (white shoes, a blue half-slip, white panties, a bra, an ankle-length yellow print dress, and two hair scrunchies) was placed in evidence bags to be turned over to the crime lab for inspection. The following day, those items, along with swabs taken from Jensen's vagina and a white envelope marked "suspected semen from body" were shipped via UPS to the Forensic Sciences Division of the Georgia Bureau of Investigations.

In the early stage of their investigation, Savannah police telephoned Simmons's friend Elliot Mitchell to get his version of what happened that night. "It's all bullshit," he insisted, when informed that Simmons had been accused by Jensen of rape. He maintained that any sex that occurred was consensual.

There was corroboration that some kind of sexual act had occurred. In addition to the items received from the hospital, the crime lab also received three vials of Simmons's blood, which he turned over at the request of prosecuting attorney David Locke. According to a Forensic Sciences Official Report dated November 18, 1997, "Chemical examination of the panties and dress reveals the presence of seminal fluid." DNA tests performed on the semen taken from Jensen's panties and dress were compared to the DNA testing performed on Simmons's blood sample. The conclusion? "No more than 1 in 10 billion individuals in the Caucasian or black populations will exhibit the DNA banding pattern which is shared between Wayne Simmons and the semen stain(s) from the dress." The report went on to conclude: "With a reasonable scientific certainty, it can be concluded that the DNA obtained from the semen stain(s) from the dress which matches Wayne Simmons originated from him or his identical twin." Wayne Simmons does not have a twin.

At the direction of his lawyer, Simmons did not give a statement to police, nor did he submit to police questioning. However, his close friend Elliot Mitchell did. In his interview with authorities, Mitchell revealed that he asked Simmons whether he had intercourse with Jensen. According to Mitchell, Simmons replied, "No. I tried to but couldn't get it in. She jacked me off and gave me a blow job."

Mitchell told authorities that Simmons, after learning he had been accused of rape, later called him on the telephone and repeated his innocence. "No. I didn't rape her," Simmons said, according to Mitchell. "Do you see any scratches on me? And I sure didn't bruise her. Did anyone hear any screaming?" According to the investigative summary of Mitchell's interview, "Simmons also stated that he tried to put it in but couldn't because she was too small. He said he got on top a couple of times but couldn't get it in."

The police were originally left with a classic "he-said, she-said" scenario. Incidental facts were important to the investigation. Thus Simmons's insistence that he had difficulty penetrating Jensen supported Jensen's claim that she was a virgin, as did Dr. Pohl's finding that Jensen suffered a tear at the six o'clock position of the vagina, an injury that was also consistent with someone who had never engaged in intercourse previously. While none of this proves that Jensen was raped (she could have consented), her status as a virgin was crucial to how she might be perceived in front of a jury—so crucial that Simmons hired a private investigator to dig up evidence that she was not a virgin. He found none. In fact, there was no evidence that Jensen had any sexual history whatsoever.

Also informing the investigation was the location of the incident. It happened in a stairwell, as opposed to a hotel room, athlete dorm, or player's bedroom. Would a teenage girl who went through high school as a virgin agree to have sex for the first time in a dingy, debris-filled, concrete stairwell that stank of vomit? And once there, would she willfully lie bare back on the cement steps while a man twice her size and whom she had never met previously lay on top of her while trying repeatedly to penetrate her—tearing her vagina in the process?

As prosecutors assessed whether to bring this case to a grand jury to seek an indictment, Simmons had another factor working against him—his own history. A background check performed on him in South Carolina and in Georgia turned up the following allegations:

• On June 25, 1989, Simmons was arrested and incarcerated for assault and battery after striking a girl "because she was ignoring him." After the victim's mother learned of the incident, she drove her daughter over to Simmons's house to find out why he struck her daughter. "Simmons began to curse them and ordered them to leave his yard and at the same time shoved the victim with his hands," according to the report.

• On June 23, 1991, Simmons, according to a Clemson University police report, was cited for assault and battery after allegedly striking from behind a Domino's Pizza delivery man. Gao Xing, a foreign student attending Clemson and working part-time delivering pizzas, had to have his rights to safety and other freedoms explained to him by the police. He declined to press charges against Simmons.

• On September 17, 1992, Simmons was arrested on charges of assault and battery after striking a fellow student at Clemson. According to the police report, the student was approached on campus by Simmons, who was with a group of fifteen of his football teammates. "Wayne Simmons was in the middle of the group pointing at me and moving his hand as if he was acting out a person sucking a penis," she said in her police statement. "He had his hand in a circular fashion around his mouth moving it back and forth away and closer to his mouth. He continued doing this and laughing with the rest of his friends." The student alleged that when she confronted Simmons about his conduct, "He then took his hat off and his football friends started holding him as he was going to hit me. He then took his hat and smacked me in the face with it. . . . Then one of Wayne's friends said that I better leave before I get hurt." She told authorities that as she walked away, "I heard Wayne yelling, 'You sucked his dick, dick sucker. . . .' I heard him yell this continuously until I walked out of the door."

• On April 11, 1993, Simmons was charged with assault and battery after he and three friends tried to gain access to a South Carolina bar without paying the cover charge. When the doorman required payment, Simmons began shouting at the man that he was "white trash" and a "pussy." Spitting on other patrons who were entering the club, Simmons and his crew started screaming, "F---- this. We are going back in there to kick every white mother f---er's ass," according to the police reports. As they approached the door, some men who were in the parking lot stepped between Simmons's group and the doorman in an attempt to explain that no one wanted any trouble. Simmons, who had retrieved a pair of brass knuckles from underneath the seat of his car, jumped over the shoulder of one of his friends, striking in the face the man who was trying to prevent an incident. The blow dropped the man to the ground and, according to the police reports, left a "severe laceration" and a scar on the left side of the man's face and nose. Simmons and his group then ran to their car, squealing tires as they sped out of the parking lot.

• On March 11, 1996, Simmons was arrested for breach of peace and failing to stop for police. When police responded to a noise complaint coming from a house occupied by Simmons and another man, Simmons refused to answer the door. Finally, Simmons and his friend emerged from the residence, walked right past the police, and climbed into a vehicle to leave. While one officer approached the driver's side to order them to stop, the other officer stood behind the vehicle to prevent them from backing out. "But the subjects still disregarded him and continued to go in reverse toward him at an accelerated rate of speed," according to the police report. "Both myself and Sergeant Toman got in our vehicle and tried blue lighting the subjects to no avail."

[The dispositions of most of these cases were not obtainable from the public record.]

In early January of 1998, prosecutor David Locke took his case against Wayne Simmons to a grand jury, seeking to have Simmons indicted for kidnapping, rape, and sexual battery. If he were at the trial stage, Locke would have to convince jurors beyond a reasonable doubt that Simmons committed these crimes. But in order to persuade the grand jury to indict Simmons, Locke needed only to prove probable cause (more evidence for than against). And he had at his disposal all the police complaints previously filed against Simmons. "We generally would make a grand jury aware of it [previous criminal history]," said Locke in an exclusive interview for this book. "Arrest records can be properly brought before the grand jury."

The witness list of those scheduled to testify before the grand jury was short: Detective Y. Strahle, Susan Jensen, and Elliot Mitchell. Grand jurors also had access to video-taped copies of numerous police interviews with individuals connected to the case.

Jensen was the star witness. An attractive, petite girl, she told eighteen grand jurors what happened in a stairwell at The Zoo. Her status as a virgin on the night of the incident went unchallenged. And on January 7, 1998, the grand jury reached its decision on whether there was probable cause to indict Simmons. "NO," wrote jury foreperson Errol F. Rhett on the form.

Why not?

"I think it basically had to do with the victim's credibility," said Locke in an exclusive interview. "The victim's statement conflicted with most of the other witnesses about what happened immediately prior to the sexual attack."

According to police reports, The Zoo's owner, and Simmons's friend, George Murphy, told investigators that when they were all at The Rave, Jensen said "she would 'f--- Wayne for two million dollars.'" He also told police that "the girl was all over Wayne, especially on the ride back from The Rave. . . ."

While her friend Emily disputed that Jensen was "all over" Simmons in the car, she did confirm that Jensen told her she wanted to sleep with Simmons.

Emily thought the comment was a joke, but Cyndy Johnson's boyfriend told authorities that he witnessed "Susan telling Wayne, 'I want to f--- your brains out.'" He said that he saw Jensen "sitting on a sofa with Simmons and she was touching all over him." Even Cyndy claimed that she, too, heard Jensen say that she would "f--- Simmons for two million dollars." Worse yet, more than one witness vaguely questioned Jensen's general credibility.

Jensen vehemently denied these charges, both to investigators and to the grand jury. "I'm not saying she wasn't telling the truth," said Locke. "It's just that it would be hard to get twelve jurors to convict the defendant of rape, knowing the trial standard is 'beyond a reasonable doubt.' It gets to whether you believe the victim consented to it or not. It is different from Joe Q. Citizen because the interaction between the victim and the football player was controlled by the fact that he was a football player. And some of the things that she is alleged to have said have to do with the fact that he was a football player. A lot of the victim's actions could be tainted by the fact of his status."

Locke offered a second, more technical explanation for why the grand jury may have declined to indict Simmons. The physical evidence didn't prove that Simmons actually penetrated Jensen's vagina with his penis (which is required to prove rape). Further, no semen was found inside her vagina. "The physical evidence supports that there was some penetration," said Locke. "But it also supports Simmons's story to his friend [Mitchell] that he couldn't enter. The sperm was found on her panties, not inside her. I'm not saying that he didn't penetrate her, I'm just saying that some of that story is supported by the physical evidence."

At the time this book went to press, Susan Jensen had made no attempt to sue Wayne Simmons or elicit a financial settlement from him. Nor has she attempted to sell her story for pay. In fact, she never as much as told her story to anyone, other than the doctor at the hospital, the authorities, and eighteen grand jurors. Still, apparently it was her credibility that could not pass the test.

In Kansas City, Simmons played a crucial role in the

Chiefs' defense as the team went on to post the AFC's best record in 1997. Although Simmons declined to be interviewed for this book, his business manager, Tom Gardo, spoke to the authors about the rape allegations.

"Wayne had a DUI and in college he got into a couple of fights," said Gardo. "But that's it. This particular crime [the rape allegation], he was exonerated. He ended up having a situation. He knows better than to get himself in a situation where he would be lured into a compromising position with a female in a place like that [The Zoo] when both of them have been drinking.

"But he's not any different than a lot of the other guys. He's a highly emotional kind of person, like a lot of ballplayers. You don't become a professional football player without a high level of testosterone running through your body."

When the authors called, Chiefs President Carl Peterson declined to discuss what he knew of Simmons's past. Team spokesman Jim Carr went one step further, taking the unusual step of denying the authors access to the publicly available team photographs of Simmons and Barnett. "I'm a PR guy," Carr told the authors. "Why would I want to help you put our guys in a negative light? I don't see any good for the Chiefs that can come out of telling these stories."

4

Born Again

People hate to say it, but what you are around is what you're going to be. At 13 years old and you're around crime, you're going to be a criminal.

New York Jets wide receiver Keyshawn Johnson, who served time in a youth detention center in California before attending the University of Southern California on a football scholarship.

Although the authors did not treat NFL spokesperson Greg Aiello's reference to "half of our players" being criminals as any sort of actual confession on his part, it is nonetheless true that the NFL has a much greater handle on the scope of its players' criminal histories than anyone else does. Consider that despite all of the crimes reported in Chapter 1, the authors did not have access to crimes committed by NFL players in their juvenile years—the fastest growing age group category for violent crime in America. It is virtually impossible to determine how many NFL players have serious juvenile criminal records. Few states collect reliable juvenile crime statistics, and even fewer states make juveniles' criminal histories a matter of public record. "Public access laws governing juvenile records will prevent you from finding out the number of NFL players who have criminal records as juveniles," explained Linda Szymanski, director of legal research at the National Center for Juvenile Justice. As a result, it is very difficult for reporters or researchers to estimate, much less pinpoint with accuracy, the number of NFL players who were involved in serious crime as teens.

Who holds the key to this information? The NFL. Equipped with resources that would rival those of any law enforcement agency, and in a position as a prospective employer to access otherwise privileged information, NFL security surely must learn not only which players coming into the league are criminals, but when, where, why, and how the crime was committed.

"The league does a lot of background work," Minnesota Vikings President and NFL Properties Chairman Roger Headrick explained in an exclusive interview. "We can go back to age twelve in the city where they have gone to school and get their criminal record. Occasionally you'll be able to get some records of things like substance abuse. That is transmitted through the medical side to the individual teams. So we know who is a drug-related risk. We also try to find out if they are related to any gang background. That is sometimes harder to find out, but you can check into where they lived, what kinds of cities they came from, particularly inner cities."

All of this information is funneled down to the individual teams, who themselves conduct further investigation, primarily in the form of interviews with probation officers and others personally familiar with those few players whom teams are most interested in drafting.

Since neither the NFL nor the individual teams are itching to reveal the extent of the criminal behavior they discover in predraft investigations, the authors asked player agent Leigh Steinberg if there were any criminal offenses that would altogether bar a player from playing in the NFL. "Murder," he replied, before qualifying his answer. "But even then there may be exceptions. You have to look at each case individually."

He wasn't kidding.

The authors compiled a list of nineteen players who played during the 1996–97 season and who grew up and attended high school in the Los Angeles area. They are: Karim Abdul-Jabbar (Dolphins), Chad Brown (Seahawks), Joe Cain (Seahawks), Curtis Conway (Bears), Aaron Craver (Chargers), Rick Cunningham (Raiders), Bernard Dafney (Steelers), Mark Fields (Saints), Deon Figures (Jaguars), Darick Holmes (Bills), Charles Jordan (Dolphins), Lamar Lyons (Raiders), Willie McGinest (Patriots), Mark McMillian (Saints), Anthony Miller (Cowboys), Chris Mims (Chargers), Charles Mincy (Buccaneers), Johnny Morton (Lions), and Marcus Robertson (Oilers).

Although all of these players have either more than five years' experience in the league or have been starters, most fans will only recognize a few of these names. Players like Lawrence Phillips and Keyshawn Johnson, both of whom also grew up and attended high school in Los Angeles, were purposely left off the list. Their histories have been well documented elsewhere, and the purpose here was to examine players who, while playing key roles, have not had their backgrounds scrutinized in the press.

The authors then turned the list over to a Los Angeles-based firm which specializes in doing legal research for law firms and private companies. Vickie Francies-Siedow, president of the firm, ran the names through a computerized criminal index that accesses all thirty-four municipal courts in Los Angeles County, as well as the Los Angeles County Superior Court. Of the nineteen players whose criminal histories were checked, seven showed up in the index as having been indicted: Mark Fields (DUI), Charles Jordan (murder, controlled substance—two times, false imprisonment, gambling, drugs, robbery, dissuading a witness through force or threat, auto theft), Darick Holmes (grand theft property), Bernard Dafney (forgery), Chad Brown (felony controlled substance), Joe Cain (prostitution), and Aaron Craver (forgery, grand theft auto, grand theft, making false financial statements, auto theft).

As startling as this list is, the most celebrated player on the nineteen-player list, Patriots star linebacker Willie McGinest, didn't show up on the extensive computerized search of court records.

While attending USC on a football scholarship, McGinest, who grew up in Pasadena, was accused along with two teammates of dragging a twenty-three-year-old graduate student into a dormitory room and sexually molesting her. The 1991 trial, which resulted in all three players being acquitted, received daily press coverage in the *Los Angeles Times*. Yet no record of McGinest ever having been charged with a crime showed up on the court's computerized records.

Francies-Siedow later discovered the case while searching, with the assistance of a court records clerk, through files that had been archived. "It's conceivable that we are only scratching the surface when turning up these cases involving NFL players," explained Francies-Siedow. "If you're a criminal in L.A., and clearly some of these players were, there's a good chance that there's little record of it if the case is more than five years old. There are simply too many crimes and too little storage space for keeping old records at the courthouses. So a lot of records are purged after five years. The rest is put on microfiche and those records are incomplete and sparse at best."

In an attempt to see just how far teams will go to overlook a player's juvenile criminal record, the authors went north to Seattle. Since Washington state law allows public access to juvenile criminal case files, the authors selected Seattle native Corey Dillon, a second-round draft choice in 1997 and the AFC Rookie of the Year, as a case study. Our discoveries convinced us that if the Corey Dillon case is any indication: 1) the popular press is barely scratching the surface in reporting on the criminal backgrounds of players who are entering the NFL, and 2) NFL teams are severely minimizing the prior bad acts of players when explaining their draft choices to the press and the fans.

Cinergy Field, Cincinnati, Ohio, December 4, 1997

"Corey . . . Corey . . . Corey," 49,000 Bengals fans cheered with two minutes remaining and Cincinnati leading the Oilers, 41-14. Boomer Esiason handed the ball off to rookie running back Corey Dillon, who plowed for ten yards, breaking Jim Brown's 1957 rookie record for yards rushed in a game. Most fans watching the game on TNT had never heard of Corey Dillon. Few would forget how he rumbled over the Oilers' third-ranked defense for 246 yards on thirty-nine carries and scored four touchdowns, breaking or tying six Bengals team records.

While Dillon's "coming out" performance dazzled those who witnessed it, the Bengals' brass were well aware of their rookie back's capabilities. In Dillon's only season of Division I-A football at the University of Washington, he broke school records in rushing yards (1,555), carries (271), touchdowns (23), all-purpose yards (2,185), and scoring (138 points)—*and he started only eight games.*

Knowing this, Cincinnati almost took him in the first round. When he was still on the board when their second-round pick came up, Bengals management knew they had a steal. Originally slated to back up Ki-Jana Carter, the first pick overall in the 1995 draft, Dillon had earned the starting position halfway through his rookie season. He finished the year with 1,129 yards rushing on 233 carries and scored ten touchdowns. Impressive statistics by anyone's standards, Dillon's numbers were largely compiled in the second half of the year. After carrying the ball only forty times through the first eight regular-season games, Dillon piled up 933 rushing yards in his final eight starts.

NFL scouts who saw Dillon run at the University of Washington had little doubt that he was a big-time player. With such remarkable potential, the question was how such a gifted runner was still available at the forty-third pick. Answer: he had a long and distinguished criminal record.

Given that Lawrence Phillips was picked sixth overall despite a far more notorious criminal background, there's obviously more to the story, however. Especially since Dillon's past transgressions, unlike Phillips's, were hardly known to the press.

While a prior history of crime will not prevent a player from getting drafted, certain types of offenses more than others may affect *where* in the draft a player is picked. Such was the case with Phillips and Dillon.

While in college, Phillips had pleaded guilty to assaulting

his ex-girlfriend. Savage as the beating was, Phillips went high. Coaches seemingly don't view domestic violence as a distraction to a player's on-field performance. And in their own way of thinking, they're right. To date, there is no evidence that guys who beat their wives or girlfriends are any less capable of showing up on Sunday and beating their opponents.

On the other hand, Dillon, whose record also includes a conviction for a violent incident involving an ex-girlfriend and a conviction for assaulting a woman, was linked to something that the NFL views as a far greater threat to its commercial reputation—drug dealing.

During Dillon's only season at the University of Washington, *Seattle Times* writer Percy Allen reported that Dillon got into "fights and mischief" as a juvenile, hardly the kind of thing that would scare off NFL teams. Allen's article, nevertheless, also revealed that Dillon "once was arrested for selling narcotics." However, the report did not specify what type of narcotics, nor did it indicate whether Dillon was ever convicted.

After the Bengals selected Dillon, Allen's article spurred Cincinnati reporters to question the team about Dillon's past. "He did have the juvenile record," Bengals first-year special teams coach Al Roberts told the *Cincinnati Post*. "He did not sell crack cocaine. That is poor information."

Roberts should know. Another Seattle native, Roberts was Dillon's running backs coach at the University of Washington. Further, his son played against Dillon in high school. "I assumed the role of a surrogate father to Corey at Washington," said Roberts in an exclusive interview. "I took him under my wing. Corey came in nice and soft, and he took me on as a dear friend or father figure. And he needed help and I needed to help him."

Within a week of Dillon announcing after his junior season that he was leaving school to enter the draft, Roberts likewise announced he was leaving the team. A seasoned NFL assistant coach who, prior to his brief stint with the Huskies, had coached in Philadelphia, Houston, Phoenix, and New York, Roberts accepted an offer from Bengals head coach Bruce Coslet to coach Cincinnati's special teams. Roberts had previously coached under Coslet with the Jets.

Once on staff, it was Roberts who convinced the Bengals to use their second-round pick on Dillon. "I did not think Corey would be available in the second round because he's a big-time running back," Roberts explained. "When our pick came up at forty-three, [Bengals team president] Mike Brown looked at me and I said, 'Take him.' He said, 'What do you think?' I said, 'Take him.' We discussed all the other problems, I said, 'Mike, *take him.*' And we took him. I didn't think Mike was going to do what he did. He just handed it over and said, 'Dillon. Washington.'"

A respected coach with an uncanny interest in the off-the-field well-being of his players, Roberts took the lead role in downplaying to the Cincinnati press corps some of the charges levied against Dillon in the *Seattle Times* article.

"I asked Roberts about the troubles Dillon had in the past," explained *Cincinnati Post* writer Todd Archer in an interview for this book. "But Dillon had denied any of the drug stuff, and we didn't push it too far."

After both Roberts and Dillon refuted the *Seattle Times* story, Archer, like the rest of the Cincinnati press, reported that Dillon's past included "juvenile offenses." Archer also wrote that, "Dillon told the *Times* he did not sell drugs."

So let's get this straight: a Seattle writer reports a drug case in Dillon's past; the Cincinnati writers catch wind of this and confront the Bengals about the report; and the Bengals go on record denying the charge. Simple enough. Case closed.

Not so fast. In the same article where Roberts was quoted denying the drug charge, Archer also quoted him as saying: "When you look at Corey Dillon and the Bengals, this fits. Cincinnati is great for him. I'm glad he's here and not in L.A., Chicago, or New York. When a young kid is trying to be born again, this is a great place to be."

Sounds like Roberts knew a little more about Dillon than he was telling the Bengals' beat writers.

As it turns out, he did. Not only did Roberts have extensive firsthand knowledge of Dillon from college and high school, but Bengals running backs coach Jim Anderson had traveled to Seattle before the draft and conducted his own thorough investigation into Dillon's past. "Jim Anderson knew all there was to know about Corey Dillon," explained Roberts in an interview for this book. "He had done all the reporting on all his behavior on field and off the field. Jim Anderson had gone to the 'hood of Seattle to find out about him. So he knew all the information that I had known. He got records from the high school. He went to the police stations. Some things he couldn't get ahold of because Corey was under age at the time. But he talked to the kids around the neighborhood.

"And Jim's report was that there were some early childhood things, but that all the other people hadn't had any hassles with him. So Jim was more than willing to draft him. His exact words were, 'He's the real deal physically and we should take a chance on him.' This kid was an okay kid. And it's not taking that big of a chance because the kid hadn't gotten in any trouble lately. I mean, he had little ruffles on the edge and he needed some smoothing out like all kids do, but he hadn't got into any of that drug-related stuff lately."

Lately?

In an attempt to learn what the Bengals knew but weren't saying, the authors spent a week in Seattle interviewing law enforcement officials, court officers, and criminal records managers. Most of the time, however, was spent culling through files and digging through archives at four courthouses (the City of Seattle Municipal Court, the Seattle District Court, the Seattle Superior Court, and the King County Juvenile Court).

At the municipal court, which handles misdemeanors and traffic violations committed within the city itself, a records supervisor confirmed that Dillon had five cases on file, three of which were driving offenses. The files for the two non-traffic cases included a May 21, 1994, charge in a four-count case that included reckless endangerment and resisting arrest (both of which were dropped as part of a plea bargain), assault (which he pleaded guilty to and was issued a "no contact order" against the victim), and obstructing a public officer, to which he pleaded guilty. The file also included a June 13, 1994, charge of theft. The case was later dismissed on condition that Dillon refrain from further violating the law.

The district court, which handles all misdemeanors committed in King County (other than those committed within the city proper) contained no records on Corey Dillon.

The superior court, which handles all felonies committed in King County, had one case on file against Dillon. On September 21, 1992, he was indicted for second-degree malicious mischief. Michelle Reed, a former girlfriend of Dillon's, reported to police that on June 8, 1992, Dillon confronted her and some friends after she drove into an AM/PM gas station to fill up just after midnight. According to a letter Reed wrote to the court dated June 9, 1992, Dillon came up to her car and began berating Reed and her girlfriends who were in her car. Referring to them as "bitches," Dillon started an argument with Reed. When she called him "bitch" back, Dillon opened the driver's side door and threatened her.

"What, what," he said, challenging her.

"I didn't ever say anything," Reed replied in fear.

"Yeah, that's what I thought."

Dillon then vandalized the car while the girls were inside it. More than $700 damage was done before Dillon stopped and threatened to throw a rock at them.

The charge was ultimately reduced to third-degree felony malicious mischief and Dillon was sentenced to perform community service, undergo counseling, attend anger management classes, and pay restitution to his ex-girlfriend's mother, the owner of the car.

Despite our discovering that Dillon had numerous misdemeanor cases and a felony case on his record, none of the three Seattle courts turned up any evidence that Dillon was ever involved in an illegal drug transaction. However, juvenile offenses are generally not kept in any of the three adult court databanks. In a meeting with a records clerk at the juvenile court, the authors discovered that for up to six years after a juvenile becomes adult, any information on file pertaining to juvenile crimes was public record—if one wanted to take the time to look through reels of microfiche.

A computer search of the juvenile court database proved that the Bengals were right about one thing: Dillon "did have a juvenile record." That was putting it mildly. His name showed up in the system eleven times between 1987 and 1992.

But claims that the *Seattle Times* report on Dillon's drug arrest "was bad information" turned out to be *bad information*. Not only was Dillon charged with a felony for selling drugs as a juvenile, he was convicted—and that was just the beginning. Below is a sampling of the entries as they appeared in Dillon's juvenile case file:

December 7, 1987, indicted on the charge of possessing stolen property.

December 5, 1988, indicted on the charge of theft in the third degree.

February 13, 1989, indicted on the charge of violating the uniform controlled substance act (selling drugs to an undercover cop).

April 21, 1989, indicted on a charge of fourth-degree assault.

January 11, 1990, indicted on charges of reckless endangerment by "recklessly engag[ing] in conduct which did create a substantial risk of death or serious physical injury to another person," and obstructing a public servant.

July 31, 1990, indicted on charges of obstructing a public servant and resisting arrest.

March 23, 1992, indicted on two counts of assault in the fourth degree and one count of criminal trespass in the fourth degree.

June 6, 1992, indicted on a charge of malicious mischief in the third degree.

The outcomes of most of these cases are detailed below.

According to the indictment contained on reel No. S8236, Dillon "on or about 11 February 1989, unlawfully and feloniously did have in his possession with intent to manufacture or deliver a certain controlled substance, and a narcotic drug, to-wit: cocaine." Court records confirm the following:

On the evening of February 11, 1989, Officer Paul Leung, an undercover cop on the Seattle police force, set himself up in the downtown area and attempted to purchase drugs. At approximately 9:30 P.M., he was approached by Corey Dillon and two other males. In exchange for cash, the three gave Officer Leung a small brown envelope containing a rock of cocaine.

At approximately 9:35 P.M., uniformed officers Ed Maser and D. Tichi, who were working in concert with Leung, arrested Dillon and the two men. In frisking the men, the officers discovered three additional rocks of cocaine in one of the other young men's underwear.

On January 19, 1990, Dillon, who was fourteen years old at the time, was ordered by the court to serve ten days' detention, undergo nine months of state supervision, perform forty hours of community service, and have no use or possession of drugs or alcohol. Dillon's juvenile status saved him. Had he been an adult at the time of his arrest, he would have been facing twenty-one to twenty-seven months in state prison.

Dillon's agent, Marvin Demoff, declined to return repeated calls made by the authors in an attempt to interview Dillon for this book.

* * *

Despite the seriousness of Dillon's felony drug case, this was hardly the most dangerous offense he had committed. Court records reveal a series of violent altercations with law enforcement authorities over a four-year period that culminated in a 1994 incident that nearly spilled over into a riot.

First, on March 30, 1990, Dillon pleaded guilty to obstructing a police officer. The plea stemmed from an incident on January 11, 1990, in which Dillon chased a man and threatened to beat him with a large stick. He was charged with creating "a substantial risk of death and serious physical injury." When Seattle police officer C. Bonner intervened, Dillon "hinder[ed] and ostruct[ed]" her from performing her duties. The government agreed to drop the charges against Dillon for reckless endangerment in exchange for his plea of guilty regarding his conduct toward the police officer.

Then on November 16, 1990, the court convicted Dillon of obstructing a police officer and resisting arrest. This incident occurred on July 31, 1990, when Dillon fought three Seattle police officers to prevent them from arresting him.

After investigating Dillon's juvenile criminal history, the authors went to Cincinnati coach Al Roberts and asked him: "How would you describe Dillon's juvenile record?" His response was: "Corey is a follower. As a kid he was always with the guys, but he never did it himself. He would be there and be around it, but he wouldn't do it. . . . All the little distinctive things that Corey was supposed to have done, I'm sure he was in the area. Did he actually put his hands in it? I'm going to say no. Was he around it? Yes."

Granted, Dillon ran with a pretty tough crowd (more on them later), but the record hardly squares with Roberts's

portrayal of Dillon essentially being guilty only by association. Further, Dillon's conduct didn't change when he
reached legal age.

On May 21, 1994, at approximately 1:00 A.M., Seattle police received a telephone call from Pier 57, a popular tourist
spot along the Seattle waterfront. Pier 57 manager John E.
Nelson requested help controlling a party that had drawn far
more visitors than the restaurant could hold. The Multi-
Greek Council from the University of Washington had
booked a party at one of the Pier's establishments from
10:00 P.M. until 1:30 A.M. The door counters stopped counting at 432, and Nelson estimated to police that at least 600
people were inside, far exceeding fire safety regulations.

Due to the Pier's location on Alaskan Way (the main thor-
oughfare running through the waterfront district of downtown Seattle) and the fact that upward of 600 people would
be turned out into the streets all at once, Seattle police responded by sending foot patrolmen, as well as officers who
were on bicycles and in patrol cars. In all seventeen officers
and three sergeants showed up. The Alaskan Way was temporarily closed down in both directions, as were the major
streets coming in and out of the waterfront area. With traffic
at a standstill, the police shut down the party and cleared the
building.

In their attempt to safely move a large alcohol-enhanced,
somewhat rowdy crowd safely out of the Pier 57 restaurant
and across the busy streets, officers witnessed a violent incident flare up on a sidewalk and spill into the street. In the
plain view of four Seattle police officers, Corey Dillon, then
a nineteen-year-old adult standing six foot two and weigh-
ing 200 pounds, punched a woman in the face. The blow

dropped the woman to the ground, at the feet of the pressing crowd.

While officers intervened to aid the woman, Dillon escaped by pushing his way into the sea of people. The crowd was so hostile toward the woman whom Dillon had assaulted that police had to form a human shield around her.

Suddenly, Dillon bolted back out of the crowd and broke through the police barricade in an attempt to further attack the woman. As four officers tried arresting Dillon, he turned on them. Dillon's aggression easily incited his friends in the crowd, who quickly surrounded the officers. One officer, who was trying to handcuff Dillon, was assaulted by one of Dillon's close friends. Shaking off the friend's blow and attempting again to handcuff Dillon, the officer was again struck by the friend, this time in the chest.

With Dillon and his group physically challenging the police and a crowd gathering in the middle of the main street, police sensed that the scene was on the verge of being completely out of their control. Officers responded by spraying aerosol pepper spray at Dillon and his friend. The pepper spray momentarily subdued the friend, but it only enraged Dillon, whose strength proved too much for the four officers trying to pin him down. Ultimately, six officers were required to physically restrain Dillon, apply handcuffs, and get him in the back of a police cruiser.

On July 11, 1994, Dillon pleaded guilty to assault and obstruction.

"He used to have a chip on his shoulder toward authority," explained coach Al Roberts. "Corey walked around with that chip when he was younger. And did he like to fight? Yeah. He's a big strong kid. Somebody would start a fight and Corey would finish it. And when people asked,

'Who did it?' people would say, 'Corey Dillon.' Because when you're talking about 'hoods, you are going to see Corey. He's a massive man and he walks with pride. Look at what he did on the field in his first year with the Bengals. Imagine him walking around the 'hood doing this."

On at least three occasions, Dillon's so-called fights were with *police officers*. Nonetheless, Roberts insists that Dillon's animosity toward authority dwindled after he started playing for the Huskies. "When he got to the University of Washington, some of that chip fell off his shoulder because he was exposed to more young kids and started going to parties where the good kids were," Roberts explained. "Not that his old buddies were bangers, they just weren't graceful. Suddenly, he was hanging around with people who have more grace about them."

Yet with his childhood neighborhood just minutes from the Washington campus, Dillon did not stop hanging around with his old friends from the 'hood. "I'm not going to change who I am," Dillon said in an interview while attending Washington. "If you were cool with me before, you're cool with me now."

One evening, Dillon's friends from the 'hood clashed with his new friends on campus, namely fellow scholarship football players. According to Roberts, one evening in the fall of 1996, a bunch of football players and women were partying on campus. Dillon invited some of his friends to attend. One of Dillon's friends, whose girlfriend was supposed to meet him at the party, arrived late. Upon entering the party, he discovered his girlfriend dancing with one of the football players.

"The guy [Dillon's friend] comes in and sees his girlfriend bumping with one of the ballplayers," Roberts explained. "He pulls out a gun and fires it. The athletes jumped out of a two-story building to get away from the gunfire."

Wonder if the "good kids" at the college party would describe Dillon's friends as "bangers" or merely "less graceful"?

In any event, Washington's star running back Rashaan Shehee sustained a season-ending injury to his foot when he landed awkwardly after jumping out of the second-story window. As a result, Dillon took over the starting position. Hey, what are friends for?

Given Dillon's extensive juvenile record, the obvious question is: How did he qualify for an athletic scholarship to Washington in the first place? The root of this answer stems back to his 1994 conviction in the incident where he assaulted a woman and then turned on police officers outside the Seattle waterfront restaurant. Facing up to 365 days in jail and a $5,000 fine, Dillon was spared jail time by the court due largely to his opportunity to attend college and play football at Garden City Community College in Kansas in the fall of 1994.

When deciding on a criminal sentence, it is not unusual for courts to take into account a young offender's proven intention to attend college. Why? Criminal justice research suggests that persons who go to college are less likely to be arrested as adults. Many juveniles who end up in the criminal justice system either don't have the chance or the desire to go to college. For those who do, judges will often tailor sentences to accommodate the individual's effort to gain an education. Community service, for example, can be performed in the state where the prospective college is located, which is exactly what happened in Dillon's case.

This courtesy, while helpful in supporting those whose primary objective is to obtain a college degree, is exploited in some instances by college football players and their coaches. First, football-friendly adults are often assigned to monitor a convicted player's community service, and then vouch for his completion of the terms with the court back in the state where the crime was committed. Consider the following letter written by F. James Gush, Dillon's academic advisor at Garden City Community College, to a Seattle probation officer on July 19, 1995:

"This letter is to serve as verification for community service that Corey Dillon performed during the 1994-95 school year at Garden City Community College.

1. Buddy day: Worked with area youngsters on football skills. (3 hrs.)
2. Project Read: Visited an area elementary school and read to the school children. (8 hrs.)
3. Senior Citizen's Banquet: Along with other team members, served food at the Senior Citizen's banquet and later attended the Senior Citizen's dance.
4. Career Day: Participated (as a college football student-athlete) in a career day seminar at a local junior high school. (4 hrs.)
5. Served as a volunteer referee for college intramural basketball games. (30 hrs.)
6. Participated in the college work-study program as an office assistant. (120 hrs.)"

Welcome to Criminal Justice 101—football star style. It's hard to imagine other convicted criminals receiving a sentence that involved refereeing intramural basketball games or being used as a role model to talk to schoolchildren about career choices. Ironically, in Washington state, Dillon had been barred from stepping on the grounds of the school next door to his home after he was arrested for barging into the school one afternoon with his loose-knit gang of friends and assaulting two students on March 23, 1992.

All of this combines to convince players like Dillon long before they reach the NFL that the rules are different for them.

As far as the courts' belief that imposing flexible sentences will allow convicted student-athletes like Dillon to earn a degree, that too is a farce in most instances. Often, the goal of making it to the NFL is not compatible with graduating from college. According to the National College Athletic Association's most recent statistics, only 52 percent of Division I-A scholarship football players graduate from college. Dillon is a prime example. After two seasons at separate junior colleges (Garden City Community College in Kansas and Dixie College in Utah) and just one season at Washington, he withdrew from school and declared himself eligible for the NFL draft.

And if he gets in trouble with the law again? "If the market calls for spending $5 million on a running back, and he steps on us by going out and smoking dope and gets caught, we punish them and give them another chance," Roberts explained. "When you take chances on these guys, sometimes you get hit in the mouth. Jim Anderson [Bengals running backs coach] has gotten hit in the mouth a lot of times. Check the history of the Bengals' running backs prior to Corey Dillon." Previous Bengals running backs who ran into trouble with the law included Ickey Woods, Larry Kinnebrew, Stanley Wilson, Derrick Fenner, and Jeff Cothran.

"Yet the first thing Jim did was stand up for Corey and say, 'Let's take this chance again.' "

The authors asked Roberts if there was a risk involved in drafting players with histories like Dillon's and paying them millions of dollars to play professional football. His answer came with one condition: "I'll tell you if you print this correctly."

Fair enough.

"I'm an adult," Roberts began. "When I was a kid I wanted adults to take a chance on me when I messed up. At twenty-four I was not the most graceful person in the world. At fifty-four I can tell you that I have some grace about me. So I turn around and take chances on young kids. As adults, we should take chances on kids, or this same kid is going to grow up and be foul. Then the same adults who stuck their feet out there and held that kid down instead of putting their hand out there and helping him up will say, 'Well, look at this degenerate generation.' As adults, we have to put that carrot out there and say, 'This is what you do, and this is not what you do.' "

The carrot here is a million-dollar salary, hero status, and the chance to play a boys' game for a living. Not bad for a guy who has a serious criminal record, no college degree, and no professional training to speak of. Yet it's tough to dispute Roberts's philosophy. The NFL, unlike any other business of equal reputation, is offering an opportunity to young kids who, in some cases, would otherwise be castoffs in society, written off as criminal teens who will one day end up behind bars for life. Some players, as a result of that opportunity, never again have contact with the criminal justice system.

"In prison the message is 'no, no, no, no,' " said Roberts.

"We, as adults in society, can't put that kind of concrete approach on a twenty-two-year-old. We have to give him chances, and go back and forth and teach them what to do. And although we see guys out there socking coaches and smoking joints, some kids are being saved by the system of professional athletics."

Will Corey Dillon be saved by professional athletics?

Early indications looked promising. Dillon completed his one season at Washington and his rookie season in Cincinnati without a single incident involving the law. On January 15, 1998, he was named AFC Rookie of the Year.

However, on March 3, 1998, while back home in Seattle, he was arrested for driving under the influence and driving on a suspended license. According to the police report, Dillon was "very hostile and uncooperative. He was yelling and would not comply with our requests for information." Hours after being released from the same county jail in which he had spent time as a juvenile, Dillon insisted, "I was harassed, the whole nine yards."

On June 3, 1998, Dillon pleaded guilty to negligent driving and was sentenced to 90 days in jail with 89 days dismissed. He was also placed on probation for two years and ordered to attend a drunk driving victims panel.

5

Arrested Development

At the end of January of 1998, three weeks after Baltimore Ravens running back Bam Morris was carted off to a Texas state prison to serve a ninety-day sentence for violating his probation in a felony drug conviction, Ravens owner Art Modell decided to cut him from the roster. "He became a major distraction for the team," Modell told the *New York Times,* "and a major distraction to the city of Baltimore." When asked why an athlete like Morris, who seemingly had everything, would throw it away, Modell replied, "I just think that, sadly, he did not display sufficient responsibility in his everyday life. I think he always thought people would take care of him."

Modell failed to mention his role in contributing to Morris's belief that "people would take care of him." Modell also didn't mention his team's role in Bam Morris's probation violation. The authors obtained a sworn affidavit signed by Art Modell on October 9, 1997, the same day Texas authorities secured a warrant to arrest Morris for failing to attend mandated meetings with his probation officer. In the affidavit, which was sent to Rockwall County prosecuting attorney Ray Sumrow, Modell stated under oath, "On or about August 21, 1997, Mr. Morris was required to be in Baltimore in regard to his employment. Given the complex nature of Mr. Morris's position on the club, it was vital that Mr. Morris not miss any time from work from July 15 through August 31. Therefore, he could not leave Baltimore to attend a probation meeting in Texas."

Knowing full well that Morris was at risk of going to prison for missing appointments with the probation department, the Ravens apparently saw his presence at training camp as being more important than his appointments with the probation department. Worse, this was while Morris was under league suspension for failing a urine test and therefore unable to play in the first four games of the season anyway. Sumrow was stunned by Modell's admission that football practice had caused Morris to violate probation. "And here's the reason why he missed appointments, I wouldn't let him go. The hell with your probation," Sumrow said, summarizing his opinion of Modell's view. "It signifies how they look at reality. The NFL has this same attitude, 'We're the NFL. Who the hell do you think you are, trying to take us on?' Talk about brazen." Prior to receiving Modell's affidavit, Sumrow had requested results of Morris's failed urine test, but the NFL refused, insisting the results were privileged information since they are part of a voluntary substance abuse program and they were barred from releasing the results by the players' collective bargaining agreement.

"What other company or reputable business would attempt to block the state from verifying that one of its employees may have violated the terms of his probation in a felony case?" Sumrow asked. "Experience has shown me that we have never had this problem with another company. The NFL is trying to hide behind a rule that was not intended to act as a shield for persons who have violated terms or conditions of probation. The NFL is big business. That's all it is, it's just a business. They want to protect their interests as much as possible. But their interest in making money and my interest in seeing that the government is effective are certainly different."

These never-before-reported aspects of the Bam Morris case are but two in a series of events that made his arrest far more than just another simple case of a highly successful athlete being caught with a few pounds of drugs in his car.

When the final gun sounded at Sun Devil Stadium in Tempe, Arizona, on January 28, 1996, the scoreboard read: Dallas 27, Pittsburgh 17. All that remained was for Commissioner Paul Tagliabue to award the Super Bowl hardware to Cowboys owner Jerry Jones and head coach Barry Switzer.

Amidst the euphoria, an NFL Films crew huddled around Cowboys star running back Emmitt Smith as he walked triumphantly off the field, his family in tow. He had just led the team to its third Super Bowl victory in four years. But long before the game was played, Emmitt had agreed to appear in the annual postgame Walt Disney commercial.

"Emmitt Smith, you just won the Super Bowl. What are you and your family going to do now?" the famous voice asked.

"We're going to Disneyland," Smith responded with a scripted line, the brim of his new championship hat already drenched in sweat.

This was Smith's second appearance in the Disney ad. NFL players began appearing in the "I'm going to Disneyland" commercials in 1988. Smith, along with Steve Young, Troy Aikman, Jerry Rice, and Joe Montana, represented the select few who have been featured in the ads after careful consideration by Disney. There is a general misconception that the Disney ads automatically feature the Super Bowl MVP. Not so. In addition to representing the NFL's talent elite, each player must pass a scrupulous litmus test screening out all but the most articulate, noncontroversial players with public appeal. Smith and the others represent the NFL's rare blend of superstar talent and model citizenry.

But while Emmitt Smith went off to Disneyland, his Super Bowl counterpart, Steelers running back Bam Morris, left for the Gulf of Mexico's South Padre Island, a resort town twelve miles offshore from one of the hottest drug-trafficking spots on the Texas-Mexico border. Drug enforcement officials estimate that 75 percent of the marijuana, along with a substantial amount of the cocaine and heroin, entering the U.S. passes through Texas. With local law enforcement powerless to stop well-connected Mexican drug cartels from using their small border towns as distribution houses for massive quantities of drugs, the federal government, through the U.S. Drug Enforcement Administration, beefed up its presence on the border. As a result, towns within driving distance of Padre Island sometimes resemble occupation zones where local farmers and ranchers tote automatic weapons and Border Patrolmen wear bulletproof vests.

Weeks after playing in the biggest game of his life, Morris chose to vacation at ground zero of America's war on drugs. Unlike Emmitt's, this was one trip that was sure not to be featured in NFL Films.

Records from South Padre Island's Radisson Resort verify that Morris and his boyhood friend Rodney Reynolds checked in on March 17. According to phone records, fifty-eight phone calls were placed from Morris's room during their four-day stay. Many of the calls were placed repeatedly to the same telephone numbers. Criminal background checks performed on the individuals to whom those phones were registered revealed that six of them were convicted felons, most for drug-related offenses.

One of the individuals whom Morris was calling had recently been released from prison after serving time for possession with intent to distribute four tons of marijuana.

A second phone pal had been arrested by federal authorities in Corpus Christi for intent to distribute forty-five kilos of marijuana and had recently been released from the federal penitentiary in Forth Worth, Texas.

"My question is how does a guy such as Bam Morris know these people?" Ray Sumrow asked rhetorically in an interview for this book. "How does he know to pick up the phone, much less even have the phone numbers, of such individuals?"

According to bank transaction records, on March 19, Morris wired money from his bank in Pittsburgh, Pennsylvania, to an institution in Donna, Texas. Morris and Reynolds picked up the money from the Donna bank that same day. A town of 14,000 that is saddled with poverty, Donna has seen drug smuggling gain acceptance as an escape. Corruption spread as far as the town's chief of police, Clemente Garza, Jr., who, along with six of his officers, was arrested and charged with conspiring with smugglers who were ferrying shipments of drugs across the river from Mexico into Donna without police resistance.

The day after their bank pickup in Donna, Morris and Reynolds checked out of the Radisson and headed for Dallas. Two days later, Mark Spears, a Drug Interdiction Task Force agent, was stationed along Route 30, approximately twenty miles east of Dallas, when Morris's shiny black Mercedes passed him. Spears, whose business card reads, "In God We Trust, All Others We Search," was suspicious of the out-of-state plates and unusually dark tinted windows. Unable to see in the car windows, Spears began tailing the Mercedes. When Morris veered over the white line into the shoulder, then back into the passing lane, Spears pulled him over.

The Drug Interdiction Task Force is a specialized unit of agents and investigators which patrols the Texas highways for the transshipment of illegal narcotics, contraband, weapons, and money. Their business is to recognize and intercept drug traffickers. Spears's unit, which patrols a small geographical area northeast of Dallas, seized over $1 million in cocaine, crack, and other narcotics during fiscal year 1996–97, plus over $1.5 million worth of marijuana, distinguishing them as the top drug task force in the state.

At Spears's request, Morris got out of the vehicle and produced his license. "I'm Bam Morris," he said as Spears examined his license, which read, "Byron Lekee Morris."

"Where are you coming from?" Spears asked, still unaware that the man he had pulled over was an NFL star.

"Edinburg, Texas, at an autograph session," Morris responded. "I'm a running back for the Pittsburgh Steelers."

An NFL fan, Spears finally realized who he had. Having watched the Super Bowl weeks before, he remembered seeing Morris run up and down the field. But when Morris said he was on his way from Edinburg, red flags went up in Spears's mind. He had been assigned to train drug agents in Edinburg. As a safety precaution, Spears and his team were required to drive inconspicuous cars and remain behind curtain-drawn motel room windows when not working. "Edinburg is almost like Mexico," said Spears. "It's a major source city. You don't want anyone to know you are police.

If you're off-duty and they find out who you are, it's not going to be very good. They'll kill you in a heartbeat down there on the border."

"Where are you headed?" Spears asked Morris.

"Cooper," Morris said nervously.

After talking briefly with Morris, Spears returned to the car and privately questioned Reynolds, who claimed, contrary to Morris, that the two were on their way back from a vacation in Padre. He said nothing of any autograph session in Edinburg.

"They had conflicting stories," said Spears. "So I asked Bam for consent to search his car."

The automobile had been leased to Morris by Mercedes for $86,000. In the trunk were various pieces of luggage, including a black and blue Reebok gym bag. Spears unzipped the Reebok bag and discovered six one-pound bales of marijuana, a pair of size 13 Reebok basketball shoes, and some Pittsburgh Steelers T-shirts. Each marijuana bale had been carefully wrapped in Saran wrap, then covered in axle grease to mask the odor, and covered in a second layer of Saran wrap. Some of the bales had also been wrapped in aluminum foil. Cling Free dryer sheets were placed between the bales to further conceal detection by smell.

Morris denied that the drugs were his, suggesting to Spears that he ask Reynolds who the marijuana belonged to. But Reynolds likewise insisted the drugs were not his. "Bam was thinking his friend was going to take the fall," said Spears. "But his friend wasn't going to do it."

Bam's shoe size was the same as the sneakers found in the bag alongside the drugs and the Steelers shirts. Reynolds's feet were five sizes too small to fit in the Reeboks.

Sensing the potential for this arrest to become a publicity magnet, Spears radioed to task force headquarters.

Within minutes, Task Force Commander Patsy Williams and Assistant Commander John Davila were on the scene.

Davila brought along a video camera and carefully filmed the condition of the car and the contents of Morris's gym bag. "This was not the doing of a rookie," said Davila, referring to the manner in which the drugs were packaged. "Whoever wrapped the dope had done it before. It took some forethought and some knowledge of how to wrap it up. It was done as well as anything we find on the highway."

The sheer amount of marijuana seized, which is underscored by the fact that it was compressed, made it obvious these drugs were not for personal use, Spears said. When asked what alternatives there were for having this amount of drugs if they weren't for personal consumption, Spears replied, "For sale."

In Edinburg, seven pounds of marijuana can be purchased wholesale for as low as $1,000. But the going street price for marijuana in northern Texas where Morris was stopped exceeded seven times that amount, a nice profit.

After arresting Morris and Reynolds, the task force turned the case over to District Attorney Ray Sumrow, no stranger to the techniques employed by drug traffickers. "Most people don't carry fabric softener sheets around in their vehicle," he said in reference to those pulled from Morris's trunk. "People trafficking in narcotics do, quite often."

For Sumrow, Morris's arrest triggered vivid memories of another case with striking similarities. On January 30, 1972, Dallas Cowboys running back Duane Thomas was stopped along the same Route 30, within miles of where Morris was pulled over. Like Morris, Thomas was arrested for possession of marijuana right after playing in the Super Bowl.

"It happened right after the 1972 Super Bowl," said Sumrow. "When he was booked into jail, he still had his Super Bowl bonus check in his property. He had never cashed it."

On January 30, 1972, one week after Thomas graced the cover of *Sports Illustrated* following his ninety-five-yard rushing performance against the Miami Dolphins, Texas authorities pulled him over for driving a car matching the description of one reported stolen earlier that day.

Thomas's car, it turned out, was a loaner from a Dallas dealership. But he was arrested after the patrolman noticed a strong odor of marijuana coming from the car window. A joint was found in the ashtray, along with a package of Zig Zag papers in the seat. "Probably less than an ounce," Sumrow said. "He was charged with possession of marijuana. At that time, any quantity of marijuana was a felony in Texas."

Facing two to ten years in the state penitentiary, Thomas pleaded guilty to possession of marijuana just twenty-one days after his arrest.

"He was placed on probation for five years and immediately traded by the Cowboys," said Sumrow. "In those days, Tom Landry and Tex Schramm didn't tolerate anyone who brought dishonor to the Dallas Cowboys."

As a former police officer, Sumrow conceded that arrests of professional football players were rare in the early 1970s. He recalled how professional football players were often afforded preferential treatment in that era. Much like fellow police officers, players pulled over for routine violations such as speeding, or even drunk driving, were rarely issued citations.

Jay Ethington, Bam Morris's Dallas-based criminal defense attorney, was a prosecutor in Dallas between 1972 and 1982. "In the old days, it was like a courtesy," said Ethington. "Players would be pulled over for violations and let go when officers learned who they had stopped."

When asked what would have happened had Roger Staubach been pulled over during his career, Ethington responded, "The cop would carry him on a silk pillow to his house. But now, if Michael Irvin gets pulled over for speeding, he gets two tickets. The suspicion of favoritism has pretty much swung the other way."

While insisting that some police officers in the 1990s are unduly aggressive in trying to "make the case" against a famous athlete accused of a crime, Ethington admitted that ballplayers share responsibility for the change in the way the game is played. "It may be the fault of the players themselves," he said. "They get out of hand. There have been a lot of tragedies among sports figures because of bad behavior and dangerous behavior—athletes getting drunk, driving fast and killing somebody or killing themselves. That has a cumulative effect. A cop who is just trying to do his job, after reading about three of those reports in the paper decides he better snatch some of these guys off the street rather than let them go down further and kill themselves or somebody else."

Morris's agent, Steve Zucker, selected Ethington to represent Bam, a logical choice given Ethington's extensive experience handling high-profile litigation, particularly cases involving Dallas-area athletes such as Cowboys players Rafael Septien, Tony Hill, Michael Irvin, and Jay Saldi. In addition to his exceptional skill and reputation in the Dallas legal community, Ethington became particularly seasoned in representing players with drug-related problems through his long-term representation of Dallas Mavericks forward Roy Tarpley. The NBA barred Tarpley from the game in 1991 for cocaine use. After being reinstated at the start of the 1994-95 season and signing a six-year, $26 million contract with the Mavericks, Tarpley was banned for life in December of 1995 after using alcohol in violation of his aftercare program.

In representing more than two dozen professional athletes (predominantly Cowboys) in his career, and handling over a thousand criminal and civil cases, Ethington said, in his opinion, players arrested for substance-abuse-related crimes are often the ones least equipped to handle fame, wealth, and the illicit temptations that come with them. Severely undereducated, in many instances these unsophisticated athletes lack the discipline necessary to avoid the people and places where drugs are found, he said.

Like Cowboy Duane Thomas and Dallas Maverick Roy Tarpley, Ethington insisted that Morris fit this category. Unable to achieve the minimum score required on the ACT for college admission, Morris spent six months with a tutor hired by Texas Tech just so he could qualify for admittance. "They need more guidance, more direction than the ordinary person," Ethington explained. "These athletes are put on a pedestal in high school. They're spoiled in that their emotional development is arrested. They are childlike. It is almost like dealing with a twelve-year-old rather than a twenty-year-old. They don't have a mind of their own."

Sumrow, who was sympathetic toward Morris, agreed that Morris fell into a category of NFL players who are sucked into illicit behavior by a system which engineers champions without regard to developing social and moral character. "I think Bam was in over his head," Sumrow said in an exclusive interview. "He's always had people to handle things for him, to make every move for him. In actuality, he's immature. A kid in a man's body."

Morris was not the only NFL player in Texas facing drug charges after the 1996 Super Bowl. At the same time Ethington began preparing Bam's defense, his law partner Kevin Clancy was retained by Michael Irvin. A Dallas County grand jury was charged with deciding whether to indict Irvin after police found him in a motel room with cocaine and other drug paraphernalia. One day while Morris was in Ethington's office, Irvin telephoned in to talk to Clancy.

"Michael happened to call in," Ethington recalled. "He was on the phone, so I said, 'Hey Mike, I want you to talk to this guy Bam.' They knew each other because Morris had scored a touchdown against them in the Super Bowl."

Both facing felony drug charges and league suspensions, Ethington thought it would be particularly beneficial for Morris to speak with Irvin. "Both of them were in a jam," said Ethington. "Both of them had the same position in the community and league. It was like a younger brother talking to a much older brother—Bam, of course, being the younger. It was like a fifteen-year-old talking to a thirty-year-old."

Unlike Morris, Irvin was much more self-assured, astute, and extremely street-smart. The popular press largely underestimated Irvin's intelligence when he arrogantly entered the Dallas County Courthouse wearing a mink coat and tinted sunglasses to answer cocaine charges in 1996.

"I told Michael, 'Do not wear that mink coat to the grand jury. It's not going to look good,'" said Ethington, exasperated by his and Clancy's failed attempts to stop him. "He turned to me and said, 'Jay, I have a different audience than you do.'"

At first, Ethington and Clancy failed to understand Irvin's attitude. But through their intimate relationship with him, both soon came to understand Irvin's actions. "There's a whole segment of society out there who thought it was cool," Ethington said. "Now, the authorities didn't. But he didn't have much concern about the authorities. He cared more about public perception. And his public is different than mine. I'm an old white guy. He's a dandy. The guy knows what he's doing. Most everything he does is calculated for the public perception."

There is a consensus among prosecutors and defense attorneys familiar with Irvin's case that the cause behind his run-ins with the law is starkly different from that of players like Morris. Irvin represents a second category of NFL players who are cognizant of their power and know how to exploit it to their advantage. Players of this type who violate the law often share a brazen disrespect for authority and distrust of the justice system.

"Irvin wasn't wearing that mink coat because it just happened to be lying by the door when he left his house," said Ethington. "He wanted to project a certain image when he went to the courthouse. That image was, 'You're not going to put me on my knees.'"

Shortly after arresting Morris, Agent Spears took the seized drugs to the state crime lab in Austin for fingerprint analysis. A laser was used to examine the plastic wrapping around the marijuana. Through his attorney, Morris was maintaining that the drugs were not his.

In addition to turning up Morris's fingerprints on the outside of the Saran-wrapped bales, the lab found five positive matches of Morris's fingerprints on the inside layer of Saran wrap. "The marijuana had been opened, unwrapped, the dryer sheets placed next to the marijuana, and then rewrapped," said Sumrow. "Morris wrapped the marijuana. He's the one who put the fabric sheets in it and wrapped it because his fingerprints are not only on the outside of the containers, they're on the inside."

Reynolds's fingerprints, meanwhile, were not found on any of the plastic wrappings. Morris, authorities were convinced, was solely responsible for packing the drugs.

There was more. On the day Morris was booked into the Rockwall County jail, he asked Agent Spears, "Is marijuana all you found?" Spears, then, was not surprised when officers who were inventorying the contents of Morris's car four days later discovered a small rock of cocaine hidden underneath an ashtray located in the console between the bucket seats.

Although possession of less than one gram of cocaine is a state jail felony in Texas, Sumrow decided not to add a cocaine possession charge to the indictment. "The cocaine wasn't discovered until after the car was in police custody for four days," explained Sumrow. "Besides, the marijuana charge is treated as a more serious offense in Texas due to the amount he had."

On July 11, 1996, after a series of testy negotiation sessions between Sumrow and Ethington, Morris pleaded guilty to a felony—possession of five pounds of marijuana. Teachers and residents of Morris's hometown came to offer character testimony in his behalf at his sentencing hearing. "What they're seeing in him is what Bam Morris was in Cooper," said Sumrow. "What they don't understand is that in the NFL, when you're put up on that shelf, there are all those things—the drugs, the sex, and the things that go along with it—that change people. It's sad. They want to remember him as the Bam Morris that grew up in our community. Not what Bam Morris has let himself become." A potential ten-year prison sentence was suspended in favor of probation. It was made clear to Morris that violation of his probation could land him immediately in jail.

Morris received no jail time, but was not as fortunate with the Steelers. His felon status cost him his job in Pittsburgh. "We have always felt that to win you have to have good people, people that related to the moral judgment and proper conduct," said Steelers team owner Dan Rooney. "In any season there is adversity. And people with character are going to stay the course. They're going to be there when things are tough."

Rooney's approach reflects a throwback to a previous era when NFL teams showed less tolerance for crime. While most teams have come to accept the use of convicted criminals in the pursuit of victory, Rooney has tried to honor the values established by his father, longtime Steelers owner Art Rooney.

"My father was a hands-on person," said Rooney. "If there was a problem [with a player's off-field conduct], he would get into it. He would come and discuss it and look at it." Rooney said that his father rarely got rid of any players for off-the-field issues, instead opting to help them in any way he could.

Admitting that his father took a Father Flanagan approach with some of his players, Rooney estimated that in over 90 percent of the cases where he took a troubled player, he helped correct the player's problem through discipline and hard work. "He was a fella that gave people a chance," Rooney reminisced of his father with a chuckle. "He always believed in the good in everybody."

But Rooney Sr.'s fatherly approach was during the 1960s and 1970s when fewer NFL players were arrested and convicted of crimes. And the Steelers, while capturing four Super Bowl titles, were led by respected veterans who exhibited the character Rooney cherished and who policed themselves. "We had players on the Pittsburgh Steelers," Rooney recalled, "who said, 'If you catch a guy, throw him out forever. First offense—throw him out!' Andy Russell,

Jack Lambert—I know they felt that way. I know that Joe Greene felt that way. Mark Malone felt that way."

Amidst a climate of inflated salaries, free agency, and increasing off-field problems, top players no longer want any part in policing teammates. Rooney sees little place for Father Flanagan types in the 1990s version of the NFL. "I don't go as far as my father did," said Rooney. "He believed he could do it with anybody. I think that there are some who you are better off not having."

From the moment Morris was arrested, Rooney was actively involved in the case. "I talked to him after he was arrested," said Rooney. "There were others in the organization who talked to him also." Head coach Bill Cowher made clear to Morris back in June that he was not welcome at the team's minicamp due to his pending case. And once he was convicted, the Steelers released him.

"We don't want to run away from a guy who's in trouble," insisted Rooney. "And we didn't run away from him. But we felt because of [his conviction] and other things that occurred prior to that, he was someone who we were better off not pursuing. It wasn't just that incident."

Although Morris had no criminal record reflecting drug use, there was no shortage of intelligence linking him to drugs. The Drug Task Force, in the course of their criminal investigation of Morris, received intelligence from the Drug Enforcement Agency in downtown Dallas that Morris had a reputation as a regular marijuana user. In a report filed with the DEA and subsequently turned over to the Rockwall County prosecutor's office, a Dallas woman claimed that Morris had been a marijuana supplier.

Both the Drug Task Force and the district attorney's office received numerous unsubstantiated reports that Morris was a supplier to Paris, Texas, a small town located twenty miles from Cooper.

However, the most compelling evidence of prior drug abuse by Morris came from his own admission. In a presentence investigation report contained in Morris's criminal case file in Rockwall County, he admitted not only to smoking marijuana since high school but to regular use of marijuana throughout his college football career at Texas Tech. Morris indicated that he was never caught or punished while on scholarship, supported by reports received by the Drug Task Force from Texas Tech.

Rooney believed that Morris would have little incentive to address his problem if the Steelers simply allowed him to return to the lineup. Although it required letting go of their best running back, the Steelers believed the decision to be in Morris's best interest, as well as the team's. "Number one, it might wake him up," said Rooney. "Number two, if he would have returned here, it could have been that kind of situation where, 'Well, I beat it this time, I'll beat it the next time.' Then there's no real regrets or sentiments for overcoming a problem."

After the Steelers cut Morris, the NFL imposed a four-game suspension on him for violating the league's substance abuse policy. The NFL took four games away from a guy who admitted to regular illegal drug use since high school and who, at the time of his arrest, was found transporting a small rock of cocaine and enough marijuana to get the entire league high. The street value of the drugs in Morris's gym bag was worth more money than Morris lost in four games under his salary with the Steelers.

Then on September 22, 1996, the Baltimore Ravens, Pittsburgh's division rival, signed Morris to a two-year contract worth $1.8 million. Morris's annual salary with Pittsburgh had been $185,000.

"We took a stand," said Tom Donahoe, Steelers director of football operations. "This is a guy who might have been the Super Bowl MVP if we win the game. But what he did, we felt was wrong. We weren't interested in having that type of player on our team. Now it seems as if he gets rewarded for what he did. What type of message does that send?"

Morris's second chance helped the Ravens. Over the final seven weeks of the 1996 season, Morris rushed for more yards than any other back in the AFC. He also scored five touchdowns and caught twenty-five passes.

"People who make mistakes should get a chance to redeem themselves," said Ravens owner Art Modell, who took the high road in justifying his decision to pay a recently convicted felon $1.8 million. But he too wanted the public to believe that he had no tolerance for crime. "If [Morris] shows me I made a mistake, he's gone."

The right-to-redemption approach is a favorite theme for coaches, general managers, and owners who hire talented player-criminals. But players with Morris's skills are scarce commodities. Thus regardless of character deficiencies, the ability to rush for 1,000 yards is guaranteed job security in the NFL.

In order to avoid his prison sentence, Morris agreed to a strict set of probation terms. In addition to neither possessing a firearm or using illegal drugs, Morris was barred from consuming any alcoholic beverages for six years. Further, he was to avoid entering any establishments where intoxicating beverages are sold, to avoid association with persons previously convicted of a crime or currently on probation. Additionally he had to attend mandatory monthly meetings with a probation officer in Maryland. Violation of any one of these terms could land Morris in a Texas prison for ten years.

The likelihood of the average law-abiding citizen going six years without as much as taking a drink, much less entering an establishment that sells alcohol, is remote. For a young millionaire living life in the fast lane, it was simply unrealistic. Even Ravens personnel were skeptical of Morris's ability to fully comply with these terms. "You're always wondering," admitted Ravens running back coach Al Lavan. "He has to show you he is taking the right steps in his preparation, and he has to do it over a long period of time. Until that happens, you're always holding your breath, wishing, hoping, cajoling. You're never lulled to sleep thinking that it's going to change unless you absolutely see a change over a long period of time."

In January 1997, just weeks after the season ended, Morris failed a league-administered urinalysis test. The failed test came as no surprise to his teammates, some of whom shared their frustration with the *Baltimore Sun*.

"I can't say I'm really surprised," said quarterback Vinny Testaverde. "I love Bam—he is a good guy to have in the locker room—but until he shows otherwise, you can't count on him. Until he returns, I won't count on him. If there is a problem, he needs to address it."

"I don't think it was a shock," echoed kicker Matt Stover.

And Morris's backfield partner Earnest Byner was likewise aggravated by the failed test results. "He has to learn from this," said Byner. "He has to grow up as an individual."

The NFL slapped another four-game suspension on Morris. Modell, meanwhile, backed away from his earlier threat to dismiss Morris if he made any more mistakes. Bottom line: Morris was far too valuable to the team as a running back to take him out of the lineup for an extended period of time. "He's going to come back, providing he's clean of mind, clean of body and in condition," Modell told the *Baltimore Sun.* "A prudent young man will come back fit as a fiddle to play football here." In short, it was status quo for the NFL and the Ravens.

News of the failed drug test prompted Ray Sumrow to request the test results from the NFL's front office. If the news was true, Morris had violated the terms of his probation. As part of the Texas Probation Department's authorization for Morris to leave the state to pursue his playing career in Maryland, Morris had to sign a waiver granting consent to Texas authorities to search any records pertaining to him, including medical records, as long as he remained on probation.

However, the NFL rejected the attempt by the prosecutor's office to see the file. NFL spokesperson Greg Aiello said that the test results were privileged under Texas law due to their being part of a voluntary substance abuse program.

With Morris's test results locked away by the NFL in New York, Morris served a second four-game suspension and again returned to the Ravens' lineup. Were it not for the NFL's refusal to turn the records over to Texas authorities, Morris in all likelihood would have been in prison instead of on the football field.

"It's a given that Mr. Morris does not want me to revoke his probation," said Sumrow. "And so long as the NFL can protect him, he's probably pleased that the NFL is doing what they are doing. Anything otherwise would be fatal to him. But this is the state of Texas that's trying to get this information because we've got a person who's on probation. It is against public policy [for the NFL to withhold test results] when it is the government who is trying to get this information in order to carry out its function."

Even Morris's attorney viewed the NFL's stance as having a self-serving element. "The primary interest they have is public perception of them," said Ethington. "They want to be held in the highest regard by the general public. So, if for appearance purposes, it is better that they severely discipline somebody, they're going to do it. If it is in their interest to let some guy slide, they're going to do that."

In the short term, Morris benefited from the NFL's refusal to cooperate with Sumrow, just as he did when Modell first offered him a contract on the heels of losing his job in Pittsburgh. "The reality is that they may not be helping Mr. Morris," insisted Sumrow. "If he has a substance abuse problem and he doesn't get help, he's going to continue to have a substance abuse problem.

"I don't really like the league dictating how we practice law. Their job is entertainment and ours is practicing law. And I take issue with their policy. They are obstructing the process. There's no question about it. They hold documentation that's certainly discoverable and relevant to the matter down here."

Morris rushed for a combined 128 yards on thirty-two carries and scored a touchdown in his first two games back. Meanwhile Sumrow verified that Morris had missed nearly half of his monthly scheduled probation appointments since signing with the Ravens.

Morris's neglect to comply with the more simple formalities of his probation, such as checking in on a monthly basis with a probation officer, were sufficient for Sumrow to issue a warrant for his arrest. Aware that a warrant was imminent in Texas, Morris made a revealing public admission at the Ravens' camp in Maryland.

"I always thought I had an attention problem when I was growing up, but it was just something we never pursued or checked out," Morris told reporters. "The doctor explained it as a part of your brain that didn't develop—you don't think clearly. I said, 'Yeah, I can see times I can be talking about something and jump off that and start talking about something else.' "

In the same statement, Morris conceded that he had little self-discipline. "Even when I was growing up I'd do things I know I shouldn't do," he said. "Good or bad, I did it because I can. Discipline was always a problem."

There were many aspects of Morris's probation that Ravens management could not help him meet. But when signing a player whose failure to satisfy all the terms of probation could land him in prison for up to ten years, the Ravens certainly had a moral obligation to help persuade Morris to keep his meetings with his probation officer.

On October 10 Morris surrendered to Texas authorities and was jailed. The following day he posted $500,000 bond and returned to Maryland. He had two months before a judge would conduct a hearing to determine his fate.

On October 26 he was back in the Ravens' lineup, leading the team to victory over the Redskins, 20–17. In the game he set career highs in attempts and yardage, running the ball thirty-six times for 176 yards and a touchdown. The following week in a loss to the Jets, he ran the ball thirty-one times for 130 yards.

"They [the Ravens] care about his performance on the field and his availability to perform on the field for a reasonable cost to them," said Ethington. "I don't know Art

Modell, but I know that he's a practical guy. And I know that he would want to have the benefits of Morris's talents on the field. This is business."

"It's real disheartening," insisted Drug Task Force Commander Patsy Williams, referring to the Ravens' decision to continue playing Morris. "Do you know how many kids look up to Bam? In all my speeches at the high schools, the immediate question is 'Aren't you the ones who got Bam Morris?'"

As Williams glanced proudly at the picture of Troy Aikman and the framed Aikman football card atop her desk, she recalled Cowboy players showing up in Oklahoma City after the bombing to aid victims. "They have such an avenue to reach people," she said. "When those players—Moose Johnston, Emmitt, Troy—visited the hospital, those kids will remember that for the rest of their lives."

Then Williams glanced at the table across the room from her desk. The six bales of marijuana seized from Morris's Mercedes two years earlier covered the tabletop. Still packed in the original foil and Saran wrap, red markers indicated spots where the crime lab detected Morris's fingerprints. A little plastic bag with a white rock of cocaine lay next to the pot. "But for one of them to ruin his career like this, it has such a negative impact on kids. Football is so big. The kids look up to that profession, and they are the leaders.

"I'm out trying to teach kids that involvement with drugs and people who use drugs will ruin their lives. But they point to Bam and say, 'Well, he got in trouble and he's still playing football.'"

The Ravens' approach with Morris remained unchanged even after he was arrested on November 17 and charged with assaulting a woman, just thirty days after being released from his brief overnight stay in a Texas jail. Morris was arrested while attending a party for Ravens teammate Orlando Brown. Alcohol was present and people were intoxicated. A police report filed after officers were dispatched to the club indicated that the alleged victim had red marks on her neck and sustained scratches on her chest and face.

When Ethington received word of the arrest in Maryland, he knew Morris would be sent to prison in Texas. But while the legal ground was shifting beneath Morris, his ability to keep suiting up and running the football on Sundays maintained a false sense of security and invincibility.

Even Sumrow was distressed over the inevitable consequences that awaited Morris after his arrest in Maryland. Morris had faithfully reported to Rockwall the previous summer and diligently mowed lawns to fulfill his community service obligations. He even visited Sumrow in his office, talking openly about how he was remorseful for letting his parents down by his actions. "The prosecutor and the probation office have personal feelings that are sympathetic to Morris," Ethington confirmed. "But they feel a strong obligation to do their job."

On December 22, the Ravens lost their last regular season game to the Bengals, 16–14. Morris carried the ball thirteen times for twenty-two yards and caught five passes for twenty-five yards.

On January 12, 1998, District Judge Sue Pirtle accepted Sumrow's recommendation and sentenced Morris to 120 days in prison for violating his probation. "I know that you have many agents and other people who try to protect you, but if you come back here, there will be no one who can protect you from this," said Pirtle. "If you don't think you can stay straight for 10 years, you're making a big mistake."

Pirtle also sentenced him to 300 hours of community service and ruled that Rockwall officials had the right to demand any future NFL drug tests should Morris return to the league after his release.

Tears welled up in Morris's eyes as the bailiff tried unsuccessfully at first to apply the handcuffs around his large wrists. Finally, court officers escorted Morris out of the courtroom and into a police cruiser for transportation to the jail.

"When these guys are used up and can no longer run and get the yardage or throw the passes or do the things that they're paid to do, does the NFL care about them?" Sumrow asked rhetorically. "I can show you a lot of former NFL players who are in pretty sad shape. And I don't see the NFL coming around and helping them after they're out of the league. It's a business. Call it what you want."

6

The Maverick

Jim O'Connor had never written a letter to anyone in the NFL before. He certainly had never written a letter like the one he penned on April 25, 1996. But when O'Connor, a career educator and high school athletic director, read the story in the *Boston Globe* about an NFL owner who took a stand, he couldn't help himself.

"Congratulations on your decision regarding Christian Peter," O'Connor's letter began. "Your decision will have an impact on our efforts to teach citizenship, responsibility and accountability to our high school student-athletes. Thank you very much."

Sitting in his office overlooking Foxboro Stadium, New England Patriots Owner Robert Kraft read the letter and smiled one of those awkward smiles. If O'Connor and the dozens of other coaches and athletic directors around the country who wrote similar letters were correct and Kraft's decision to cut Christian Peter sent a message to young athletes, the cost to his team would have been worth it. "Only time will tell," the dapper owner said, nestled in an overstuffed chair in his office. "Only time will tell."

The controversy began with an otherwise nondescript selection during the latter half of the 1996 NFL draft. Most reporters were focused on the team's first-round debate, where coach Bill Parcells had demanded the team draft defensive help. But Kraft wanted to take the immensely talented receiver Terry Glenn out of Ohio State. In the end, the owner won. Parcells was so upset over losing control of the choice, that he began making disparaging references to Glenn—he deliberately referred to him as a "she" in one widely publicized incident—once the receiver was chosen.

With the soap-opera-like debate over Glenn grabbing all the headlines, it was a couple of days before attention turned to the team's fifth-round pick, defensive lineman Christian Peter from Nebraska.

But when the attention turned, it did so in a big way. Boston area media reported that while at Nebraska, Peter's off-field behavior could, at best, be described as boorish. During his college career, Peter was arrested eight times and convicted four times for a variety of offenses. His rap sheet included a May 1994 conviction for assault of a former Miss Nebraska (during which he twice grabbed her between her legs), and a charge in another assault against a twenty-one-year-old woman (he lifted her from the ground with his hands around her neck). Peter was sentenced to eighteen months' probation in the first assault and ten days in jail and a $300 fine for disturbing the peace in the second. Additionally, he was arrested on charges of refusing to comply with the order of a police officer and third-degree assault for threatening to kill a parking attendant. Finally, the University of Nebraska settled a civil lawsuit in which a former Nebraska student alleged Peter twice raped her.

Yet at his workout for NFL scouts at Nebraska's Cook

Pavilion, the six-foot, 300-pound lineman flashed his biceps—complete with a Peterbilt truck logo—and wowed onlookers with his speed and agility. Though Peter's bad-boy status was well known to the stopwatch-toting scouts, the attention paid to him and his criminal record paled in comparison to that of college teammate Lawrence Phillips. That is, until the Patriots drafted him.

When Kraft picked up his morning paper a couple of days after the draft, he learned for the first time what most everyone in the NFL had known much earlier—that they had committed his team to hiring a convicted sex offender.

Kraft didn't hesitate. He called Player Personnel Director Bobby Grier and College Scouting Director Charlie Armey into his office, asked a few questions, and within twenty-four hours took the extraordinary step of cutting Peter loose before even offering him a contract. NFL insiders said they had never before heard of an owner doing such a thing. Especially when Kraft made it known he had done so *on principle!*

The Patriots' press release was short and simple. It read in part: "Based on information we obtained in the last 48 hours following a review of his past actions, we concluded this behavior is incompatible with our organization's standards of acceptable conduct."

Kraft lightheartedly said he made his decision to cut Peter because he "couldn't explain hiring a man with his record to my wife."

Imagine that becoming the NFL's new standard. Imagine owners having to explain to the ones they love why they would want to surround themselves with men convicted of assaulting women.

Peter, who blamed his problems on too much alcohol and

too little maturity, proved the latter by blasting the Patriots, telling reporters he "wouldn't want to play for someone without enough guts to defend a player he selected, who then comes up with some cockamamie story he wants to give the public. I feel hurt and somewhat betrayed. I feel I was made an example of for every bad thing that men in athletics have done."

As one might expect, Kraft's office was flooded by letters of congratulations from high school and college coaches.

"I just felt that it was a great example of what a professional team could do to set the tone for, not only colleges, but also for the high school coaches and principals who are trying to set some standards for kids today," said O'Connor, athletic director at Framingham High School in Framingham, Massachusetts. "Too often, the message to kids is that if you're a good player, like Christian Peter, you can do anything you want and never suffer for it. What Mr. Kraft did said that's not always true."

Noticeably absent among the scores of letters: a single note of praise from anyone else in the NFL. Maybe that's because so many of them were busy calling Peter's agent, asking about his immediate availability.

"I wasn't looking for that," Kraft said when asked about the shortage of congratulations from his colleagues. "I'm not going to sit here and preach to them because there's no one way of doing things. People have different standards."

But, Kraft was asked, will a lack of standards one day come to haunt his colleagues?

"I don't want to speak for or about them, I hope you'll appreciate that," he said. "But I worry about athletes being arrested, yes. I worry about us, I think we have a responsibility to support our athletes better. I'm not preaching to anyone else. I'm just doing what works for me and I've had good success. I know what's gotten me into trouble, and it is usually not making the right decision."

Kraft said he didn't look at his move as "bold or brave."

"I'm not saying that I'm a do-gooder and I admit that I have myself, while growing up, gone to the edge in doing things," Kraft said. "But on the other hand you establish a certain set of standards that you want to work by."

After his decision was made, Kraft was approached by several NFL teams about trading for Peter. Doing so would have allowed the Patriots to salvage something from the whole mess.

"I wasn't interested in trading him," Kraft said. "Our organization made the error. We needed to suffer for it, not profit from it. I wanted to send our organization a signal about how serious I was."

Those within Kraft's organization got the signal loud and clear. They also saw how different that was from the signal being sent by the team's competitors. Within days, as many as six teams were bidding for Peter's rights, according to sources within the league. Ultimately, the New York Giants won Peter's services.

Peter's agent, former NFL player Ralph Cindrich, said he was disappointed by the Patriots' decision, but glad the controversy didn't cost his client a career in the NFL. Through Cindrich, Peter declined to be interviewed on this subject.

"If I were on the outside, I would want him [Christian] lynched with everybody else," Cindrich said. "I'm telling you, I know the facts. Christian is a much better guy than what you've read. First off, what actually happened and what were proven results and proven facts was never grasped fully by the media. There were a lot of allegations that were simply unsubstantiated, misstated, simply untrue. You're not going to want to hear that. Nobody else is. I'm saying to you it's a fact.

"I don't believe these kinds of records should keep players from the opportunity to earn a living," said Cindrich, long one of the most respected agents in the business. "If you think that banning players with police records is going to stop players from committing crimes, well, you probably believe the death penalty has a positive effect on eliminating or decreasing murders."

For the record: Cindrich, a criminal defense attorney before he became a sports agent, doesn't believe in the death penalty, either. "I've represented murderers and had tears in my eyes and pleaded for them not to die."

Kraft did not shed any tears when he dumped Peter. Neither did New England fans, who flooded call-in shows and newspaper editorial pages with their words of support.

"I'm not in the legal profession," Kraft said, making the distinction between his vantage point and Cindrich's. "I look at myself as a custodian of a public asset. This team belongs to the fans in New England. I sat up there in Section 217 on the goal line when the stadium opened. I went through the highs and lows, a lot of lows with this team, and my dream was to own the team. I want to run this team the same way we run our other businesses and we have certain rules that we go by and these have always worked for me. To me this [the Peter decision] was good business. We have businesses all over the world, and the same rules work no matter what the culture, what the business. We hire people number one on integrity and character, number two on the work ethic, and number three on brains. And while there's a definite thrill in trying to win a championship on the field, that thrill is greater if you didn't have to compromise to do it, in my opinion.

"I don't think fans want to see players or owners or coaches who are making a lot of money, who don't sign autographs, who get into trouble, who do interviews that are smart-alec. On the other hand, I think that the people who live paycheck to paycheck and are looking to escape their problems, the team in your community is one avenue for doing that. So they all feel that they own a piece of this team and I want them to feel that. They don't want members of the family doing things that are embarrassing to them. I think maybe in other regions of the country people might be more tolerant to family members doing incidents and welcoming them back. I think the standards are a little tougher here."

Though it wasn't his goal in the days following that draft, Kraft is hopeful that some part of the message might endure.

"Those coaches [who wrote me letters] are right. If teams show certain leadership, the power of sport allows you to do things in your community and set an example that other businesses don't have. That's a very powerful responsibility. We have to understand that."

Kraft said he is sure that his staff understands. "I think people here now know that whoever might make a decision like that or allow us to bring someone in with that kind of background won't be working here," he said. "I was told it's very hard to find defensive linemen and if you want to win you've got to have defensive linemen, that's the shortest commodity. But that doesn't mean that you sacrifice your business principles. I don't care if it's hard to get defensive linemen, it doesn't really matter to me."

Yet, it was pointed out to Kraft, seven months after cutting Peter, his team was in the Super Bowl. "Well you said that, I didn't. But I'm glad you made that conclusion," Kraft said. "I believe that football is the ultimate team sport. You saw it in the Super Bowl, where a special teams player can make a run back and be the game's MVP. A team is like family. I really believe that off-field distractions can be very disturbing to a franchise and there's enough things that can go wrong in this business because it's not a business of production with machines, you're dealing with human beings and coaches and players. You have seventy-five different human beings working there who all have families, who all have bad days, who have kids who are sick or maybe talking about getting a divorce. All the problems of this world are within this family and we have to contain them and support it as best we can. Why add a problem to all that? What do you really gain?

"I hate losing any game, but I don't feel long-term this approach really costs you games," Kraft said. "I don't want to have to sell my soul to be in this business."

Kraft said he was sorry that the incident had caused so much embarrassment for Peter and his family.

"I actually wrote the gentleman a letter and sort of apologized for our organization not handling itself in as professional a manner as I would like," he said. "On the other hand I hoped that it would be a signal to him to maybe try to get some help and do things that would allow him to be productive."

All signs indicate Kraft's hope may have come true. Peter joined the Giants under a restrictive agreement that delayed his playing days for a year while he attended counseling sessions with team psychologist Joel Goldberg. Nearly two years into the plan, Peter had made the team, made two tackles in seven games . . . and made no appearance on a police blotter.

"It was a good move for both the Giants and for Christian," Goldberg told the authors. "We're a very conservative organization. But we believed he was capable of getting his life under control."

Goldberg said he made the recommendation that the Giants sign Peter after meeting with the player and understanding what made Peter tick. He compared his investigation to the work done by a good broker.

"How do you decide to invest in a stock?" Goldberg asked rhetorically. "You study it and decide what its growth potential is. You look at risk-reward, you look at availability of cash, you look at the industry, you look at history, you look at management. Those are the ingredients that you make a decision about. If you're studious you don't react out of emotion. You try to be deliberate. You try to be thoughtful. But the odds are, more often than not, if you follow your intellectualized process, you'll be okay. To me it's the same methodology. I try to understand the basic ingredients and then evolve from there.

"Christian had issues he needed to deal with. A lot of people do. Obviously, it helped that he was a talented athlete, because it meant people were willing to help him grow. I think it has worked."

Only time will tell.

Kraft and New England's community standards were put to the test again in early 1998 when fan favorite Dave Meggett was arrested in Toronto and charged with sexual assault and robbery. On June 23 Toronto authorities dropped the sexual assault charge. No matter. After his arrest, Patriots brass determined that Meggett no longer represented the standards set for their players and they cut him from the team. The robbery charges were ultimately dropped.

7

Wanted

When training camp opened for the St. Louis Rams under new coach Dick Vermeil in July of 1997, starting quarterback Tony Banks showed up with his six-month-old rottweiler named Felony. Banks and his teammates loved having Felony around. The coaches didn't. Vermeil ordered Banks to send Felony home. It wasn't the name Felony that was the cause of concern. No, the Rams were used to having felons in camp. It was the dog that was prohibited.

On March 24, 1997, special agent Larry Fox of the Drug Enforcement Agency paid an official visit to the St. Louis Rams' front office to subpoena the Rams as part of a federal probe into a drug trafficking conspiracy. With management under attack for the repeated crimes of star running back Lawrence Phillips, news of another player under investigation was not welcome. Fortunately for the Rams, the press would not learn of the investigation until the middle of training camp, four months later.

Fox was shown to the office of Rams executive vice president Jay Zygmunt. After identifying himself, Fox served

Zygmunt with the subpoena. Addressed to the St. Louis Rams, it read, "Pursuant to an ongoing official investigation being conducted by the Drug Enforcement Administration of a suspected felony, it is requested that your company furnish the following information: Copies of any and all checks or payments for the length of employment fronts and backs, made to the following person: James Harris."

One month earlier, the Rams inked Harris to a $2.9 million contract and paid him a $700,000 signing bonus. Now the team was on notice that the DEA suspected Harris of being implicated in a drug investigation. Eager to obtain more information about Harris's alleged role in the case, Rams officials called the DEA office, but were only told that Harris was suspected of supplying currency to a drug dealer. It would be early summer before authorities were ready to turn the matter over to a federal grand jury.

The uncertainty of Harris's legal status could not have come at a worse time. He was signed with the expectation that he would compete for the starting defensive end position. Instead, Harris now faced the prospect of prison. Meanwhile the NFL draft was just weeks away, and recently hired head coach Dick Vermeil had been on the job just two months.

On top of all this, just two weeks earlier, on March 11, a Nebraska judge sentenced Phillips, the team's first-round pick in 1996, to twenty-three days in jail for violating the terms of his probation. After pleading no contest to charges of brutally assaulting his ex-girlfriend in 1995, Phillips was spared jail time pending no further brushes with the law. However, on June 13, 1996, just two months after the Rams drafted him, the California Highway Patrol arrested Phillips for drunk driving. He was driving eighty miles per hour in a car that had a flat tire. His plea of no contest in California triggered the jail sentence in Nebraska.

Phillips's problems were well documented, and Vermeil came into the job anticipating that one of his major tasks as a football coach would be to work with the criminal justice system. "The Rams had invested the sixth pick in the draft overall," Vermeil told ESPN, explaining why getting Phillips in the lineup was among his top priorities. "That's the sixth player in the draft. That's a real commitment by an organization. I felt it was my responsibility to do everything I could to get him to play up to his ability and make that investment a good investment."

On February 20, St. Louis authorities charged Phillips with a series of motor-vehicle-related violations after he drove his Humvee into a pillar and then left the scene of the accident. Four days later, Phillips was again arrested, this time in Omaha, Nebraska, where a woman alleged she was assaulted, battered, and falsely imprisoned by him at a party. After arriving at the hotel, police charged Phillips with disorderly conduct.

Yet, on April 12 Vermeil was standing outside the jail doors in Nebraska when Phillips emerged with a grin and a garment bag draped over his shoulder. Extending his hand, the coach then escorted his troubled star through a sea of cameras and into the back of a yellow taxi cab. He used the flight back to St. Louis to get more personally acquainted with his number one back and impress on him his value to the team.

Despite his commitment to Phillips, Vermeil admitted to reporters that he would not have drafted him had he been the head coach in 1996. Yet, just one week after escorting Phillips from jail, Vermeil used his fourth-round pick in the draft to select Texas Christian University All-Conference lineman Ryan Tucker (see Chapter 1).

With Tucker's criminal past showing a resemblance to Phillips's, Vermeil tried to dispel any comparisons between the two players. "The problems [of Phillips and Tucker] are different," Vermeil said, insinuating that alcohol as opposed to upbringing was the source of Tucker's violence. "They aren't maybe as deep and may be easier to control [for Tucker]. When a guy drinks a beer and gets in fights, that's a little easier to control than environmental things in a young man's process of growing up."

However, Vermeil conceded that he was taking a chance with Tucker. "I think I know what I'm doing," he said. "He's not a thug. He's a youngster who got in trouble and was out of line and he himself will tell you he's embarrassed about it."

Rams assistant coach Johnny Roland used similar rationalizations to minimize the seriousness of Phillips's criminal conduct shortly after they drafted him. "Everybody deserves a second chance, sometimes a third and a fourth," said James, justifying the selection of a twice-convicted criminal. "What Lawrence did had nothing to do with drugs. It was harassment. He didn't kill anyone. He didn't stab anyone."

By the time the Rams opened training camp in Macomb, Illinois, on July 15, federal prosecutors were presenting their case against James Harris and four other men to a grand jury. On July 24, Anthony "Fat Head" Washington, Stanford Riley, Jr., Andre R. Hogan, and Dwight "Chip" Flowers were indicted on charges of conspiring to "knowingly and intentionally distribute and possess with intent to distribute cocaine and cocaine in the form of cocaine base (commonly known as 'crack')." Harris was indicted on charges of aiding and abetting the conspiracy by allegedly supplying over $50,000 to Washington for the purchase of cocaine.

Word of the indictments swept through training camp, prompting a quick response from Vermeil. "My first thought would be he's not guilty until he's proven guilty," he told reporters. "I'd feel lousy if I said, 'You can't play, you can't be a Ram,' and they acquit him of whatever the charge may be, and it's cost him the opportunity to make a living."

In light of the fact that Phillips and Tucker continued to play despite allegations of criminal conduct, there was little doubt that Harris would remain in uniform unless carted off in handcuffs—or his on-field skills deteriorated. However, the investigation into Harris and his alleged co-conspirators demonstrated just how far a team will go to protect its player, despite how bad things looked.

Investigators traced the trail in the Harris case back to the night of February 6, 1996, with the homicide of Eugene Vincent Birge, an East St. Louis drug dealer. When Birge answered a knock on his front door at 11:35 P.M. that evening, three men forced their way into his home with shotguns and 9mm semiautomatic weapons. They shot Birge once in the abdomen, twice in the chest, and once in the head with the shotgun at point-blank range. Less than thirty minutes later he was found lying in a pool of blood and pronounced dead. Anthony "Fat Head" Washington, who Harris was accused of supplying with money, emerged as the primary suspect in the ambush killing.

With so many murders annually in East St. Louis, area newspapers did not bother to report Birge's death, dismissing him as another nameless casualty in the drug trade. However, Birge was no ordinary drug pusher. He was a dealer-turned-informant who was secretly working with the DEA. His government contact was Larry Fox, the same agent who served the subpoena on the Rams. At the time Birge was murdered, Fox was coordinating the investigation into a national cocaine ring that stretched into all geographical regions of the United States. Prosecutors had already indicted eighteen people in connection with the case. In addition to being an informant, Birge was a potential government witness in the federal trial of the eighteen conspirators. Authorities would later claim in federal court that Washington had Birge executed when Washington discovered that Birge was cooperating with the government. "He [Washington] middled the hit on the informant," Fox said in a telephone interview.

Identified in court papers as "a distributor in the East St. Louis, Metro East area," Washington was also suspected of participating in a kidnapping-for-ransom plot investigated by the FBI. "In 1995, Mr. Washington allegedly kidnapped an individual from St. Louis, brought him to Illinois and demanded $50,000 from his relatives to have his son returned alive," Fox testified at Washington's detention hearing.

Harris and Washington are close friends, their relationship stemming back to childhood when they grew up as neighbors. When Harris returned to the East St. Louis area in April 1996 after the Rams signed him as a free agent, he renewed his ties with Washington. Their renewed friendship led directly to Harris's indictment. According to prosecutors, Harris knowingly gave Washington cash to purchase a shipment of cocaine.

Harris denied the charge. "I come home and I hang out

with some old friends of mine, and because I'm hanging out with some old friends, the DEA expects me to be a drug dealer," complained Harris in an interview with the authors. "Why? Because I go back to my old neighborhood to make sure everybody's doing okay?"

Bob Shannon, Harris's high school football coach and a longtime resident of East St. Louis, spent years using football as a carrot to lead kids out of the crime- and drug-infested neighborhoods that were Harris's and Washington's home. Other kids Shannon coached who went on to play in the NFL include Bryan Cox (who played with Harris for one season under Shannon) and Tennessee Oilers linebacker Dennis Stallings.

Shannon recalled a character-defining moment in 1984, Harris's sophomore year of high school. With the team clinging to a lead late in the state championship game, Shannon's team was pinned down inside their own ten-yard line. Shannon put Harris in at quarterback. On the next play Harris pivoted to hand the ball to the fullback, who cut too wide. Harris overextended himself attempting to make the handoff. He fumbled. The other team recovered and scored.

"When James came to the sideline," Shannon recalled, "I said, 'Why'd you try to give him that ball?' He said, 'Coach, it wasn't my fault, it was his fault. He went too wide.'

"I said, 'James, you had the football. All you had to do was keep it and we wouldn't have fumbled.'

" 'It wasn't my fault, coach. It was his fault.'

"I tried to get him to see one more time that he had made a bad decision. But he never did see it. And I knew right there with that incident with James Harris that it was going to be difficult for him to play quarterback for me because he didn't realize that he made a bad decision."

In Shannon's view, the poor decision making of Harris, along with other NFL players, stems back to their decision-making processes developed as youths. "It has something to do with people being able to recognize and have a clear definition of right and wrong," he said. "Some guys in the NFL are talented athletes but they come from backgrounds where they've been around gangs, been around gang members, or have been in gangs. It gets back to making good decisions. There are guys who have been able to walk away from those types of situations and be productive and say, 'Hey, that was wrong. That was a period of my life when I could have gotten in serious trouble, but I didn't.' And they see the light.

"James Harris is a guy who had the wrong kind of friends and was not able to divorce himself from them after he had had a certain amount of success, came back into the community, still associated with those guys, and didn't have a clear understanding of what's right and what's wrong."

Tipped off by an informant, the DEA pulled Washington over on March 19, 1997, while he was en route to meet a drug courier. According to the informant, Washington was to deliver cash in exchange for one kilo of cocaine. Unaware that he was under surveillance, Washington stepped out of the car while agents conducted a search. In the driver's side door, they discovered a Boatmen's Bank bag containing $52,000 in cash.

Not at all surprised to find the cash, the agents were nonetheless puzzled by the amount. The approximate wholesale price for one kilo of cocaine was $17,000, leaving authorities to speculate that the additional $35,000 was for additional kilos and courier fees.

Under questioning, Washington denied knowing that the

money was in the car and insisted that it belonged to his friend James Harris. When agents escorted Washington to his home, they found Harris, who claimed ownership of the cash. Bank records confirm that Harris withdrew $50,000 cash from his account on the nineteenth. Harris said the other $2,000 was cash he was carrying in his pocket. But he denied the money was to be used to purchase drugs, claiming instead that he withdrew the money earlier that day to purchase a Porsche 911 at BW Motors in Belleville, Illinois.

"Anthony didn't even know the money was in the car," Harris insisted in an interview for this book. "He knew I had some money, but he didn't know the money was in the car."

According to Harris, he arrived at Washington's house on the nineteenth with the intention of going to purchase a Porsche. But when it got too late in the day to travel to Belleville, he postponed the purchase until the next day. In the meantime, he said he hid the $52,000 for "safekeeping" in a car parked in Washington's driveway while he temporarily left Washington's house to run an errand. When he returned two hours later, Harris claimed that Washington had left in the car containing his money.

The DEA did not buy any of this. Although they did not arrest Harris at that point, they seized his money and initiated their investigation into him as a co-conspirator. While the DEA did not bother to check, Harris did in fact have a deal arranged to purchase a Porsche from BW Motors. However, interviews with Harris, his attorney, Ron Norwood, and Brad Stubbs, the owner of BW Motors, leave many questions.

Stubbs confirmed that on March 18 he spoke by telephone with both Washington and Harris and reached a verbal agreement to sell a Porsche 911. For over ten years Stubbs had been building made-to-order Porsche 911s for professional athletes. His clients include Scottie Pippen, Charles Oakley, John Starks, Anthony Bonner, and Al Toon, among others.

The Porsche he agreed to sell to Harris actually belonged to New Jersey Nets forward Kevin Edwards. Stubbs had customized the car for Edwards in 1992. After owning the car for five years, Edwards asked Stubbs to assist him in selling it. One afternoon in early March, Anthony Washington, who Stubbs admitted would infrequently stop by his shop to browse, entered the garage and said he had a close friend who would be interested in Edwards's Porsche.

On March 20, the day after the DEA seized his money from Washington's car, Harris returned to his bank and withdrew $35,000. This time the money was in the form of a cashier's check made out to Kevin Edwards. He then drove to Belleville and bought the car.

When asked why he initially withdrew $50,000, Harris said, "I was going to spend $15,000 on my stereo, on my alarm system, my tires and my rims."

However, when Stubbs was asked if he had quoted Harris a price for installation of a stereo and the purchase of new tires, he responded, "We had never discussed that. There was talk about doing a stereo and what-not. But I know nothing about the fifty-two thousand. That was not going to come to me."

The surplus of money found in Harris's bank bag was the same amount Washington was supposed to pay for one kilo of cocaine. When asked about this troubling coincidence in an interview for this book, Harris said, "I can't explain it because I didn't know nothing about no dope. I never knew what was going on in the beginning."

When asked if Washington would have involved him in a drug deal, Harris said, "Anthony wouldn't put me in no circle like that. I don't care what he was doing and I don't know what he was doing. Don't care to know. But whatever he was doing, he would never have put it in my face."

When the indictments against Harris, Washington, and the others were announced by the U.S. Attorney's Office, Vermeil told reporters he was "surprised and disappointed." Surprised? Vermeil had known the troubling aspects of Harris's case for months. "One day Vermeil called me in the office and said he needed to talk to me about something," said Harris. "I just told him the truth." According to Harris, that meeting took place in the spring. "He knew. He knew long before anybody else."

In addition to receiving assurances from Vermeil that the team would support him, Harris also had a private meeting with Rams vice president of football operations Lynn Stiles. In that meeting, Stiles, according to Harris, asked him point-blank, "Were you involved in this?"

"I told him no. He said, 'Well, we're going to stick with you all the way through this, and we'll see you through.'"

Harris took the unified support from coaches and management for granted. Given his experience in the NFL, he expected nothing less. When the Rams signed him they were fully aware that he was on probation for a felony assault conviction from his days with the Minnesota Vikings.

On January 26, 1996, Harris had pleaded guilty to third-degree assault and was sentenced to ten days in the Hennepin County Adult Correction Facility in Minnesota. The case stemmed from a domestic violence incident on December 29, 1995. Police arrested Harris after he left his wife at the emergency room with a broken nose and fractured collarbone.

Prior to that, Harris had pleaded guilty to fifth-degree assault on December 15, 1992, after police reported finding blood under the left eye of his first wife. The police report indicated that Harris hit his wife with a closed fist and kneed her in the stomach and chest. It also noted that this was not the first time police had been dispatched to the Harris house on a domestic violence call.

"There are a lot of players that end up in the National Football League," admitted Vermeil in an interview, "and a lot of people have told them, 'You do that one more time and you're not going to play anymore.' And they don't believe you because they've played one more time. And they did it in high school, they did in junior college, they did it in college and they get in the National Football League and they do it anyway."

Harris had every reason to believe Vermeil's endless definition of "one more chance." His own experience with the Rams had proven the point.

Less than two months after signing Harris in April 1996, the Rams were notified by St. Louis police that a felony arrest warrant had been issued against Harris in Minnesota on July 11. He was wanted for failing to make court-ordered payments in conjunction with his conviction for assaulting his wife.

Patti Cohen, a police clerk in the warrant office of the Hennepin County Sheriff's Department, answered the telephone when a person identifying himself as a Rams coach called to resolve the matter. "Just wanted to know what the warrant was for and how much it was to pay it off," said the coach.

"Three thousand and thirty dollars to pay it off," Cohen responded.

The coach then indicated that he would take care of it, and Cohen provided him with a number to call to inquire about getting an extension on the fine. The records indicate that an extension was obtained and the warrant was squelched. Although the records do not reveal by whom, on October 2, 1996, the fine was paid in full.

The week that Harris's federal indictment was handed down, representatives from the FBI paid their annual training camp visit to the Rams. As part of the NFL's efforts to educate its players on the dangers associated with being a wealthy celebrity, FBI agents visit every team prior to the start of the regular season. Their presentation to players and coaches warns of the influences of organized crime and illegal gamblers, and the dangers of drugs and other illicit behavior.

Many of the players being warned about these dangers have had extensive contact with law enforcement, some of them for carrying out the very crimes that the league is attempting to insulate them from. Besides Harris, Tucker, and Phillips, Rams in attendance included:

• Linebacker Percell Gaskins, who was arrested at Kansas State University in November of 1995 in connection with an assault that left two people and a dog injured. The charges against Gaskins were ultimately dropped.

• Running back Craig "Iron Head" Heyward, who pleaded guilty in February of 1991 to disorderly conduct and public drunkenness after slamming a police officer's hand in a car door during a fight with officers who were trying to arrest him. Heyward had used his car to push another vehicle out of a parking space he wanted.

• In February of 1992 Heyward was convicted and received a suspended sentence after being arrested for assaulting two women at a fund-raiser. Heyward, who was drunk at the time of the incident, head-butted one of the women.

• Offensive lineman Gerald Perry. On November 22, 1988, Perry was charged with raping a woman at gunpoint. A jury later found him not guilty.

• On June 15, 1989, Perry was arrested for soliciting a prostitute and subsequently convicted and ultimately served a fifteen-day jail sentence.

• On September 7, 1989, Perry was arrested for soliciting a prostitute, assault and battery, false imprisonment, and impersonating a police officer. He was convicted on the prostitution charge and served another fifteen-day jail sentence.

• A jury acquitted Perry of assaulting a man on May 9, 1990.

• On May 24, 1991, Perry pleaded guilty to sexually assaulting the fiancée of one of his teammates on the Denver Broncos. Perry was sentenced to 180 days in jail and served sixty-five.

• On May 9, 1994, Perry agreed to an out-of-court settlement with an Anaheim, California, woman who filed a suit against him, alleging that he threatened to kill her if she did not have sex with him.

Harris said he knew going in that the FBI would not talk about his case. "I wasn't uncomfortable," Harris told the authors. "My incident never came up. The agent knew that I was in the room, so they never said anything about it. But they said something about Darryl Henley's case."

Carefully choosing an example of a player whose career was prematurely ended due to crime, the FBI selected former Rams defensive standout Darryl Henley. In 1994 he was indicted on federal cocaine charges, accused of recruiting Rams cheerleader Tracy Ann Donaho to carry twenty-five pounds of cocaine from Los Angeles to Atlanta. The same Rams administration had permitted Henley to continue starting games for the Rams while free on bond. Citing the familiar "innocent until proven guilty" theme, the Rams played Henley until he was sent to federal prison after a jury convicted him in March 1995 (see Chapter 16).

Ironically, Henley was incarcerated in the maximum security prison in Marion, Illinois, located just 100 miles from the Rams' new home in St. Louis.

The FBI's discussion of the Henley case makes clear that only prison will prevent a player from playing. Unfortunately, this compelling account did nothing to persuade players to change their criminal ways. "A lot of them are just unreachable," said Harris in a December 1997 interview for this book. "They just don't care. 'Man, I'm not listening to what you're talking about. I'm not trying to hear that. I'm my own person.' That's their attitude about it.

"The players usually sleep through the sessions. They don't care. It's just something that has to be done. It's not a good use of time. The only reason guys ask questions is to try and make the meeting go longer so they don't have to go to practice or go watch films."

Harris knew what was coming when federal agents arrested him on July 28. Rams vice president of player development and legal counsel Kevin Warren was hastily dispatched to Peoria, Illinois, to testify at Harris's detention hearing. The

Rams were hoping to persuade the judge to allow Harris to remain free on bond so he could remain in camp.

Warren made it to the courthouse to hear federal Judge Michael Mihm open the proceedings. "This indictment charges four people with the offense of conspiracy to distribute and possess with intent to distribute cocaine and cocaine in the form of cocaine base," said Judge Mihm in a very deliberate, matter-of-fact tone. "This defendant James Edward Harris is charged in that indictment as an aider and abettor.

"If the information I have is correct, this offense upon conviction carries with it a minimum mandatory sentence of at least ten years in prison and up to life and a fine of $4 million and a period of supervised release of at least five years and it could be for the rest of the defendant's life."

Harris sat in stunned silence. Suddenly the immediacy of getting back to practice was unimportant. He was staring at the prospect of spending the rest of his life behind bars.

Although no stranger to criminal proceedings, never before did his presence in the courtroom jeopardize his career, much less his liberty. However, he now was in federal court being aggressively prosecuted. The game had forever changed: Harris was not fighting for a job, he was fighting for his life.

Federal prosecutor Randy Massey argued that Harris should be jailed until his trial. Citing Harris's felony conviction for assault in Minnesota, as well as his prior domestic violence case, Massey insisted that his record in conjunction with his current role in a felony drug case qualified Harris as a danger to the community.

Warren's job was to refute the government's arguments

that Harris should be detained pending his trial because he was a risk of flight and posed a danger to the community.

"With regard to his risk of flight," said defense attorney Kevin Green, "what is your opinion? Is Mr. Harris a risk to leave?"

"He just signed a three-year, $2.9 million contract sometime in February," answered Warren. "If Mr. Harris were to leave camp, he would probably be forced to refund his signing bonus. And quite naturally, if he's not playing, he's not going to get paid his salary. He would run the heavy risk of not being a member of the team. So as far as risking flight, I see no reason why he would do that. He would have no means of income if he did that."

Warren went on to explain that Coach Vermeil's strict minute-by-minute scheduling regimentation left no time for players to get into trouble away from the field. According to Warren, players were subject to curfews, bed checks performed by security guards, and fines for missing or being late to meetings and practices. Harris had done everything expected of him by the coaches during camp.

"Would you consider Mr. Harris to be a danger to the community?" Green asked.

"Based on what I've seen during training camp, no," testified Warren. "He has too much at stake in the National Football League. This is a once-in-a-lifetime opportunity."

"What would be the impact if he's detained?" asked Green.

"It would have a negative impact on him if he's detained for any period of time," answered Warren. "The detention of James Harris today would ultimately cost him his job with the St. Louis Rams."

Warren's testimony carried the day. Convinced that Harris had tremendous financial incentive to remain in St. Louis, Judge Mihm released Harris on an unsecured $750,000 bond. Warren then drove Harris back to camp and he was in uniform the following day. All other defendants arrested in the conspiracy were denied bond and detained in jail pending their trial.

Harris received repeated assurances from coaches and administrators that they would support him throughout the proceedings. Warren, who was assigned to assist Harris, also repeatedly reassured him that the team was behind him. "He kept telling me they wasn't going to let me go," said Harris. "They're not going to let you go because Les Miller [the team's director of player development] is a good guy. He's going to stick with you."

But even the friendly confines of training camp could not erase the voice of Judge Mihm saying "life in prison." Adamantly maintaining his innocence, Harris nonetheless appreciated the reality of prison. Sleepless nights followed and soon he stopped eating. During the next two weeks of training camp he dropped twenty pounds. Lethargy set in on the field and drowsiness was obvious in film sessions and team meetings.

"James Harris was not the same football player because of all the problems on his mind," confirmed Harris's agent, Harold Lewis. "He just couldn't go out there and be the same James Harris when it came to practice. He was not paying attention in meetings. His mind was not there."

On August 17, just nineteen days after Warren assured the court that Harris's contract provided a structured environment and job security, the Rams summarily cut Harris. At that point, Harris had yet to be paid a penny of his $2.9 million contract, which was not guaranteed but was conditional on his playing the 1997 season. Although he had received a signing bonus, he had already chewed up $200,000 worth paying for his lawyers.

Harris learned that he was cut the same way fourteen other players did, by reading his name on a list tacked up on the team bulletin board. "They called me in the office," said Harris. "But I knew when they called me in."

While the Rams' dismissal of Harris appeared a turnabout, reflecting a decision to finally draw the line with players and crime, Harris was cut for one reason—his performance declined in camp. Both his mental concentration and physical prowess were suddenly lacking, and he was therefore no use to the team. "He didn't get around the quarterback as much as you wanted to see," said defensive line coach Carl Hairston.

Coach Vermeil made clear that his decision to cut Harris was not designed to send any messages. "I did not make the decision to release James Harris based on his off-the-field problems," Vermeil said. "I do think his off-the-field problems influenced his play. I don't see how a guy can play football with things like that hanging over his head, and concentrate on what he has to do to be a good football player."

Bottom line: if Harris could have maintained his on-field aggressiveness—like Henley, Phillips, Tucker, and others— there is little question that he would be on the opening day roster.

Unemployed and running short on money, Harris was without all the safeguards that the Rams had provided him. More importantly, his incentives to appear in court, as described by vice president and legal counsel Warren, were gone.

When Warren was questioned by the authors about his testimony given under oath, he downplayed his statements to the judge. "The big thing that I was trying to stress was the fact that, when the judge asked me, while he was at training camp, how much free time," said Warren. "Basically, that's what they wanted to find out because they were concerned about 'Is he gonna flee?' All I was saying is 'Hey, this is his schedule. They gotta be at meetings at 7:00 A.M. and they get done at 11:00 P.M.'"

Now Warren echoed Vermeil's explanation for letting Harris go. "He was just released like twenty-five other people were," said Warren. "It didn't have anything to do with [his pending case]."

Privately, Warren disagreed with Vermeil's handling of the Harris situation. On the day Harris was cut, Harris and Warren talked after Harris cleaned out his locker. Harris recalled the following exchange:

"I expected this," Harris said, looking into Warren's eyes.

"Man, they are giving you a raw deal," Warren responded.

"I expected it," repeated Harris.

"I didn't expect it," Warren replied.

Ironically, the Rams retained players whose cases involved far more conclusive evidence. The evidence against Harris was tenuous at best. And on October 23, Judge Paul E. Riley found Harris not guilty of aiding and abetting the other co-conspirators.

More striking was that Judge Riley announced the acquittal before the defense even put their case to the jury. Citing an absence of evidence, Riley granted a defense motion for a directed verdict after prosecutors rested their case. It was the first time in his twenty years on the bench that Riley granted such a motion. Jurors agreed with the judge's decision, telling reporters that they too would have acquitted Harris.

His friends were not so lucky. On December 8, a jury convicted Anthony Washington and Andre Hogan. On May 29, 1998, they were both sentenced, Washington to 188 months in prison and Hogan to 121 months in prison. Stanford Riley, the fourth co-defendant in the case, was acquitted of all charges. And Dwight Flowers, the informant who arranged the drug deal with Washington, was sentenced to seventy months in federal prison.

His legal problems behind him, Harris received inquiries from numerous teams, including the Chicago Bears and Miami Dolphins. The Denver Broncos, in search of another pass rusher to shore up their Super Bowl run, went as far as to fly Harris to Denver and put him through a workout. But two months out of action and the stress of the trial left him far from being in game day condition. No offers materialized. While the 1997 season came to a close, Harris spent his days sitting idly in his East St. Louis apartment, watching repeat broadcasts of ESPN's *Sports Center* and waiting for a call from an NFL team. On March 11, 1998, he got the call. That day he signed a free agent contract with the Oakland Raiders.

8

What to Expect When You're Expecting

Miami Dolphins team headquarters, Davie, Florida: "It's a matter of anytime that there's talent available you continually try to upgrade the bottom four or five spots on your roster," Miami Dolphins head coach Jimmy Johnson told a group of reporters gathered at the team's headquarters on December 2, 1997. He was explaining his decision to offer a contract to troubled running back Lawrence Phillips. "There's a large upside," Johnson insisted. "If Lawrence does all the things we ask in a highly disciplined program, then he can realize what his talents might be and realize the success that you probably thought he was going to have in the first place."

Less than two weeks earlier, the St. Louis Rams suddenly cut Phillips after he was reportedly fined fifty-six times for violating team rules. In his nineteen-month tenure with the Rams, Phillips was arrested three times, served a jail sentence for domestic violence, and was twice sued by women—once for domestic violence and once for sexual assault. Having received a "second chance" at the University of Nebraska following a brief suspension for brutally assaulting ex-girlfriend Kate McEwen, the Rams also gave Phillips multiple "second chances" before finally releasing him.

Johnson assured the media that he and the Dolphins had thoroughly investigated Phillips, and that he was not the menace often portrayed in the popular press—all words that had been used by the Rams two years earlier. "Actually I expected all of the worst, with all of the rumors that you hear," Johnson said. "And I can say this for a fact, all of the rumors that you hear are not true. We have checked out in factual information and the things that you hear are highly, highly exaggerated."

Exaggerated? Although the attack on McEwen which landed Phillips in jail had received excessive media play, the scope of Phillips's abusive behavior was kept hidden from the public. McEwen, despite requests from countless national publications and television networks, never spoke publicly about her violent relationship with Phillips. But on August 16, 1996, she did file a civil complaint at the Jackson County Federal Court in Kansas. In it, she revealed a brutal litany of assaults suffered at the hands of Phillips while the two attended the University of Nebraska.

Although civil law suits are typically a matter of public record and available to the press, McEwen's complaint was filed under seal. To the liking of Phillips and his lawyers, reporters were unable to view its content. However, on September 3, 1996, federal judge William F. Mauer surprisingly lifted the seal. In effect, Judge Mauer's decision left the painful details of McEwen's civil complaint available to any reporter who showed up at the courthouse and requested to see the file. Wanting desperately to conceal the details, Phillips's lawyers acted promptly and were able to secure a court order placing the document back under seal within twenty-four hours.

But during the brief window when the case file was open, *Kansas City Star* court reporter Joe Lambe was at the federal courthouse and he made a copy of the complaint. He is the only reporter in the country to have seen the case file. Lambe reported these details from McEwen's complaint:

• October 1994, "Phillips shoved her head into a wall so hard it broke through the wall, then choked her and would not allow her to leave his apartment."

• April 1995, "Phillips asked her whether she was dating anyone else and threatened her, saying, 'I'm going to shoot you in the kneecaps and then shoot you in the elbows. This is Los Angeles gang style of dealing with people.'"

• May 10, 1995, "Phillips slashed her car tires and threatened to kill her. That came after he demanded a glass of water and McEwen told him to get it himself."

• August 24, 1995, "McEwen agreed to drive Phillips, who was drunk, home to his apartment. He forced her to stay there and sexually assaulted her."

• September 10, 1995, "Phillips beat her and kicked her while she was at a friend's house. She contends he then grabbed her hair 'caveman style,' pulled her down three flights of steps and slammed her head into a wall."

Phillips reached an out-of-court financial settlement with McEwen, which required that she neither discuss the nature of her complaint nor the details of the payoff.

Maybe the reason Johnson could so comfortably claim Phillips's record was "exaggerated" stemmed from the comparison of Phillips's record with some of his other players who had either served time in jail or been convicted of a violent felony. Yet these players were never scrutinized by the press like Phillips. For example, Johnson signed little-known free agent wide receiver Charles Jordan in 1996, who developed into one of Dan Marino's most reliable receivers in 1997. As a teen growing up in Los Angeles, Jordan was an active member of the Bloods. The authors discovered that his criminal history made Phillips look like a choirboy.

On June 27, 1990, Kenney Jones was gunned down in a hail of bullets while walking down a sidewalk near the intersection of 79th Street and Avalon Boulevard in Los Angeles. A five-block area between 76th and 80th Streets around Avalon Boulevard is home turf to a local gang calling themselves the Swans, a subset of the Bloods street gang. Jones, at the time he was shot, was wearing blue, the colors of a rival gang.

Neighbors were initially reluctant to cooperate with investigators' search for the killers. But a week after the shooting, Officer Jerry Pierro received information linking Swan gang members Charles Jordan, aka "Chucky," Tyrone Jordan, aka "Whitey," and Glen Jones, aka "Glayball," to the murder. According to a witness, the three were seen speeding away from the scene in a white Oldsmobile. Then on July 3, a man who lived at the corner of 79th and Avalon went to the police and revealed that his twelve-year-old son had been outside at the time of the murder. According to court documents, the boy also saw a white Oldsmobile speeding away from the scene.

When police finally questioned Charles Jordan about his whereabouts on the night of the killing, he claimed, according to court documents, that he was at home, one block away on 78th, along with Glen Jones and knew nothing about the murder. Police then separately questioned Tyrone Jordan, who pinned the murder on fellow gang members John Davis and Maurice Stevens. However, Tyrone admitted that Charles and Glen Jones *were* at the murder scene and that Charles "made comments about the victim wearing the wrong colors just before the victim was shot."

When police tracked down Maurice Stevens, he admitted that he and Davis were at the scene as well, but insisted "that Chucky and Tyrone did the shooting."

In follow-up questioning by the police, Jones admitted that he and Charles had concocted a story about their where-abouts the first time they were questioned. In a September 13 interview with police, Charles Jordan said that he lied about his whereabouts because "he knew that the word out on the street was that he committed the murder," according to court documents. The officers then asked Jordan if he would submit to a lie detector test. After failing it, Jordan re-fused to cooperate further with police in their investigation.

In addition to being the prime suspect in the murder of Kenny Jones, Jordan had to appear in court on September 27, 1990, for a pretrial hearing on an unrelated matter. He had been charged with threatening to kill Warrena Wilson and Wilbur Holloway when they showed up to testify at the pretrial hearing of Swan gang member Craig Williams, who was himself facing two counts of attempted murder. Ac-cording to court documents, on August 13, 1990, Jordan confronted the two witnesses in the hallway outside the courtroom in an attempt to scare them from going inside. Jordan's brash intimidation tactics were witnessed by Los Angeles Deputy Sheriff Shaun McCarthy, who was in charge of the Williams investigation.

"When I walked into the hallway after I got off the eleva-tor, I saw two males [Jordan and Williams] standing having a verbal conversation with both Ms. Wilson and Mr. Hol-loway," McCarthy testified at Jordan's preliminary hearing on September 27. "They were approached by those two males, and they were encouraged just to leave court and drop the whole incident. . . . The defendant in the attempted murder case [Williams] offered $500 to the victims if they would leave court."

McCarthy testified that when the witnesses rejected the hush money, Jordan issued his threats. "At that point," said McCarthy, "Charles Jordan made the statement, 'Then it is your life that you're messing with.' At that point, the victim, Holloway, said, 'Mr. Jordan, is that some kind of threat?' Mr. Jordan responded by saying, 'No, that's a promise.'"

The threat worked. Williams and Holloway ultimately left the courthouse without testifying that day. The sheriff's attempts to bring them back at a later date were unsuccessful. "I have been told by Mr. Holloway's family that he has moved out, that he is afraid to testify and that they don't know where he has moved," McCarthy testified at a subsequent hearing. "I have contacted Warrena Wilson's family, and I was told that she has moved to San Bernardino and that they don't know where."

On October 11, Jordan was indicted on two felony counts of dissuading a witness by force or threat. (He later pleaded guilty on March 8, 1991, and received probation.) Then on October 31, Jordan was finally arrested and charged with the murder of Kenny Jones. He was jailed and denied bail. Two other Swan Blood gang members, Maurice Stevens and John Davis, were also jailed and charged in the murder.

Jordan's stay in the Los Angeles County Jail, however, was far shorter than that of Stevens and Davis. On January 25, 1991, Jordan was released and the murder charges against him were dropped. Just days before Jordan's release, Tyrone Jordan and Glen Jones, who were originally spotted driving away from the murder scene with Jordan, testified at Jordan's pretrial hearing. In their testimony, they exonerated Jordan and implicated another man, John Davis.

"These witnesses kind of changed the way they thought about things to where Charles Jordan . . . was no longer involved," said Davis's court-appointed attorney, Matthew Kaestner, in court documents. Kaestner suggested in court that Jordan may have placed collect calls from the county jail and told Tyrone and Glen Jones what to say at his pretrial hearing. "They're involved in a conspiracy, number one, to put these two men [Stevens and Davis] away," Kaestner suggested to Judge Clarence Stromwall. "The second conspiracy was to get Charles Jordan out of jail. This was a three-defendant case. The man who failed the polygraph is the shooter. He gets dismissed out at preliminary hearing. That's Charles Jordan. He's the leader of this gang. He puts out orders to these two witnesses, this is what you are to say at preliminary hearing."

Kaestner's theory was that his client (Davis) and Stevens were taking the fall for Jordan. "I want to know, is there anything in the group dynamic of this gang that when someone has to go down on a shooting, a couple people get pointed out and they do the time and go away because they were lower in the pecking order," Kaestern said to Judge Stromwall in his attempt to get a court order giving him access to the jail's pay phone records. The judge did not appear to be buying Kaestner's argument.

On January 9, 1992, the murder charges against Maurice Stevens were also dropped, leaving only Davis in jail. Witnesses had told police that he was seen with a handgun at the scene. On January 17, Davis pleaded no contest to reduced charges of voluntary manslaughter in the death of Kenney Jones and was sentenced to three years in prison. It was Jordan, however, who insisted during a December 1997 interview with ESPN that he was the one who had willfully taken the rap for another gang member by sitting in jail for nearly four months. He added that he would do the same thing again for a fellow gangster if the opportunity arose. Jordan declined to be interviewed for this book.

According to the authors' research, Jordan's life as a gang member before entering the NFL involved a wide range of other run-ins with the law. The following list was compiled from the criminal court docket at the Los Angeles Superior Court:

• August 3, 1988, charged with taking a vehicle without owner's consent. Pleaded no contest to theft of property and sentenced to thirty days in jail.

• August 21, 1988, charged with felony robbery and jailed. Bail was set at $16,000. The case was later dismissed.

• January 1, 1989, charged with illegal gambling. [No disposition records were available.]

• February 20, 1992, charged with reckless driving and driving with a suspended license. Pleaded no contest and was placed on probation and sentenced to either pay a fine or serve ten days in jail. He was also ordered to attend alcohol education classes. On January 1, 1993, he was found in violation of his probation and sentenced to serve five days in jail.

• Jordan was also charged on three separate occasions with possession of a controlled substance and in 1990 he was indicted for kidnapping.

Although he said he is no longer actively involved with the Bloods, Jordan nonetheless still considers himself a part of his gang family. "I may not be active, but I still consider myself as one," he told ESPN. Further, Jordan continues to

give proceeds from his Dolphins paycheck to the Swan
Bloods in Los Angeles. "Once I give it to them, it's theirs. I
don't really ask what it's about. I just hand it to them."

The Dolphins' willingness to employ a gang affiliate is not
extraordinary. In a groundbreaking 1997 report, ESPN's
Outside the Lines chronicled the climb of numerous NFL
stars who made the transition from the Bloods and Crips to
the gridiron. Redskins defensive end Chris Mims, Bengals
running back Eric Bieniemy, Jaguars defensive back Deon
Figures, and Bills running back Darick Holmes discussed
their early exposure as teens to street gangs. Holmes, whose
brother is on death row for three gang-related homicides,
said he owned his first gun at age thirteen.
　How many former gang-bangers play in the NFL? Chris
Mims estimated "dozens."
　"The basic conclusion was that professional athletes are
increasingly coming from the inner city, and the inner city is
where gangs predominate," explained Matt Morantz, who
produced the ESPN report on gangs. Morantz spent four
months researching the connection between professional
sports and gangs. In the process, he interviewed approximately 300 people, among them gang experts, law enforcement officials, and NFL players. "The consensus of the
players was that you can't grow up in that environment
without having your life touched in some way by gangs," he
explained in an interview for this book.

Given Jordan's track record, it is little wonder that Jimmy
Johnson would embrace Lawrence Phillips when no other
NFL teams were as eager to do the same. Phillips had not
been implicated in murder cases. Nor had he confessed on

national television to supplying financial support to a violent street gang. Domestic violence was the biggest mark against Phillips, which hardly distinguished him from his new mates. Miami's other running back, Irving Spikes, pleaded no contest to battery for beating his wife in 1996. And wide receiver Lamar Thomas had been arrested multiple times for domestic violence during 1996 and 1997. A closer examination of the Thomas case reveals why it is no surprise that Johnson would give Phillips another chance.

On October 13, 1997, one day after the Dolphins defeated the Jets at Giants Stadium, Jimmy Johnson cut veteran wide receiver Fred Barnett. Lamar Thomas, who caught five passes against the Jets for seventy-five yards—including a crucial reception on the team's game-clinching drive—took Barnett's position in the lineup. "Fred does everything you ask," Johnson told reporters. "But had I not made the release I would not have been fair to our team as a whole."

A consummate veteran with a favorable off-the-field reputation, Barnett was replaced by the younger, faster, and criminal Thomas, whose domestic violence record was more prolific than his pass-catching statistics. "The bottom line is production," Johnson said candidly days before making the formal announcement. Indeed, production was the priority when Miami signed Thomas the year before on the heels of a vicious series of domestic violence attacks.

Much of the following account is based on court records and police reports obtained by the authors from the Office of the State Attorney in Fort Lauderdale, Florida.

On July 4, 1996, Thomas, then a member of the Tampa Bay Buccaneers, and his pregnant fiancée Ebony Cooksey attended a private pool party and barbecue at the home of Dr. and Mrs. Edmund Darroux in Plantation, Florida. At the time, Thomas was living in Tampa and Cooksey was still in Miami. She was completing her last year of college at the University of Miami, where the two met while both were on athletic scholarships.

The two were spending the week together in the Miami area before Thomas had to go north for training camp. The Darrouxes' son Richard, a friend of Lamar's and Ebony's, invited the couple to his family's Fourth of July celebration. Shortly after arriving, however, Thomas left the party briefly to visit his uncle in nearby Fort Lauderdale. When he returned, Thomas brought a cousin with him, and immediately insisted that Cooksey, who was relaxing in the pool, get out so he could introduce them.

"Lamar's very impatient," Cooksey would later say to a police officer in her attempt to reconstruct the sequence of events leading up to her assault at the hands of Thomas later that day. "I was trying to dry off and he kept say[ing] 'come over here, come over here.' It went from asking me to demanding me to come over."

Tired as a result of her pregnancy, Cooksey left the pool area altogether shortly after meeting Thomas's cousin. Inside the Darrouxes' house preparing to take a shower, Cooksey was fully undressed when Thomas barged into the bathroom unannounced to urinate. Despite the availability of other bathrooms in the house, Thomas insisted on using the one occupied by Cooksey. Wrapped only in a towel, she waited in the hallway for Thomas to finish before reentering the bathroom, locking the door behind her this time.

Minutes after Cooksey began showering, Thomas realized that she locked the door and began knocking, demanding that she let him in.

"Look, I'll be out," Cooksey responded from the shower.

Dissatisfied with Cooksey's response, Thomas located a clothes hanger and picked the lock.

Cooksey was unaware that Thomas had entered the bathroom until he jumped into the shower fully clothed and attacked her.

"He was enraged and demanded to know why I wouldn't let him in," Cooksey said in her police statement. "He opened the shower door and began strangling me and . . . I guess for about five seconds I couldn't breathe."

Dripping wet, Thomas stepped back out of the shower, leaving his pregnant fiancée cowering and crying. However, he wasn't finished.

"The next time I knock, you better f---ing answer it, you know," he shouted as he sprang back into the shower. "It doesn't make sense for you not to answer." He then grabbed Cooksey's head and began slamming it into the shower wall.

"The glimpse that I did catch in his eye," Cooksey later recalled to police, "it was like nobody was there." The violent assault was finally interrupted when a female guest at the barbecue entered the bathroom after hearing the commotion. Thomas again climbed out of the tub, his clothes now drenched. He ran out of the house still wet, jumped in his truck and drove off.

Naked, wet, bleeding, and battered, Cooksey was aided by the female who interrupted the assault. When barbecue host Mrs. Darroux learned what took place, she brought Cooksey upstairs to her bedroom so she could rest. A cup of coffee was brought up, along with Cooksey's clothing.

"Some domestic batterers don't have the social and psychological makeup to create other vents for their emotions," explained former Miami Dolphins offensive lineman Ed Newman, who is now a domestic violence judge in Dade

County, in an interview for this book. "They don't know how to take time out or channel emotions elsewhere, how to obtain solutions. They act without thinking. This is a dysfunction. These batterers are a wellspring of emotions. This leads to impulsive actions, and the actions are totally inappropriate."

Approximately thirty minutes after being attacked in the shower, Cooksey looked out Mrs. Darroux's second-story window only to see that Thomas had returned. His truck parked in front of the house, Thomas was standing outside talking to Richard Darroux. Scared, Cooksey decided to place a call to her father, and asked Mrs. Darroux to escort her downstairs to the library where there was a phone.

While Cooksey talked by telephone to her father, Thomas entered the library. With both Mrs. Darroux and Richard in the room, Cooksey was confident that Thomas would not harm her.

Suddenly, while Cooksey was in mid-sentence with her father, Thomas snatched the receiver from her hands and hung up the phone.

"I'm talking to my father," she pleaded.

"Shut up," Thomas demanded.

"Why are you acting like this?" Mrs. Darroux interjected. "Come on, Lamar. Sit down."

With all eyes on him, Thomas paused, sat down, and insisted to those in the room that Cooksey's fear of him was not sincere, but rather an act. Then, as Cooksey attempted to exit the room, Thomas leaped lightning quick to his feet. "At that point I knew I wasn't gonna get out of that room because he's Lamar and she's [Mrs. Darroux] who she is," said Cooksey, who quickly retreated behind a large desk for protection.

Meanwhile, Richard and his father, who had just entered the room, gingerly approached Thomas while Mrs. Darroux positioned herself between Thomas and the desk. None of this, however, deterred Thomas.

"He came toward me [as] if I was an offensive lineman and pushed me towards the window," Cooksey said. "And the window shattered on the lower right hand side. I feared for my life because I was imagining my head or something going through the window. And it was a thick window."

Mrs. Darroux later corroborated Cooksey's account to a criminal investigator. "The moment she picked up the phone, he sprang out of the chair, jumped across me," said Mrs. Darroux in her police statement. "It was like a football tackle. Straight across me, straight into her and push[ed] her into the window."

Both Richard and his father went to Cooksey's rescue, pulling Thomas off her. In the struggle, the library was trashed. Cooksey climbed back under the desk, hiding in fear as the men tried to restrain Thomas. A 911 call was placed for police assistance. Before the dust settled, Thomas's rage left red marks on Cooksey's throat, scratches on her left biceps, a large bump and bruise on her right triceps, and a red bruise on her right arm. He also caused over $700 in property damage, putting a hole through the wall, shattering a window, breaking a lamp, and destroying various objects on and around the desk.

Realizing that police had been called, Thomas tried to reassure everyone that there was no longer any threat of danger to Cooksey. "I'm calm," Thomas said unconvincingly. "I have it under control." He then exited the house and hurried toward his truck. Mrs. Darroux followed him outside while one of her children placed a second 911 call, trying frantically to get police to come quicker.

"Where's he at now?" the 911 operator asked.

"Sir, I hope he's outside of the house," Mrs. Darroux's son said.

"What does he look like?"

"Oh though, he's with my mother and I don't want to leave him alone with my mother, so could you just please get somebody here?"

"Someone's on the way out there. But what does he look like?"

"Um, he's 6'4, his name is Lamar Thomas. He plays football for the Tampa Bay Buccaneers. He's 170, 75 pounds, a goatee. He's medium to dark skin. He's wearing a pair of blue jeans."

Five days after the attacks, Cooksey gave her formal statement over the telephone to Detective Cindy Costanza of the City of Plantation Police Department. By then Cooksey's bruises had darkened, looking much worse than they did when the police photographed them on the day of the incident. However, Cooksey's primary concern was the fetus she was carrying.

"I spoke with my doctor on Saturday regarding my pregnancy and whether or not it should be terminated or whether or not it still lived," Cooksey told Officer Costanza.

"You did?" asked Costanza.

"It's just that it's a big decision that I'm gonna have to make in terms of whether or not I want him to father this child," said Cooksey.

Costanza's chief concern related to the fetus as well, but for reasons different than Cooksey's. While domestic violence is treated as a misdemeanor in Florida, assaulting a pregnant woman is classified as a felony. "Can you tell me about the pregnancy?" asked Costanza. "Did [Lamar] know that you were pregnant?"

"Oh yeah, yeah," said Cooksey. "He even bought me the book called 'What to Expect When You're Expecting.' Lamar had wanted a baby for quite some time and that was sort of a problem that we were having in our relationship. . . . I have a year of school to go. We're not married yet."

On July 10, a warrant was issued for Thomas's arrest on two felony counts of aggravated battery against a pregnant female. One week later, the Buccaneers released Thomas. A player who wished to remain unnamed told the authors that the Buccaneers dropped Thomas as a result of his arrest. Buccaneers officials, when contacted by authors, refused to confirm that there was a relationship between Thomas's case and his release. "We're not going to talk about that," said communications director Reggie Roberts. "We have no comment."

Not ten days passed before Dolphins newly hired head coach Jimmy Johnson signed Thomas to a contract. Johnson had coached Thomas in college at the University of Miami and insisted that he deserved a "second chance."

"Jimmy Johnson recruited Lamar to the University of Miami," explained Thomas's defense attorney and agent, Howard Weinberg. "Jimmy Johnson left when Lamar got there, but Jimmy was aware of the type of person that Lamar was. Jimmy realized that Lamar was the type of guy who was worth saving. Lamar was lucky because there wasn't just Jimmy there, Gary Stephens was there too. And they are both well aware that of all the receivers who have played at the University of Miami, and it's quite a distinguished list, Lamar is the all-time leading receiver in the history of the University of Miami."

After her physician determined that the fetus had not suffered any fatal injuries, Cooksey opted to go through with the pregnancy. The Darrouxes, meanwhile, received a call from Thomas's attorney, Howard Weinberg. "He [Weinberg] apologized," Darroux told the police, "and said that he [was] gonna make sure the bills get paid and he's going to take care of it, see that [Lamar] gets counseling and . . . make sure it doesn't happen again," according to court documents.

However, it did happen again—and the problem was not taken care of. After appearing in nine games for the Dolphins in 1996 while his lawyers successfully delayed the disposition of his case until after the season, Thomas was sentenced to eighteen months' probation for aggravated battery on a pregnant female on February 24, 1997. He was also ordered to spend ten days in Broward County Jail, which was to be served on the weekends, and to complete a thirteen-week Batterer Intervention Program at LifeLine in Miami.

The Dolphins then offered Thomas a new contract on March 11, 1997. Three weeks later, Thomas assaulted Cooksey again. On March 29, Metro Dade police were dispatched to the couple's Coconut Grove home. Cooksey, at this point, had given birth to a baby boy who was now six weeks old.

Upon arrival, the officers found Thomas holding the newborn. Cooksey was discovered in the couple's bedroom crying. Her underwear was torn and there were scratches on her right hand, left shoulder, and neck. After she told Officer Grass that Thomas tore her underwear three times and choked her, he was arrested, issued his Miranda rights, and escorted to the back of the police cruiser.

After Thomas's arrest, probation officers learned that he had yet to begin the counseling program that was part of his probation. A subsequent report signed by correctional probation supervisor Jasmine V. Seligman and correctional probation officer Dorett Jones recommended that Thomas's "probation be extended to twenty-four months, with a longer period of counseling. Thus giving [Thomas] a chance to change his temper and be able to live as a law abiding citizen." The report also indicated that Thomas had accumulated eighty-eight total sentencing points, which carries a maximum of seventy-five months in state prison.

Johnson's initial decision to hire Thomas in 1996 came before the talented receiver had been formally convicted of anything. By the time the team re-signed him a year later, Thomas was a convicted felon. Now he was charged with assaulting his fiancée again, and found to be in violation of his probation. Did any of this change Thomas's playing status with the Dolphins? Not exactly.

There were no reported disciplinary measures taken by the team. No ultimatums laid down. But Weinberg said that the team strongly encouraged Thomas to seek counseling. "There are selfish motives [on the part of the Dolphins], arguably, because they want him to be the best player possible," explained Weinberg. "But they're saying, 'If you want to reach your full potential, then you have to be able to meet the challenge of dealing with the problems off the field.' No one is capable of completely separating his personal life with his professional life. These things bleed through."

Jimmy Johnson declined to be interviewed on his decision to continue playing Thomas.

The authors did, however, interview other former Dolphins familiar with the Thomas case. "The role of the coach to win plays a large role to how they respond to these situations," said ex-Miami Dolphin defensive back Liffort Hobley in an interview for this book. Hobley worked for the Dolphins when running back Irving Spikes was arrested for beating his wife in 1995. Don Shula was the head coach then, and Hobley saw stark differences in the way the Spikes and Thomas cases were handled.

On August 26, 1995, Pembroke Pines police officers responded to a domestic violence complaint at the Spikes residence. According to the police report, Spikes choked his wife and struck her in the face before throwing her to the floor. Stacey Spikes sustained injuries to the neck, knees, and right foot. The following day, Shula met with Spikes, who was entering his second season in the NFL. Despite not yet being convicted of anything, Spikes was informed by Shula that he was on disciplinary probation for a full year. Any more incidents, and he'd be dismissed.

"Domestic violence is definitely something that Shula would not condone," said Hobley, who actively worked with Spikes in an attempt to help him get counseling. "Shula made sure Spikes got into counseling. It was mandatory. He had to go at least two hours a week. Spikes felt threatened for his job."

According to Hobley, after Spikes met with Shula, he said, "If I get cut from here, who's going to give me an opportunity after this guy [Shula] cuts me? Everybody respects him." Spikes pleaded no contest to battery on May 16, 1996. However, as of the publication of this book, Spikes has had no further contact with law enforcement pertaining to domestic violence. He was cut by the Dolphins during the 1998 off season.

In contrast, Thomas faced no apparent disciplinary action from Johnson. Nor was Thomas required to fulfill his obligation to attend anger management courses. "Under Shula, anything that you did and got caught doing it, you were gone—no matter who you were," according to Hobley. " 'Anything happens outside the realm of this organization that I hear about, and there's no question that you did it, you're out of here,' Shula used to say."

On April 24, 1997, Judge Geoffrey D. Cohen signed a warrant for Thomas's arrest for violating the terms of his probation. It read in part, "the probationer did commit the offense of Simple Battery on March 29, 1997, as alleged in Dade Circuit Court. . . ." Thomas was again arrested and jailed pending his trial. It wasn't until Thomas was incarcerated, according to Weinberg, that Thomas started to confront his problem. One day while Weinberg was visiting Thomas at the Broward County Jail, a guard knocked on the door of their private cubicle and interrupted the conversation. "It's time," the guard said to Thomas.

"Time for what?" Weinberg asked Thomas.

Weinberg soon discovered that a group of at-risk teenagers were touring the jail in conjunction with a Scared Straight program. Thomas, when he found out about their visit, had volunteered to speak to the youths. According to Weinberg, Thomas stood up in front of the boys, wearing his jailhouse jumpsuit, and told them, "I'm locked up in here. I have a baby at home. I'm sending him the wrong signal. And I play football in the NFL, so you probably think I'm pretty tough. Well, guess what? I'm not too tough to cry. You never ever want to be in the situation I'm in."

Prosecutors suddenly dropped the charges against Thomas on May 14 and he was released from jail. Cooksey had decided not to testify against Thomas, leaving prosecutors without their prime witness.

Cooksey's reluctance is typical of domestic violence victims, but rarely understood by individuals who have not experienced violence in the home. "Sometimes victims have good reasons for not testifying," explained domestic violence judge Ed Newman, the former Dolphins lineman. "Domestic violence is like a dance. In this dance, one is the aggressor-perpetrator, the other is the victim. The victim adopts strategies to avoid the next beating. Some victims think, in the procedural context of a trial, that they will be beaten if they step forward as a witness. Sometimes they are concerned about retaliation. Sometimes the victim is financially and emotionally dependent on the perpetrator."

After playing in two Super Bowls under Shula, Newman completed his law degree and was later elected to the bench. He is one of a group of Florida judges who have been assigned to hear domestic violence cases on an exclusive basis. "When there's an apparent problem, when you see a young lady with a black eye and it happens again and again, somebody needs to intervene," said Newman. "Not only for the good of the individuals, but for the good of the image of the league and of the Dolphins."

Apparently nobody ever intervened on Ebony Cooksey's behalf. Thomas got talked to many times about the need to address his problems, but there was little incentive in the way of consequences. After his incarceration, however, Weinberg said that Thomas started to take counseling quite seriously. "A black male, particularly one who plays professional sports, does not see reaching out for psychiatric help or counseling as a viable option," explained Weinberg. "They see that as a sign of weakness. So it was of great value when Lamar stood up in front of a bank of reporters and said, 'I need professional counseling and that doesn't mean that I'm not a man.'"

According to Weinberg, Thomas, Cooksey, and their child were living together as of the spring of 1998. At that point in time, Thomas had been in counseling for nearly a year. Thomas declined the authors' invitation to be interviewed for this book.

And as far as Jimmy Johnson's motives for keeping Thomas on the roster throughout the assaults, arrests, and jail time? "They want to win games," Weinberg said. "There's no question about it. If they can get him to play his best, they've helped themselves. But I definitely noticed concern that was separate and apart from just those issues."

When assessing whether Johnson is acting out of raw self-interest or altruism, it is difficult to overlook that in 1998 Dan Marino will be throwing the ball to two athletically gifted criminals (Thomas and Jordan have both been convicted of violent crimes).* His own words from a press conference in October of 1997 seem to sum up his motives best. "The bottom line is production," Johnson said.

---

*Editor's note: Marino will not be handing off to Phillips, however, who was cut from the Dolphins on July 25. Coach Jimmy Johnson now has a number of talented running backs to replace Phillips, who'd begun fumbling the ball in training camp. Johnson explained to reporters that his decision to release Phillips had little to do with the troubled athlete's most recent brush with the law: As this book goes to press, Florida police are investigating allegations that Phillips assaulted a woman in a Miami nightclub in June.

9

Clear and Present Danger

"**V**ikings: Scandinavian warriors from the 8th century to the 10th century. They were exceedingly cruel and rapacious on their raids, and the dread they inspired facilitated their conquests."

You will not find this definition in the Minnesota Vikings media guide. Rather, it comes from the *Columbia Encyclopedia,* second edition. The authors' extensive investigation reveals, however, that this definition fits a disturbing number of the NFL's version of the Vikings. While the Dallas Cowboys have been vilified as a lawless bunch of renegades during the 1990s, the Vikings may have been the most out-of-control team in the NFL.

Eden Prairie, Minnesota, March 3, 1997

According to police reports, it was dusk when Officer Kevin White of the Eden Prairie Police Department was dispatched to a reported car accident at the intersection of Prairie Center Drive and Valley View Road. Car parts and debris lay scattered across the area. A black Toyota Camry appeared to have rear-ended a gray Jeep Grand Cherokee.

Fifty-five-year-old Corrinne Altanette, the driver of the Cherokee, was already outside her vehicle. She reported being struck from behind by the Camry while sitting at a red light.

Another officer at the scene soon informed Officer White that the driver of the Camry was acting very strange and reeked of alcohol. As White approached the Camry's driver's side window, the occupant said his name was Carl Hargrave. When asked to produce his insurance papers, Hargrave started retrieving a black bag from the glove box. After twice being asked what was in the bag, Hargrave snapped, "None of your f---in' business!" White wrote in his report that night. Hargrave then handed White an identification card and exclaimed, "This is who I am!"

The card read, "Minnesota Vikings," and identified Hargrave as the running backs coach.

Asked to step out of the car to perform sobriety tests, Hargrave asked, "Can't we work this out? Why don't you just take me home?"

Asked again to step from the car, Hargrave became indignant. "You're pissing me off," he announced to White, prompting the officer to radio for backup.

With Hargrave detained until other officers arrived, the coach went from appeals for leniency to making threats. "He advised me that I was making a mistake, and that I should know better," said White's report. "I asked what he meant by that, and he said, '[You] should know.'"

With the arrival of backup, White and another officer asked Hargrave to step from the car so they could search the vehicle for weapons. "F--- this shit!" Hargrave said. "You're starting to piss me off." Once out of the car, the officers made one final attempt to administer sobriety tests. "F---

no," responded Hargrave. "Arrest me. Arrest me, mother-f---er."

Handcuffed in the back of White's cruiser, Hargrave continued his profanity-laced threats all the way to the police station. "I'm gonna get you, you motherf---er," shouted Hargrave at White, one of the only black officers on the Eden Prairie force. "You don't know who you are messing with. You know you are going on what the white lady said to you. You motherf---er."

"Mr. Hargrave told me that 'I'm gonna find you and kick your mother f---in' ass,'" reported White.

Once at the station, Hargrave refused to let officers administer the implied consent advisory. He also refused to be photographed for booking and repeatedly interrupted officers' attempts to read him his Miranda rights. The following is an excerpt from the Eden Prairie Police Department Intoxication Report Form:

OFFICER: Do you understand these [Miranda] rights?
HARGRAVE: No.
OFFICER: Do you wish to talk with us at this time?
HARGRAVE: F--- you.
OFFICER: Have you been in an accident?
HARGRAVE: I was in no accident.
OFFICER: Tell me what happened—why did an officer stop you?
HARGRAVE: I don't know why you guys are f---in' with me.

Officer Brent Griffith was asked to enter the booking room in hopes of de-escalating Hargrave's belligerence. At six foot five and 275 pounds, Griffith's arrival temporarily quieted Hargrave. But Hargrave's sudden mood change was not due to Griffith's imposing size. Instead, it was because Hargrave must have sensed a chance to catch a break. Griffith, a recently retired NFL lineman, had played briefly for the Vikings and was familiar to the coach. "I just told him that things would be better for everyone if he just cooperated with the lead officer," Griffith explained in an interview for this book.

After agreeing to take the breathalyzer test, Hargrave falsely attempted to blow into the intoxilyzer. Repeatedly told that he was not blowing into the device, Hargrave reverted to asking if they could "work it out." When Hargrave received no preferential treatment, he again turned violent. Griffith and White were forced to wrestle him to the ground, handcuff him, and escort him to the county jail. "It was an uncomfortable situation," Griffith explained. "But it doesn't matter who you are. We can't start bending the rules just because of who you are. There were no favors given."

Hargrave was charged with five criminal counts: refusal to submit to chemical testing, driving under the influence of alcohol, obstructing legal process, disorderly conduct, and careless driving.

Hargrave, the police soon discovered, had been through this drill before. In 1994, shortly after being hired by the Vikings, he had been pulled over for drunk driving and refused to take a breathalyzer. On May 20 of that year he pleaded guilty to reckless driving and had his Minnesota driving privileges revoked. As a result of the prior refusal to be tested after a DUI stop, Hargrave was now facing jail time, since under Minnesota law, a second refusal of a breathalyzer qualified as a "gross misdemeanor."

There was a reason Hargrave didn't understand why the Eden Prairie police, and in particular an ex-Viking-turned-cop, would not cut him a break. As the authors discovered and volumes of evidence will show, Hargrave had watched his fellow coaches and players avoid accountability for their actions time and time again, often with the help of the team's head of security, Steve Rollins, an ex-cop-turned-Viking. In particular, Hargrave himself had been previously rescued by Rollins after Hargrave's relentless attempts to bed a Minneapolis-area nude dancer nearly exposed a deep, dark secret: that head coach Dennis Green had already bedded the same woman, impregnated her, and paid her to have an abortion in order to save his career. More on that later. First, some history.

Heading into the 1992 season, Vikings head coach Jerry Burns was in the final year of his contract. With management having changed hands the previous year and the recent naming of Roger Headrick as the club's new chief executive officer, Burns knew he would be replaced at season's end. Aware that players sensed his lame duck status, Burns took measures to insure no sordid off-the-field incidents tainted his last year.

Days before training camp opened in Mankato, Minnesota, Burns called a private meeting with Dan Endy, the Vikings' director of operations, to come up with a strategy. Much of the following account of what took place in that meeting is based on an interview with Endy, who was fired by the Vikings in 1993. The circumstances leading up to Endy's dismissal from the Vikings are detailed later in the chapter.

"I don't think it is any surprise that these guys know that

this is my final year," Burns told Endy in their pre-training-camp meeting. "I don't want the inmates to run the asylum. I don't want one of those Dutcher things." Jim Dutcher, ex-head coach at the University of Minnesota, was forced to resign under heavy media scrutiny after three of his players were arrested for gang-raping a woman in the team's hotel during a road trip.

At Burns's direction, Endy drafted a memo to team president Roger Headrick, requesting the creation of two new part-time security positions. "This is a great idea," Headrick wrote in a response relayed to Burns through Endy. "But instead of going with two half-time guys, why don't we go with one full-time guy." Headrick, according to Endy, added, "It has to be a minority."

Endy and former Vikings linebacker Scott Studwell, who had been recently hired to work in the front office, solicited the league office for potential job candidates. After being telephoned by Studwell, Charlie Jackson from the NFL's security division forwarded the names of two former law enforcement officers from the Minnesota area who were minorities. The league has long compiled the names of minority job candidates in a variety of fields and encourages the individual teams to hire from the list.

Endy, Studwell, and Headrick interviewed both candidates and decided against hiring an ex-FBI agent, instead offering the position to Steve Rollins. A former police officer with the St. Paul Police Department, Rollins appeared the perfect fit for coach Burns's intentions. "Burns was not a real disciplinarian," said Endy. "Jerry's idea of discipline to the team was 'I don't want to have to be a chickenshit coach. Don't put me in a situation where I have to fine you. I'm leaving it up to you guys to behave accordingly.'

"Rollins came in with the suit. He was very formal, authoritative."

Rollins may have looked good in a suit, but he did not look so good on paper. The Vikings, apparently, were unaware that the man recommended by the NFL had a history of misconduct that ultimately ended in him turning in his badge.

Citing "personal reasons" in his resignation notice to the police force dated August 30, 1988, Rollins was the subject of discharge proceedings due to recurring police misconduct. The chief of the St. Paul Police Department sought Rollins's dismissal from the force after outstanding arrest warrants were issued against him for repeated motor vehicle violations in 1985, 1986, and 1987. "Aside from the obvious concern of having an officer in the Department who is in violation of the very laws he is expected to enforce," wrote Chief McCutcheon in a December 3, 1987, letter to Rollins, "if a warrant is not taken care of, your driver's license will be suspended and you will be unable to perform your duties as a Police Officer."

Rollins was also facing a four-count indictment involving two felony charges of intent to escape taxes, one charge of unregistered use of a vehicle, and one charge for failure to transfer ownership of a vehicle. In a Waiver and Resignation statement signed by Rollins the day before he resigned, Rollins admitted to the following: "On August 29, 1988, I, Stephen Rollins . . . approached Tom Hughes, Special Prosecutor for the City of Saint Paul, and proposed a settlement of the criminal matter against me. . . . I suggested that the City dismiss charges against me in return for my resignation from the Police Department, and withdrawal of the appeal of my discharge."

Internal affairs files for the City of St. Paul Police Department reveal that Rollins was reprimanded fifteen times between 1976 and 1987 for police procedure violations ranging from improper use of force to driving with a suspended license. For example, on July 27, 1983, the deputy chief of the St. Paul Police Department censured Rollins for the "improper use of physical force to restrain" a citizen.

"I cannot agree with the technique you used to resolve what could be a haven for the individuals who you are trying to keep off of your beat," wrote the deputy chief. "Your actions came very close to false imprisonment, which is not a viable alternative for police officers to resolve conflict situations."

The NFL declined to explain how individuals with a record such as Rollins's ended up on their list of highly recommended job candidates.

Within days of Minnesota naming Rollins head of team security, reports started surfacing within the organization regarding his past record. Rollins, according to Endy, quickly quieted the rumors with his handling of an incident that could have exposed the team to unwanted negative publicity. One evening at training camp, All-Pro defensive tackle Keith Millard crashed his Corvette while driving through a Hardee's restaurant parking lot. The accident reportedly caused property damage to the Hardee's and left Millard's car undrivable. Before police arrived at Hardee's, Millard got a ride back to the team's residence hall with a teammate, leaving his Corvette at the accident scene.

According to Endy, who was at the Vikings' dorm when

police showed up to question Millard, Rollins successfully discouraged the senior officer, who was on friendly terms with the Vikings from previous training camps, from seeing Millard or administering a breathalyzer test. As a result, Millard was never charged in the incident.

One former Vikings player, who is both a friend of Millard's and quite familiar with the Hardee's incident, said that the way Rollins dealt with the situation convinced players that "this guy could cover up anything." However it was the Vikings' brass who were most impressed. "Steve was lauded, like, 'Hey, this was a great thing that he had done,' " confirmed Endy, who was director of communications before being promoted to director of team operations. "Headrick was proud. Steve was his hire. And from a publicity standpoint it may have been a great thing. But from a health standpoint, we had a chemically dependent defensive tackle who needed help, and we glossed it over."

On the surface, a simple drunk driving incident hardly seems worth the effort to cover up. However, Millard had a history of drunk driving arrests, which had been well reported in the Minneapolis press. At the time of the Hardee's incident, he had just recently come off probation for a 1990 conviction for reckless driving, which was reduced from DUI. His 1990 arrest had touched off a firestorm of criticism in the Minneapolis press that exposed a major drunk driving problem among the Vikings players. Millard became the thirteenth Vikings player in a four-year span to be arrested for driving drunk.

Thanks in part to Rollins's ability to minimize exposure this time, the team did not have to have their drunk driving problems resurrected on the front pages of the papers all over again. With the arrival in 1992 of head coach Dennis

Green and his new staff, the Millard incident was like a pre-season warm-up for the kind of public relations problems that Rollins would be asked to squelch in his capacity as director of team security.

In February of 1992, after being named as the Vikings' new head coach, Dennis Green began assembling his staff. He offered Richard Solomon, an old teammate and roommate at the University of Iowa, the job as defensive backs coach. Solomon, who had no prior coaching experience at the pro level, accepted and immediately moved to the Minneapolis area. Along with a group of other new assistants who needed temporary housing until they could purchase new homes and relocate their families, Solomon moved into a hotel in Bloomington, one of a number of Minneapolis-area hotels where the Vikings maintained a business account. The hotel, which was used primarily by the team to accommodate players and coaches while in transition, used a number of representatives to personally oversee the Vikings' account. One of Dan Endy's responsibilities as director of team operations was to work directly with the hotel's representatives. It was in this capacity that Endy quickly became embroiled in a controversy that would ultimately cost him his job.

Within weeks after the coaches moved in, Endy started receiving reports from a certain sales representative, a young single woman, that Solomon was making unwanted sexual advances toward her. Over time, the reports increased both in frequency and in severity. "I had known the woman for a couple of years," Endy said. "During the season, we'd talk on the phone at least twice a week for business-related matters. It was in this context that she made me aware of

Solomon's actions. She wasn't asking me to do anything about it. She wanted our business. She was just making me aware because we had a mutually respectful relationship."

But Endy did do something with the information he was receiving. He forwarded the reports directly to his superior, team vice president Jeff Diamond. Endy estimated that at least once a month throughout the spring and summer, he would meet with Diamond and convey what this woman was reporting. Each time they met, Diamond would take notes and would ask Endy if he had ever witnessed firsthand the reported harassment. "I was always up front with Jeff," Endy said. "I told him that I never personally witnessed this stuff, but that I was merely forwarding along this woman's reports. I had known her for over two years and had no reason whatsoever to doubt her."

Then in the preseason, the nature of the woman's complaints changed from mere verbal harassment to physical assault. "When she called me she was crying," Endy said, referring to a call the woman made to him in August of 1992. "It was the first time that had ever happened. She went on to tell me that Solomon had come into her office, thrown her up against the wall, grabbed her breasts and tried to force himself on her. To me, that was an assault. And it was the first time I ever asked her, 'Do you want me to do something?' "

Endy had been to Diamond's office so many times in the previous seven months with less than flattering reports of Solomon, that when he arrived to report the latest, Diamond looked up and said, "What did he do now?"

"This guy's dick is going to get us in trouble," Endy flatly stated, as he closed the door and sat down.

Endy was not sure what Diamond was doing with all the

notes he was taking about Solomon. But as soon as the regular season started, the sales representative from a Minneapolis hotel began reporting unwanted sexual advances as well. Only the subject of these complaints was not Solomon, but Green.

The Vikings stayed at the hotel every Saturday evening prior to home games. One of the people who handled the Vikings' hotel account, a very attractive woman in her thirties, began reporting to Endy that coach Green was requiring her to meet him at 6:00 A.M. for breakfast on Tuesdays during the regular season. She said that Green, who was married at the time, would always conclude the breakfast session by kissing her on the lips. "Maybe that's a term of affection," the woman said to Endy. "But I'm an employee of the hotel. He's doing this around other employees and customers. I don't think he meant anything by it, but there's a restaurant full of people who might assume I'm some other woman."

"So don't meet him for breakfast," Endy suggested.

"I have to," she said.

"Why?" asked Endy.

"I don't want to lose your business," she said wryly. The Vikings were renting 100 rooms per weekend from the hotel during the winter months.

Neither of the sales representatives at either hotel asked Endy to forward their reports to Vikings management. Moreover, by going to Diamond on his own, Endy, who had been with the club for over a decade and had aspirations to become the assistant general manager, was risking that he might alienate himself among the new coaching staff. So why did he bother reporting the accounts?

"My motives were *not* altruistic," Endy said candidly. "I was afraid there was going to be a scandal. I had heard enough from these women to know that a scandal was not unlikely. And I was petrified that if any of these women filed a lawsuit against the organization, I'd be fired in a heartbeat if the team discovered that I knew about these women's complaints and never passed them along to executive management. The team would have been justified, in that case, in saying, 'Here's a guy who knew things that could have helped the club protect itself from liability. But he didn't bring it to our attention.' That was my real reason for forwarding the complaints against Solomon and Green to Jeff Diamond. I was trying not to get fired down the road. I was trying to cover my butt, *not* be Mr. Hurrah for Women's Rights."

Endy's calculated risk resulted in precisely what he was trying to avoid. As soon as the season was over, President Roger Headrick directed Diamond to terminate him. Endy's dismissal prompted a backlash against Headrick in the press. Endy was formerly a public relations assistant for the Vikings and had a well-respected reputation among the local media. "This is a matter that nobody can understand except me and the people involved," Headrick insisted to the press, when asked what prompted the decision. "I don't think it's appropriate to make my case in the press. We're doing what we feel is right for the organization."

In fact, even individuals at the highest level of management did not understand the decision to fire Endy, even the guy who had to do the firing. "You know everybody around here loves you and thinks you do a great job," Diamond said, unable to look Endy in the eye as he paced around Endy's office. "But two people around here [Headrick and

Green] don't share that opinion. And unfortunately, those are the two people with the power." Diamond declined repeated requests on the part of the authors to answer questions regarding Endy's dismissal.

When the authors met with Endy in Minneapolis in early 1998, he turned over folders full of letters and cards he received following his dismissal (over 100 in all). The sentiments of the letters ranged from a bewilderment over his firing to rage. Many of the letters were from Vikings players and personnel. Most notably, there was one from Diamond himself, written on Vikings letterhead, crediting Endy with being "a diligent, hard working, employee who was dedicated to the team."

There was also a letter from Vikings owner Wheelock Whitney, who had been part of the decision to hire Headrick. Whitney's letter, dated May 22, 1992, was written to Minneapolis mayor Donald Fraser, in behalf of Endy, who was then searching for a new job. Below is an excerpt:

"I want to put in a good word for my friend, Dan Endy. Dan is applying for a new position as Media Specialist with the Minneapolis Police Department—and I'm sure he'd be someone you'd be proud of as an employee of the city. . . .

"And I'll keep my fingers crossed that Dan gets the job. He's a *good* one [emphasis in the letter]."

Headrick was probably right in his speculation that people would not understand the reasons behind his decision to fire Endy, not to mention that full disclosure would unleash a serious investigation by the press into the allegations coming from the hotels. By firing Endy, the allegations would be silenced. It was a good bet that the two sales representatives were not going to go public on their own (they wanted the business). And in Endy's severance package, the Vikings made him agree not to discuss anything negative about the Vikings as a condition of the payout he received from the team (worth approximately $75,000).

Endy was not the only apparent casualty of Green's and Solomon's alleged sexual exploits. When others within the organization raised allegations of sexual impropriety, they also were terminated and paid off.

On the heels of Endy's dismissal, the Vikings held a mandatory sexual harassment seminar in May of 1993. Shortly thereafter, an attractive intern who had been assigned to work with the Vikings alleged that Solomon had been harassing her and pressuring her into a sexual relationship.

Days later, the intern was let go by the organization. She retained Minneapolis attorney Lori Peterson, who specializes in litigation involving sexual harassment in the workplace.

In preparation for suing the team, Peterson obtained a sworn affidavit from Dan Endy. The intern, having worked with Endy for nearly a year, suspected the reasons behind his dismissal and asked if he'd state them under oath. In his affidavit, dated September 1, 1993, Endy detailed the series of sexual harassment reports made to him. He also confirmed that each report he had received was passed on to Jeff Diamond. His affidavit also included the following particulars:

"Green frequently phoned a woman during the middle of the night and once even offered to come over and help keep her warm."

"Coach Green often made suggestive remarks to a woman. He told her he and his wife had an 'arrangement.' "

"Coach Green repeatedly told her 'You want me' and 'You'll realize you really want me.' "

Shortly after Peterson secured the affidavit, the Vikings offered the intern $150,000 to settle the matter out of court. According to Peterson, she had yet to file the lawsuit when the Vikings made their offer. The conditions of the settlement required, among other things, that the intern could never discuss her allegations, and the documents pertaining to the case, the affidavit chief among them, were placed under seal.

"We have a very clear and very well-defined policy on sexual harassment," said Headrick when discussing the issue with the authors. "And that can be anything from language to physical contact or anything—even innuendo. But I'm getting a little bit callous to just wildly alleged 'I feel uncomfortable' in this essentially male environment. When somebody knows that this is going to be 90 percent male and they don't like to hear people swear, go work for a church of some sort."

Yet, the crux of the complaints coming from the intern and the two sales representatives had nothing to do with swearing. Nevertheless, his point is well taken: sexual harassment is a broad term with ill-defined parameters. But in April of 1995, Headrick received word that the team had been sued again. This time, the allegations, if true, described a clear-cut case of sexual harassment. Former Vikings cheerleader Michelle Eaves, eight months after being fired, sued the team and franchise player Warren Moon. In her suit, Eaves, who was an exotic dancer before being hired by the Vikings, claimed that shortly after she was hired by the Vikings in April of 1994, Moon began making unwanted sexual advances, and that she had consulted with her husband on how to deflect them.

Then, according to the suit, while the team was in Tokyo to play the Kansas City Chiefs in an exhibition game in August of 1994, Eaves said that Moon summoned her to his hotel room. She asked fellow cheerleader Amy Kellogg to accompany her, but Eaves insisted that Moon made her leave the room. Once Kellogg was gone, Moon "insisted on having oral sex with [Eaves]," according to the lawsuit. "Without consenting, [Eaves] finally relented to Moon's insistence on oral sex. Defendant Moon then attempted to coerce [Eaves] into sexual intercourse, but [Eaves] refused and finally succeeded in leaving his room." In court papers, Kellogg corroborated Eaves's account.

"That is total nonsense," Moon said in an exclusive interview for this book. "I actually knew Michelle and her husband before I became a Minnesota Viking. She became a cheerleader on the squad the same year that I came to the squad. Then she got fired from the squad when we were in Japan because she and another girl [Kellogg] were caught fraternizing with a member of the opposing team at the Hard Rock Cafe.

"She came to me and was crying to me about everything that had happened. At the same time, while the team was in Tokyo, her grandmother passed away. So she had to go back home early. So they fired her from the squad. In April of the next off-season, all of a sudden this sexual harassment thing comes up against me and the Vikings, claiming that she wanted this money. There was never nothing involved with me as far as harassment or anything like that. It just was convenient to go after me because I was the highest paid player on the team."

Despite Moon's adamant denial, he did nonetheless reach an out-of-court settlement with Eaves. Shortly after Eaves filed her suit at the Hennepin County District Court in Minneapolis, Moon's lawyer, Clayton Robinson, won a temporary restraining order on May 18 which blocked the media from obtaining copies of the complaint. However, on May 23, cheerleader Amy Kellogg's lawyer, James Wicka, surprisingly filed court documents in connection with the case and attached Eaves's complaint to his filing. By that afternoon, *Minneapolis Star Tribune* reporters had read the allegations against Moon and informed Robinson that they intended to publish them in the following day's edition of the paper. That evening, Moon and the Vikings settled their case with Eaves by paying her $150,000. She was barred by the terms of the settlement from ever discussing her complaint publicly.

"I wanted to fight them because I knew I had done nothing wrong," Moon told the authors. "But my attorneys pretty much told me that they didn't think I needed the publicity."

Moon told the authors that Steve Rollins had conducted the team's internal investigation into the merits of Eaves's allegations, which resulted in the club determining that Eaves filed the suit out of revenge for her firing. It was Rollins who also handled the investigation which led to Eaves's and Kellogg's firing in Tokyo. The Vikings cited "inadequate skills and lascivious conduct" for the reasons which led to the two cheerleaders' dismissal. Rollins's investigation determined that both women had fraternized with two Chiefs players while at the Hard Rock Cafe. "Absolutely, we have a very strict policy keeping cheerleaders away from players on a social standpoint," Vikings vice president of marketing Stewart Widdess told the Minneapolis press. "Cheerleaders sign an agreement that they will not fraternize with the players. We are very strong on them. If the policy is not followed, they are terminated." Unfortunately, as Eaves pointed out, players aren't fired for "fraternizing" with cheerleaders.

Yet one security officer who was assigned to escort the cheerleaders while the team was in Tokyo has a different recollection of what Eaves and Kellogg did. Eaves and Kellogg were indeed at the Hard Rock. But so were all the other cheerleaders. They had been booked to make a public appearance there. While there, they were asked to go around to all of the tables and pass out cheerleader calendars to the patrons. Two Chiefs players happened to be in the Hard Rock at the time, and they momentarily conversed with Eaves and Kellogg. "But the team's claim that the girls had to be fired for fraternizing is bogus," the security official told the authors. "And there was no investigation. Rollins wasn't even at the Hard Rock. And he didn't interview any of the security officers who were. There were four of us assigned to be with the cheerleaders that day, and not one of us was ever questioned by Rollins or anyone else about what happened between Eaves, Kellogg, and the Chiefs players. It was a bogus firing."

And what about Eaves's account of what happened in the hotel room with Moon? Roger Headrick insisted that the team is governed by strict curfews that are enforced by automatic termination if players are not found in their rooms—alone—when bed checks are performed. According to a security officer hired by Rollins and assigned to monitor the players' hotel floor at night, there was an unspoken rule that filtered down from Rollins exempting Moon from the curfew. "I would sit in the hallway until six in the morning making sure none of them try to leave and that no women are invited up," said the official. "It was an unofficial policy that if you worked the hotel, the players were to stay in their rooms after eleven o'clock bed check, nobody on the floor, nobody off the floor—except for one player, Warren Moon. And he had a room to himself."

The authors asked Moon whether he received preferential treatment from security. "They just knew me," he said. "Whenever they checked my room I was lying in my bed or on the telephone or watching television. With some of the players, the security might check behind their curtains or under their bed, especially with some of the younger guys who may have had problems with people being found in their rooms. But I had never had any problems like that, so the security people just knew how to deal with me. I got checked every night like everybody else, but I didn't get my room searched. I never have anybody in my room and I never leave my room, so the security people gave me my privacy."

The security guard who spoke to the authors conceded that the timing of Eaves's lawsuit presented an appearance of revenge seeking on her part. "It sounds like sour grapes— that Eaves was fired and went after somebody," the official told the authors. "But there's more smoke to that fire."

The security officer is not the only one who disputed the Vikings' insistence that Eaves filed her suit as an act of revenge for her dismissal. "That's total bullshit," said James Harris, who claimed he was friends with Moon when they were teammates at Minnesota and who was familiar with what transpired in Tokyo. "I believe Michelle and I'm a player. The bottom line is that if you're expendable, you're screwed." And cheerleaders are expendable. The franchise quarterback is not.

In the months surrounding Moon's legal travails, the *Minneapolis Star* reported that in January of 1995, a woman who had worked under Dennis Green when he was the football coach at Stanford University had reached an out-of-court settlement in a sexual harassment suit filed against the school. According to the *Star,* while his team was in Hawaii to play in the Aloha Bowl, "Green allegedly grabbed" the woman "on a Honolulu hotel balcony after she refused repeated sexual advances."

Reporters descended on the Stanford campus in hopes of interviewing the woman following the announcement that the university had settled a lawsuit that apparently involved Green. However, the woman was reluctant to participate in interviews. She did, however, place a call to Dan Endy after reading a press report that referred to his affidavit detailing the hotel employees' complaints against Green.

"Around mid-morning one day I was sitting in my den and the phone rang," Endy recalled. When Endy answered it, the female voice on the receiver was unfamiliar.

"Is this Dan Endy?" she asked.

"Yeah," he replied.

"Is this the Dan Endy that worked for the Vikings?"

"Yeah."

"You don't know me, and I'm not going to tell you my name. But I just wanted to say thank you."

"Okay," he said, puzzled. "But what did I do?"

"I'm the woman from Stanford."

Having read the vague press reports of a woman at Stanford who claimed she was sexually harassed by Green, the woman's announcement on the phone sent a chill over Endy's body. "Well what are you thanking me for?" Endy asked, unsure of what else to say.

"For two years I've felt I was dirty, slimy, and gross," she said. "Now that you've come forward in your affidavit, I know that I'm not the only person."

According to Endy, the Stanford woman described sexual advances by Green that resembled the reports that had come from the hotel sales representative. "She said, 'I tried everything. I tried to ignore it. I tried to be mean. Nothing stopped him. He would just smile coldly. He was like the Terminator. He only knew coming forward.'"

As allegations continued to dog Green, his players were becoming increasingly out of control. Steve Rollins's job as full-time director of security required he work serious overtime. Below is a list of the players who were involved with the police in the midst of Green's off-field problems:

• November 30, 1992, defensive lineman James Harris was arrested and charged with fifth-degree assault after Bloomington police were dispatched to his home on a 911 domestic violence call. He pleaded guilty on December 15, 1992.

• October 6, 1993, running back Keith Henderson was arrested for raping a woman just weeks after being released by the Vikings. Green had previously signed Henderson away from San Francisco. Ultimately Henderson was convicted for raping three women in an eight-month span. He was sentenced to six months in jail and placed on ten years' probation (see Chapter 13).

• March 3, 1994, defensive back Joey Browner was indicted for third-degree criminal sexual misconduct. The complaint alleged that Browner raped a thirty-four-year-old woman in her home on January 15. On the eve of his jury trial, charges were dropped.

• July 20, 1995, linebacker Broderick Thomas was caught with a handgun at the Houston Intercontinental Airport. Charges were later dropped.

• July 21, 1995, quarterback Warren Moon was charged with assaulting his wife in Fort Bend County, Texas. A jury acquitted him in February 1996.

• August 16, 1995, lineman Esera Tuaolo was arrested on drunk driving charges. The case was later dismissed.

• December 29, 1995, James Harris was arrested on a felony assault charge for beating his wife. He pleaded guilty on January 25, 1996, and was sentenced to ten days in the Hennepin County Adult Correction Facility.

• January 11, 1996, linebacker Broderick Thomas was again arrested, this time for drunk driving and carrying a gun without a permit.

• March 8, 1996, defensive back Corey Fuller was arrested for domestic violence and resisting an officer with violence. He pleaded no contest on April 15, 1996, and received a suspended sentence and was placed on probation for one year.

• March 13, 1996, Corey Fuller entered a pretrial diversion program in Florida after he was charged with larceny and petty theft.

• May 7, 1996, defensive end Fernando Smith was arrested on a felony count of failing to make court-ordered child support payments. Despite earning $712,499 in salary from the Vikings and receiving $500,000 in signing bonuses, Smith had not made a single payment to support his five-year-old daughter, leaving him $42,182 behind. He previously was convicted of a felony for carrying a concealed weapon in Michigan.

• July 22, 1996, rookie free agent cornerback Jamie Coleman was investigated by Bloomington police in connection with the alleged sexual assault of a twenty-year-old woman in a hotel. No charges were filed in the case.

• September 12, 1996, ex-linebacker Walker Lee Ashley received a stayed jail sentence for stealing public funds after pleading guilty to taking money from the city of Eagan, Minnesota, by forging checks issued by the city in connection with youth development programs he supervised.

• April 30, 1997, running back Moe Williams pleaded not guilty to first-degree rape charges in Lexington, Kentucky. The alleged victim was examined at the University of Kentucky emergency room and diagnosed with contusions on her back. Charges were later dropped. In November of 1994, the year before Minnesota drafted him in the third round, Williams was charged with fourth-degree assault and threatening to kill his girlfriend. After Williams was released from jail on a $10,000 bond, the victim dropped the charges.

• June 29, 1997, safety Orlando Thomas was arrested, charged with starting a riot outside a bar in Crowley, South Carolina.

• September 2, 1997, offensive lineman Korey Stringer was investigated by Eden Prairie police after they responded to a 911 domestic violence call placed by his girlfriend. She declined to press charges.

• October 14, 1997, center Jeff Christy and tight end Greg DeLong pleaded guilty to carelessly operating a watercraft after being arrested in August for boating under the influence of alcohol.

• January 3, 1998, wide receiver Chris Walsh was arrested for drunk driving while returning home from a playoff game. He later pleaded guilty to careless driving and was sentenced to thirty days in jail. The judge, however, stayed the jail time.

Former defensive end James Harris, who was sentenced to ten days in jail after his second conviction for domestic violence while playing for the Vikings, argued that as players' lawlessness increased, Green and his coaches were in no position to lay down the law. "Everybody knew about the shit Dennis Green was doing," claimed Harris, who praised Green as one of the best coaches he ever played under. "Everybody knew what Solomon was doing. At that time, the Vikings were getting in a hell of a lot of trouble. Players getting in trouble. But Green never talked to me about my criminal cases. He wasn't in a position. He was f---in' up himself."

Nor was Steve Rollins in a position to stem the tide of player problems. He was too busy, according to a KSTR-TV report, doing Green's bidding to get involved with the players. On September 4, 1996, KSTR's investigative reporter Robb Leer, after acquiring a sealed court file detailing a secret lawsuit filed against Green back in 1992, reported that Green had paid a Minneapolis-area woman, identified in court papers as "Jane Doe," to have an abortion. Shortly after Green was named head coach in 1992, he began a six-month relationship with the woman, whom he would meet at his private apartment in Eden Prairie. According to Leer's report, the woman claimed in her lawsuit that Green urged her to "have an abortion because otherwise it would 'ruin' his career."

In their civil settlement, both Green and Jane Doe entered into a binding contract that barred either of them from ever discussing their affair or the abortion with anyone. However, in the summer of 1996, Jane Doe wrote Green an angry letter accusing him of violating the contract. Enter Steve Rollins, who Green dispatched to deposit $5,000 cash in Jane Doe's bank account in hopes of stifling the matter.

When the authors asked Green's lawyer, Joe Friedberg, about the abortion charges, he replied with a hypothetical. "Let's assume for a second that the guy had a relationship and she got pregnant," Friedberg began. "That she wanted an abortion and that he paid at least part of, probably all of the expenses of it. So what?"

Friedberg's position was that it's really no big deal, which begs the question: Why all the effort to keep it secret? Green's lawyer tried to get an injunction from a Minneapolis judge blocking KSTR from airing its report of the whole incident. The petition was denied.

In an official statement released by Green on September 5, one day after the television report aired, he said, "I today instructed my lawyers to go into court and seek to obtain an order from Judge Danielson which would permit me and my attorneys to disclose the true facts surrounding this regrettable incident to representatives of the Minnesota Vikings." Neither Green nor the Vikings, however, ever disclosed the "true facts" to the public. Why? Because it is a little more complicated than the hypothetical.

In an exclusive interview with Jane Doe, the authors discovered that the second lawsuit (for breach of contract) would never have been filed if the Vikings' coaches—two in particular—could have kept their libido under control.

In June of 1995, Jane Doe was having dinner at an Applebee's in Eden Prairie, just minutes from the Vikings' practice facility. A single mother, Doe was accompanied by her nine-year-old daughter, her seventy-three-year-old mother, and numerous other relatives. During dinner she noticed that a man sitting at the bar was staring at her. Smiling and repeatedly making eye contact with her, the man got up from the bar when Doe went toward the ladies' room. "I really hate to interrupt you," he said politely. "And I know you're with your family. But I would love to see if you are interested in maybe going out to dinner or going out for a drink with me sometime."

"Where do you live?" asked Doe, who is both attractive and outgoing.

"Right down the road at Eden Place," answered the man, who then introduced himself as Carl Hargrave.

After a pleasant conversation and discovering that they lived practically across the street from each other, Doe agreed to meet Hargrave a few nights later for drinks. Unbeknownst to her, Hargrave was Green's running backs coach. Unbeknownst to Hargrave, Doe was the same woman whom Green had impregnated and entered into a binding agreement with to never discuss the matter.

When Doe met Hargrave for drinks a few night later at Ciatti's, an Italian restaurant in Eden Prairie, he wasted little time informing her that he was a coach for the Vikings. According to Doe, he seemed pretty confident that this would impress her. He could not have been more wrong. Afraid that she might inadvertently violate the gag order she was under, Doe desperately tried to think of a creative way to prematurely end the evening. Hargrave made her job easy, however, when he admitted to her that he was married with children and that his wife was expecting in two weeks.

"I have to go," Doe snapped, angered that Hargrave, like Green, expected that she would be interested in a sexual relationship with a married man merely because he coached in the NFL. "I have to go pick up my daughter."

"Where does this stop?" Doe asked in her interview for this book, disclosing her disgust with Hargrave's attitude. "I could not believe it. You can see the mentality of not only the players, but the coaches. It's just all part of the little game. They feel they can, so they do it."

As Doe stood up to leave, Hargrave grabbed her hand and placed it on his crotch.

"He was testing me," Doe explained. "He was seeing what I would do. I stopped him."

Hargrave would not be denied easily, however. From his office at the Vikings' facility, he repeatedly called Doe's home trying to convince her to sleep with him. Angered when Doe continued to rebuff him, Hargrave finally announced, "I guess you have to be the head coach."

Hargrave's careless slip of the tongue implicated Green. How else, Doe figured, would Hargrave know that Doe had a prior sexual relationship with Green?

When Doe informed her attorney, Lori Peterson, Peterson filed a breach-of-contract suit against Green. His lawyers responded with a countersuit. The judge in the case ultimately dismissed both suits. Meanwhile, Green's lawyer, Joe Friedberg, filed an ethics complaint against Peterson, attempting to get her license revoked, for trying to sue Green. "It's our contention that Lori Peterson tried to blackmail Dennis Green," said Friedberg in an interview with the authors.

"And we refuse to be blackmailed. We told her to take her best shot.

"The rap that Dennis Green has had, that he grabs women and that kind of thing, there's never been an allegation like that. He's really gotten a bad rap, which is that he's a womanizer, puts the make on women, that kind of stuff. It's never been true. There's nobody that's ever alleged that. As to whether a guy with a fractured marriage screwed around on the side, in contemporary society that really wouldn't make much difference. And that's really what was going on. There's never been any sexual harassment or any of that kind of stuff."

In Friedberg's ethics complaint against Lori Peterson, filed at the Office of Lawyers' Professional Responsibility in St. Paul, Minnesota, Green undergoes another makeover—he received a new name. Throughout the complaint he is referred to as "John Smith." At the time this book went to press, the ethics complaint was pending.

The coincidence that two coaches pursued sexual relations with the same woman indicated the depths to which off-the-field misconduct had sunk. And Rollins's willingness to pay money to a woman who aborted the child of the head coach demonstrated what the head of security's position had degenerated to. Yet cheerleader Michelle Eaves was fired for "lascivious" conduct?

Meanwhile, the rash of Vikings players running afoul of the law led Headrick, in January of 1996, to begin publicly calling for a league-wide crackdown on lawlessness. More specifically, he instituted a termination policy for players who leave their hotel rooms after curfew and engage in after-hours activity that is not related to on-field performance. "The reason why it's subject to termination," Headrick explained to the authors, "is because if that is so important that you would allow yourself to participate in activity that would detract from your ability to play the game the next day, then you don't have enough respect for your teammates to be around."

Fortunately for Steve Rollins, the new policy did not apply to heads of security. On October 30, 1995, Rollins attacked KMSP-TV cameraman Dan Metcalfe following a Monday Night Football game between the Vikings and the Bears. According to court papers filed at the United States District Court in Minneapolis, Rollins and Metcalfe had an ongoing feud stemming from a previous game where Metcalfe was trying to get a close-up shot of Dennis Green as he was coming off the field. When Rollins spotted Metcalfe in the tunnel underneath the Metrodome following the Monday Night game, he ordered him to move and a dispute ensued.

"Rollins grabbed Metcalfe by the collar of Metcalfe's shirt and hurled him to the ground," according to court papers. Metcalfe also said that "Rollins shoved [him] against a wall causing Metcalfe to strike his head against the wall behind him."

"Who's pushing you now, motherf---er?" Rollins shouted at Metcalfe, according to court papers.

Minneapolis police officer Donald Banham, a close friend who also worked security detail for the Vikings, arrested Metcalfe and charged him with disorderly conduct. In his arrest report, Banham described *Metcalfe* as the aggressor:

"At one point Mr. Rollins placed his hand on the back of the defendant and asked him to just go up the tunnel at which point the defendant spun away from him abruptly and the camera fell off his shoulder onto the concrete floor. At this point the defendant became enraged and charged at Mr. Rollins. The defendant ran hands first at Mr. Rollins, pushing him in his chest. Mr. Rollins put his hands up in a defensive posture and attempted to push back. At this point I intervened, attempting to grab the suspect and push him up the ramp. The defendant began to resist at which time I placed him in a carotid neck restraint and began to apply pressure."

Metcalfe's arrest quickly grabbed headlines in Minnesota. Rollins, meanwhile, insisted to team president Roger Headrick that he never touched Metcalfe. As a result, the Vikings released a statement explaining that Metcalfe had refused repeated requests to move away from a restricted area underneath the Metrodome and was arrested as a result.

Within hours of releasing the statement, however, Vikings director of communications Dave Pelletier received a phone call confirming that a freelance photographer had captured the entire tunnel incident on video. The video showed a much different incident than that described in Banham's police report. When Pelletier took the videocassette into the office of Roger Headrick, the two watched it privately.

"You lied to me, Steve," Headrick said under his breath, as he watched footage of Rollins striking Metcalfe without provocation. The next day, November 1, 1995, the Vikings changed their tune. "Regardless of the provocation, there is no justification for the type of force used in the incident," Headrick told the media. "Appropriate disciplinary action is being taken with those involved . . . to ensure that there is not repetition of this type of event in the future. We regret the occurrence of this incident and do not condone and will not accept this type of behavior."

The criminal charges against Metcalfe were dropped. He then filed a federal civil rights lawsuit against Rollins and Banham.

Why didn't Headrick fire Rollins? A former Vikings security official who worked under Rollins had a hunch. "Because Rollins knows more dirt on the Vikings than anyone," the official said. "Everything ugly that has happened behind the scenes for the past seven years, he knows it. And if he were fired by Headrick, Rollins would spill it. And Headrick would never risk that. Rollins is untouchable."

Dennis Green, Steve Rollins, and Richard Solomon declined to be interviewed for this book.

On May 6, 1998, Carl Hargrave, after successfully delaying his DUI case from being resolved for over a year, pleaded guilty to the gross misdemeanor charge of refusal to submit to chemical testing. According to the prosecutor, Hargrave's driving record in Minnesota now reflects a DUI offense. Hargrave was sentenced to 365 days in the Hennepin County Adult Corrections Facility, but 335 days were suspended by the judge. The remaining thirty days Hargrave was allowed to serve on work release, meaning that he would not be locked up. According to the prosecutor, Hargrave had to wear an ankle bracelet so the state could monitor him, and he was barred from leaving the state during the thirty-day period.

"His argument about the whole conduct issue is that he minimized what he did," said assistant Eden Prairie city attorney Jennifer Inz. "I'm not someone who supports the idea that sports figures are role models or should be considered to be role models. The reason that people know who they are and choose to remember them and what they do is because of their physical and athletic abilities. That says nothing about their character."

Weeks before Hargrave entered his plea, the Vikings used their first-round pick in the 1998 draft on Marshall University receiver Randy Moss. His criminal history included a conviction and jail sentence for attacking a youth while in high school; smoking marijuana while on a work release program from jail; a conviction for domestic violence; and an additional arrest for domestic violence. His checkered past made him fodder for the predraft press coverage, sufficient to discourage many teams with first-round draft choices, who passed him up. How perfect then when Moss's slide ended with the draft's twenty-first pick, four hours after the start of the draft, by the Vikings. Dennis Green apparently overlooked Moss's criminal past, wasting less than sixty seconds announcing the choice to Commissioner Tagliabue.

"This is old news, old news," Green said in an interview moments after making the pick, making no effort to hide his defensiveness. "We're not going to dwell on what some kid did in high school in West Virginia." Green, of course, had every reason to understate Moss's history and to be defensive, given the collection of criminals already assembled in the Twin Cities.

"I know deep down inside why I didn't get picked in the top ten," Moss said. "I'm not going to worry about that. I'm a Viking. I'm in the NFL now."

Legendary *Minneapolis Star-Tribune* columnist Sid Hartman praised the choice, suggesting: "Vikings coach Dennis Green has proved he has complete control of his players and what they do on and off the field. And Green will have a great influence on Moss, who will give the Vikings the most potent passing offense in the NFL." It remains to be seen what kind of influence Green has on Moss.

P.S. On May 18, just four weeks after being drafted by the Vikings, fourth-round draft pick Kivuusama Mays out of North Carolina pleaded no contest to assault charges.

10

Dirty Little Secret

Missouri City, Texas, July 18, 1995:

911 DISPATCHER: 911 Missouri City. What is your emergency?
JEFFREY MOON (*eight-year-old son of NFL quarterback Warren Moon*): [Crying]
DISPATCHER: Hello? What's the problem?
JEFFREY: It's my . . . You need to come . . . Hurry . . .
DISPATCHER: What . . . What's the matter?
JEFFREY: It's umm . . . my daddy.
DISPATCHER: Is he OK?
JEFFREY: My daddy gonna hit my mommy. Please hurry.
DISPATCHER: OK. You need to calm down. We'll get the police there. Just a moment. OK?
JEFFREY: They're walking down the street. Please hurry up.
DISPATCHER: OK.
JEFFREY: Please hurry up.
DISPATCHER: Hold on. Now your daddy hit your mommy, right?
JEFFREY: Uh huh.
DISPATCHER: And they're walking down the street. Does she need an ambulance? Hello. Hello?

By the time the police arrived at the Moon home, Warren had sped away in his car. His wife, Felicia, according to authorities, fell into the arms of a female officer with whom she was a social acquaintance. "Mary, he beat the s—t out of me," Felicia cried. Officers responding to the scene reported, "She had blood to the right side of her face and neck. She had scratch marks on her face and abrasions on her neck."

When police asked her what caused the violent incident, Felicia, an ex-board member on the Fort Bend County Women's Center, which runs a shelter for battered women, indicated that Warren had come home that morning and attacked her while she was reading on the grounds of their home. "Warren started to slap me on the head by my ears with his open hand," Felicia told the police. "He choked me so that I couldn't talk or breathe. When he choked me I thought he was losing control and that he wouldn't know when to stop choking me. I was afraid for my life."

For the NFL, it could not get any worse than seeing Warren Moon, of all players, charged with wife beating. Moon was hardly known for volatile outbursts or criminal behavior. Nor was he some obscure, third-string lineman. Rather, the Hall of Fame bound quarterback was a former NFL Man of the Year who was widely perceived as one of the league's most exemplary citizens away from the field. After enduring a year of questions about NFL players and domestic violence following O.J. Simpson's arrest for murdering his ex-wife, the league now saw one of its most revered current players implicated for spousal abuse.

However, the spotlight ultimately did not shine on this, the NFL's most cowardly of crimes—the beating of wives and girlfriends by men who are idolized because of their strength and size. Instead, the Moon case became notorious for the conduct of Felicia Moon, the alleged victim. After filing her complaint, Felicia tried to persuade prosecutors to drop the case against her husband. When the state rejected her request, Felicia refused to testify. The state then threatened to cite her with contempt and jail her. Reluctantly, she finally took the stand and told jurors that she was to blame for the incident. She denied knowing the source of the bruises and injuries depicted in the police photographs, telling the jury, "They might have been self-inflicted."

On February 22, 1996, the jury deliberated less than thirty minutes before acquitting Warren Moon. Jurors were not aware that a restraining order had been issued against Moon in 1987 for allegedly threatening his wife. Nor did the jury learn that Fort Bend County records indicated that Moon had physically attacked his wife on at least three prior occasions during their marriage. According to court records, in one incident Moon "beat [Felicia] with close fists in the presence of the children." Each of the complaints was later dismissed "for lack of prosecution."

"The charges weren't true, but they were charged," Warren Moon told the authors, acknowledging that his wife had accused him of domestic violence in the years leading up to his arrest in 1995. "They [the allegations] had to do with a problem my wife had." Although Warren Moon did not discuss the particulars of his wife's previous allegations or the incident that led to his arrest and trial, he insisted that the intense media scrutiny of his case indicates why other players plead guilty rather than fight domestic violence charges in court. "Sometimes players plead guilty just so they don't have to go through what I went through during my trial," Moon told the authors. "But the reason I went through all that was because my wife and I were adamant about what happened in the case. There was no way I was a criminal in that whole process. We wanted that to become public and for the record to be clean.

"This was a misdemeanor case. The way the media covered it was as if I had chopped somebody's head off."

Moon also pointed out that he did not undergo any counseling as a result of the domestic violence incident. His wife, on the other hand, did. "Domestic violence calls to police happen all the time," Moon told the authors. "Some incidents are small and some are big. It could be an argument. It could be a wife throwing a pan through a window. But it's just part of life and those things are going to happen."

While Warren Moon is arguably the most famous active-roster NFL player ever to stand trial for domestic violence, he is hardly alone. Weeks before his trial began, a member of the United States Congress asked the NFL to address the "repeated tragic examples [of violence against women] involving professional football players." The authors obtained a January 24, 1996, letter written by Vermont Congressman Bernard Sanders to Commissioner Paul Tagliabue. "We are writing," read the letter, "to ask in the strongest terms that the NFL join with us and commit to work together to fashion a multi-faceted strategy to deter domestic violence, including counseling, strong disciplinary action when warranted, and a high-profile education and advertising campaign against domestic violence." The following is an excerpt from Representative Sanders's letter to the commissioner:

"We believe the time has come for the NFL to step forward . . . and assume a leading role in deterring domestic violence among current and future NFL personnel.

"Surely you recognize the enormous influence that big-time football players at the professional and collegiate levels, as role models, have upon our society. Many men identify with NFL players and look on them as both heroes and role models to be emulated off the field. Undoubtedly when instances of domestic violence receive little more than a slap on the wrists in court and go unpunished by the NFL . . . that sends an insidious and harmful message to many Americans. Unfortunately, the current message being sent seems to be that domestic violence is not to be taken too seriously and that it is not the indefensible and serious crime that it is.

"Finally, we are troubled by public comments of the NFL's Communications Director, Greg Aiello, to the effect that unless domestic violence affects the business of football, then the NFL should be reticent about taking disciplinary action against professional football players who are charged with domestic violence for fear of possible legal action. That sounds like a short-sighted rationalization to justify the NFL continuing to ignore domestic violence in its own ranks.

"We are appealing to you to make it a top priority to see to it that the men who are privileged to play professional football, as role models, help to publicly condemn domestic violence as a serious crime and do not sluff it off."

Congressman Sanders's letter perturbed league officials, who rebuffed him with an accusatory letter of their own. In it, the league warned Sanders that any attempts on his part to single out the NFL on the issue of domestic violence would be treated as racist. More on that later.

It is little surprise that the NFL resisted Congressman Sanders's proposal. After all, the league even rejected efforts from a member of the so-called NFL family who expressed interest in dealing with players' domestic violence problems. Former Dolphins defensive back Liffort Hobley successfully organized a group of current and ex-Dolphins to combat domestic violence in the Miami area. Hobley's group agreed to speak at a symposium sponsored by Women in Distress of Broward County, an organization which brings together local law enforcement officers and domestic violence counselors to combat domestic violence. Hobley, along with Irving Fryar and Troy Vincent (both of whom are currently playing for the Philadelphia Eagles) and numerous other Dolphins players admitted to and condemned their own prior abusive behavior toward women. "Domestic violence was the way of life in my home," Vincent told those in attendance. "To see my mother get beat was just part of life. It was part of the community to beat your wife, your girlfriend. It was cool. When you'd leave home and go to school, you'd hear some of the guys say, 'Man, I smacked my girlfriend three times last night.' Then one of his friends gives him a high five. That was a way of life, and it wasn't right."

The results of the players' candor was a tremendous force for good. According to Bonnie Flynn, the president of Women in Distress of Broward County, hundreds of middle and high school age children were positively impacted by hearing their heroes deliver such a strong message. "The potential for NFL players to spread a message of intolerance for domestic violence is great," Flynn told the authors in an interview for this book. "The efforts of Liffort and the other Dolphins players have influenced our community's schoolchildren in a way no other men can. Liffort, especially, has been a true leader here."

Based on the program's great success, Hobley proposed a league-wide effort patterned after the Broward County symposiums. But the idea received no support from the NFL and died. "There are a lot of programs out there that have been offered to the NFL," said Hobley in an interview for this book. However, he was careful not to criticize the league in hopes that it may someday reconsider his proposal to work with other teams. "But it is so hard to get the league to let outside entities come in. They are tough. They want to keep everything inside. They're a closed book and will not let any outside companies participate in their issues because there are a lot of issues that don't get addressed, unfortunately. As a player, you know those things. There are lot of things that happen around the league that we don't discuss because we can't. It's a personnel issue and they try to keep those things inside the NFL."

Loath to acknowledge the scope of the domestic violence problem within the league, the NFL, as Congressman Sanders and Liffort Hobley both learned, takes exception whenever anyone suggests otherwise. The league argues repeatedly that there is no statistical evidence suggesting athletes are arrested for domestic violence more than any other segment of the male population. While true, this fact alone hardly proves that there is no problem. According to the authors' research, in fact, domestic violence is the biggest problem the league faces in terms of criminal conduct among its players. Of the 109 criminally accused players in the authors' player-crime index, they were responsible for forty-five domestic violence arrests. No other crime, including drunk driving, showed up as often in players' criminal background checks. And arrests statistics only begin to tell the story.

The authors' research of police records revealed that it is not uncommon for players' wives to call 911 for help, only to decline to press charges after police have arrived and restored order. The reasons, which are elaborated on below, are primarily: 1) the excessive media attention that their allegations will attract due to the player's fame, and 2) fear that no one will believe them due to their husband's status.

In addition to the unwillingness on the part of victims to press charges, there is a unique factor at play when the abuser is an NFL player—he benefits from tactics employed by teams to repress incidents of spousal abuse from coming to the attention of the authorities, as well as the media.

"What you've got is a coddled class of people," domestic violence judge Ed Newman, the former Dolphins lineman, said in an interview for this book. "Instead of being an ordinary person on the street receiving the same punishment, the NFL player may be told 'Don't worry about it. Keep on catching the touchdown pass.' The problem is intercepted before it comes to the light of day."

Based on his experience as both a player and a judge, Newman agreed with the NFL's stand in one respect. He insisted that NFL players are no more likely than other males to be involved with domestic violence. Where they differ, he said, is in how they are treated after the fact. "These are darker shadows in the alleyways of life," said Judge Newman. "The league would rather have blinders on. They want to close that door unless it becomes a liability."

Interviews conducted by the authors with numerous representatives from NFL teams confirm that it is common for teams to take steps to both insulate players from criminal prosecution and conceal abuse from the public.

The Dallas Cowboys were one of the first teams to provide counseling to players with domestic violence problems, offering the service as far back as 1982. Larry Wansley, an ex-FBI agent, oversaw the counseling program between 1982 and 1989, during which time he met personally with players struggling with family violence. "Domestic violence was not as pervasive as drugs when I was hired by the Cowboys," said Wansley in an interview for this book. "But it was a big problem. These cases were primarily kept behind closed doors. Law enforcement rarely got involved at that time, and the cases never made it into the newspapers."

Although Wansley hesitated to give a precise number of players he saw with domestic violence problems while working for Dallas, he confirmed that the overwhelming majority of them were never known by the public. "At the time, I don't think the term 'domestic violence' existed," Wansley said. "But the crime or the events certainly did. And I had a lot of that. In some cases it was a big problem."

Since the 1980s, public awareness regarding domestic violence has greatly increased and strict law enforcement procedures for responding to family violence crimes have been instituted in many communities. The Minnesota Vikings, like many teams, have internal policies in place to discourage domestic violence complaints from getting to the police.

"We've had a couple of cases that have never been brought to light," confirmed Vikings team president Roger Headrick in an interview with the authors just weeks before Vikings quarterback Warren Moon's domestic violence trial got underway. According to Headrick, the Vikings had been successful on more than one occasion in getting players in-house counseling, thus avoiding criminal prosecution and public exposure.

In light of Headrick's admission, the authors sent the names and birth dates of over sixty current and former Vikings players to the following law enforcement agencies located in close proximity to the team's facilities: the Eden Prairie Police Department, the Minneapolis Police Department, the Bloomington Police Department, the St. Paul Police Department, the Carver County Sheriff's Department, and the Ramsey County Sheriff's Department. After soliciting from these agencies all available records on any player who had been in contact with police on a criminal matter, the authors discovered eleven reported cases of domestic violence involving seven players. Most of the cases never resulted in an arrest or a news account, due primarily to the victims' reluctance. The case of Vikings All-Pro defensive end John Randle is representative of what the authors found.

On July 24, 1990, Bloomington police responded to a domestic violence dispute at Randle's home. However, at the request of Randle's wife, no charges were filed. Then on September 26, 1991, Eden Prairie police received a 911 call from the Randle home. According to the police report, when the officers approached the house, they could hear the voice of a female inside. "This is it, John," yelled his wife. "This is the last time you'll pull this crap." Police then entered the home and discovered that his wife had sustained bruises to the facial area. After John Randle was arrested for fifth-degree assault and taken to the police station for booking, his wife informed authorities that her husband had a history of abuse, including a prior arrest in Texas. Authorities in Kingsville, Texas, confirmed that Randle had been previously arrested and forfeited his bail after failing to appear in court. Randle later left the state and the case was dropped.

Despite Randle's arrest in Eden Prairie, the charges were later dropped by prosecutors after his wife took the children and moved out of state. At the time the authors were provided these reports, John Randle was the highest paid defensive player in the NFL, and his contact with authorities due to domestic violence complaints was buried in police files.

Unlike Randle, former Vikings defensive end James Harris (see Chapter 7) is a player who did receive considerable attention in the press after twice being convicted for domestic violence crimes while playing for Minnesota. However, even he was involved in a chilling incident on file that never made it into the press. According to a St. Paul police report dated May 7, 1995, Harris and an associate, Antwon Johnson, forced entry into the apartment of Janice Kopp* and assaulted her. Harris and Johnson were searching for another woman who previously lived with Kopp. When Kopp was unable to tell the men of her former roommate's whereabouts, Johnson grabbed Kopp by the throat and demanded to know where the woman was. As Kopp tried unsuccessfully to free herself from Johnson's grip on her throat, her three-year-old son ran toward his mother out of fear. The toddler, as he reached for his mother, was quickly pushed to the ground by one of the men.

"I'll kill you if you call the police," Johnson threatened Kopp as he released her. Harris and Johnson then bolted out of the apartment and into Harris's green Lexus. After initially cooperating with police investigators in the case against Harris and Johnson, Kopp decided to drop the matter in June of 1995 out of fear, she said, for her life and that of her child's.

This incident never found its way into any Minnesota press reports.

However, the cases of Randle and Harris, like all the cases discovered by the authors, were at least brought to the attention of the authorities by way of a formal police complaint. But Vikings president Roger Headrick conceded personal familiarity with cases that never reached the attention of the public. It is this deeper, more hidden layer of domestic violence cases that holds the key to how NFL teams cover up abusive players' conduct and protect them from criminal prosecution. In order to access this most hidden sphere of violence, the authors located and talked with nearly a dozen victims of domestic violence. These victims endured years of abuse without going to the authorities for help. Only after it boiled beyond belief, some went forward, but they nonetheless still refrained from pressing charges. Their experiences have never before been mentioned in press accounts.

While willing to talk under an agreement of confidentiality, almost all of them declined to have their accounts detailed in this book out of fear of their abusers. However, one victim, the former fiancée of current Minnesota Vikings running back Leroy Hoard, agreed to speak concerning her experience. As uncovered by the authors in Ohio police records, the story offers a graphic illustration of how NFL teams work to insulate players from criminal liability.

Before joining the Vikings in November of 1996, Leroy Hoard played five years for the Cleveland Browns. During that time, he and fiancée Debbie DuBois* lived together. According to DuBois, she endured repeated incidents of do-

mestic violence, including being thrown through walls at
their home and suffering beatings that required her to undergo plastic surgery on more than one occasion. This finally came to the attention of the Browns organization
following a particularly violent episode. "I was trying to
back out of the driveway, and he kicked out the passenger's
side window," DuBois said. "The glass got stuck in my face
and I went into shock."

A couple of Hoard's teammates who witnessed the incident went to the Browns' coaching staff and recommended
that Hoard get some help. Within days, Browns head coach
Bill Belichick telephoned DuBois.

"Coach Belichick left a message on the answering machine with the name of Joe Janesz, the person who I was
supposed to contact, the therapist," said DuBois. "From that
point on, Leroy and I attended therapy sessions for a year.
The team let him leave right after practices for therapy on
the days our sessions were scheduled."

The therapist whom the Browns asked to counsel Hoard
and DuBois was Joe Janesz from the Cleveland Clinic.
Janesz was one of a small team of professionals from the
clinic who were hired by Browns owner Art Modell to counsel players with drug and alcohol abuse problems beginning
in the early 1980s. Janesz had extensive experience working
with individuals suffering from alcohol and drug abuse.

DuBois had understood that she and Hoard were meeting
with a domestic violence counselor who was trained in psychology. "The psychologist," said DuBois in an interview
for this book, "told me 'This is Leroy's lifestyle. He goes out
every week and has to basically try to punish people on the
field. He'll go after them and try to kill them. A lot of times

he can't relate to coming home and not doing that to you when he's upset.'

"I couldn't accept that, because any human being knows the difference between tackling someone on the field and hitting the hell out of a woman," said DuBois. "But Dr. Janesz was a team employee. The NFL accepts the fact that there is a major problem and they try to cover it up most of the time."

When the authors contacted Joe Janesz at his Cleveland Clinic office in February of 1998, he explained that he was hired by the Browns to assist players with drug and alcohol problems. "Then we went to a broad-brush approach," Janesz said in an interview for this book, "meaning that we began assisting players with any problem that presented itself and would impact the players' quality of life and subsequently their quality of play. That included marital problems, aggressive disorders, anger disorders, anxiety disorders, and steroid abuse."

Janesz acknowledged providing domestic violence counseling services for the Browns, and more specifically to having counseled DuBois and Hoard. Janesz was asked to explain what DuBois described above—specifically that she was told by him that Hoard would continue to abuse her because he was a man who played a violent game for a living. "I can't comment on that," Janesz told the authors. "It is moving to patient-client privilege. To indicate yes or no on that, I would be breaching her confidentiality."

"The whole process was a very embarrassing situation for me," DuBois said. "Everybody I was dealing with was in the NFL or had something to do with the NFL. They were all men and they were probably thinking, 'Honey, you know you just have to leave him.' "

DuBois's experience is not unique, as teams go to great lengths to protect players and their organizations from public scrutiny. "They [teams] try to internally police themselves before it [domestic violence] becomes public," said Judge Ed Newman. "Police don't get to the player. In effect, what management is doing is what was happening in the 1940s. They close the door. There was a man beating up his wife, everyone heard the screams, but they said it was a private matter. The NFL is in effect, at times, doing the same thing."

Hoard's therapy sessions with the Browns' in-house drug and alcohol specialist did little to curb his violence at home. Finally, on February 1, 1996, DuBois called the police. That evening, Hoard broke down the couple's bedroom door, entered the room, grabbed DuBois by the neck, and threw her across the room. The police report, obtained by the authors, noted that the bedroom door was broken. The front door to the house and the garage door were also broken.

"Tonight he told me he wanted me out of the house, unfortunately I had no money so I couldn't leave," DuBois said in a written statement to the police. "So he broke the door down, came upstairs, grabbed me by the neck and told me 'Bitch, I want you out of my house.' [He] threw me across the bed . . . [and told me] to get the f--- out of his house."

Despite police intervention and the filing of a formal complaint by DuBois, this case, like all the preceding ones, went unreported in the press. Why? DuBois was too scared to press charges, thus the police never arrested Hoard and the media remained in the dark. DuBois did, however, place repeated phone calls to Browns owner Art Modell. "I left a few messages for Art Modell," she said. "But there was no response. He didn't return my calls." Modell also declined an interview for this book.

According to DuBois, when the Browns learned that she had reported the incident to police and that a court-appointed lawyer was assigned to assist her, the team contacted the attorney and offered to settle the matter out of court—a strange proposal considering that DuBois had not even pressed charges.

"They didn't want anything to hit the papers because Leroy was a major player, a star," said DuBois. "And the public loved him. Obviously, people didn't know what he was really like."

On February 14, 1998, Hoard, while en route to a post-season vacation in Florida, drove through Ohio, where he still maintained a home. While in town, he located DuBois, who was then separated from him and seeing another man. A fight ensued and, according to a copy of the police log entry dated February 14, 1998, police were sent to the scene. The log reads: "Complaint: Male has a fire going and is throwing the female's clothes into the fire." The 911 call was placed at 3:29 A.M. by DuBois's brother, who was aware of his sister's previous abuse at the hands of Hoard. Police responded to the scene, but no incident report was filed and Hoard was never arrested.

The police reported that they were unable to locate a fire upon their arrival, but there was a "verbal altercation" underway. "If there are signs of injury, our guys are instructed to make the arrest," said Police Chief Bickan in an interview with the authors. "We like to make the arrest wherever possible in a domestic situation. The only thing that interferes with that is reluctance on the part of the combatants to file charges. It is very, very prevalent for people to call us in these situations but not want to follow through with charges." Hoard was permitted to leave the state and continue on his way to Florida. DuBois, according to one of her friends, went into hiding. The authors were unable to speak with her after this point.

While the NFL insists that its players are subjected to unusual amounts of publicity when they are arrested, many incidents, like Hoard's, do not result in an arrest and thus the press never hears of them. Fear and intimidation are major deterrents to filing criminal charges against abusive NFL players. Although predatory acts of domestic violence have become more familiar to the American public, such accounts hardly fit the image of a hero. As a result, women such as DuBois feel even less secure in taking their cases to the courts because they are rarely believed and remain exposed to further abuse.

"If I know a drug dealer who lives in an organized criminal entity," suggested Bonnie Campbell, head of the U.S. Justice Department's Violence Against Women Division, "and I go to a prosecuting attorney in New York, they're going to say, 'Well, will you testify against him?' And if I say yes, the government will put me in a witness protection program, maybe for the rest of my life. I may have a whole new identity. Conversely, we do not offer protection to battered women. Instead, they are left exposed to ongoing danger and threats. Why shouldn't they recant? We leave them out there at the mercy of someone who's demonstrated over and over again a complete will to hurt someone by battering."

One reason for the NFL's attitude of denial rests in the explosive racial implications lurking beneath the surface. Consider the following: according to the authors' research, over 90 percent of the NFL players who had been charged with domestic violence were black.

"That is a problem in getting at and around this issue because it seems to come out as an issue of racism," said Campbell. She has worked directly with NFL director of player programs Lem Burnham and is familiar with the racial issues associated with the NFL and reports of domestic violence. "The NFL is very black and I think a lot of people are really afraid to look beyond for fear it looks not like athletes and violence, but race and violence. There is real resistance to delve into that in great depth on the part of African-American leaders, especially on the part of sports officials, who just don't know how to handle the question 'Is this about athletes or is it about black athletes?' "

Far from confronting the racial implications attached to frequent player arrests for domestic violence, the NFL uses race as a weapon to intimidate journalists, researchers, and policymakers who earnestly attempt to investigate and address the issue. For example, when Commissioner Tagliabue received Congressman Sanders's January 1996 letter calling on the league to address repeated player arrests for abusing women, the NFL took three months to respond. When it finally answered the congressman, the league issued a veiled threat to charge him with racism if Sanders persisted.

In an April 19, 1996, letter obtained by the authors, the NFL senior vice president of communications and government affairs, Joe Brown, denied the existence of a domestic violence problem within the NFL, and insisted that any statements by Sanders to the contrary were inherently racist. "To single out athletes will unfavorably serve to perpetuate stereotypes—including as to ethnic and racial groups—that impair efforts to deal with these issues," wrote Brown. The letter went on: "It will also unfairly stigmatize athletes by inevitably suggesting that they have a particular propensity to engage in such behavior when there is no basis for such an implication. . . . We believe that any resolution on this subject selectively directed at athletes . . . is highly inappropriate and necessarily open to criticism as discriminatory."

Ex-Miami Dolphin Liffort Hobley and former Cowboys security chief Larry Wansley, both of whom are black and very sensitive to the negative stereotypes that can be associated with this issue, have invested years counseling players who batter. And both see the NFL's use of the race card as inappropriate and unnecessary. "If the league takes the position that by merely addressing the disproportionate number of black players being arrested you're giving some sort of tacit credibility to the claim that this is racist, I think that's irresponsible," Wansley said in an interview with the authors. "That cop-out has been around for years. Yes, there have been examples of white players not getting the same media scrutiny after committing an equally heinous crime or act. But there's always been this fascination with the cop-out: 'This happened to me only because I'm black.' I know from personal experience things that happened to me because I am indeed black, but that does not excuse this approach."

After being apprised of the authors' data on the disproportionate number of arrest reports for domestic violence among black players, Wansley said, "If someone brought me that kind of data, it would tell me that I really need to take a close look at this. There are some signals being sent that I don't understand. But I'm going to make it my business to find out."

The NFL declined the opportunity to review and respond to this information.

Hobley, who largely agreed with Wanlsey's viewpoint, said: "Probably 65 percent of the professional athletes who come into the NFL have some background where someone in their family has had a problem with domestic violence. Seeing domestic violence at home and also seeing it from neighbors, friends, and teenagers who were older than you—it can have a carryover effect to your adult relationships. Primarily, minorities have had more problems with domestic violence because of our background or because of the environment that we grew up in."

Wansley and Hobley pointed to the absence of father figures among black players as an important factor. "Fatherlessness is a common background trait," Hobley said. "Usually, in this day and age it is prevalent in minority homes. I grew up the same way. My father left when I was a five-year-old." Statistics and scholarly research support Hobley's position. According to David Blankenhorn, author of *Fatherless America,* roughly 40 percent of the children in the United States live in homes where no father is present. That number climbs to 70 percent among blacks according to the U.S. Census Bureau. "Many males who turn to violence . . . grew up without a father," wrote Blankenhorn. And criminal justice experts William Bennett, John J. Di-Iulio, and John P. Walters report that fatherlessness is disproportionately plaguing the black community.

Finally, life in the NFL can directly increase the likelihood that domestic violence problems will arise. "Mentally and emotionally, domestic violence is more prevalent throughout the entire NFL than anything because of the things that spouses and significant others have to deal with on a day-to-day basis," explained Hobley. "Players are in such a limelight and there are so many different people, not only women, but men who tend to take a lot of time away from the family. It becomes a problem. We fail to understand the concept of family time, and tend to put off the things that we should be doing with our family and close friends. You feel like you're more important than they are. We tend to not realize those things until it's too late."

As of this writing, the collective bargaining agreement between the owners and the players contained no prohibitions against or punishments for domestic violence. Why? The crime is not seen as a direct threat to the integrity of the game. Drug use, gambling, and in some cases the unlawful possession or use of a firearm authorize the commissioner to discipline a player.

The following excerpts are taken from the NFL's official policy and programs:

Substances of abuse. "Substance abuse can lead to on-the-field injuries, to alienation of the fans, to diminished job performance, and to personal hardship," according to the NFL's policy for substances of abuse. "Discipline for violations of the law relating to use, possession, acquisition, sale, or distribution of substances of abuse, or conspiracy to do so, will remain at the discretion of the Commissioner."

Guns and weapons. "Whether possessed legally or illegally, guns and other weapons of any kind are dangerous. You and your family can easily be the losers if you carry or keep these items in your home. You must not possess these weapons while traveling on League-related business. . . ." The policy goes on to say, "If you violate this policy on guns and other weapons, you are subject to discipline, including suspension from playing." Ironically, not a single player who used a gun while assaulting his wife or girlfriend— such as Patrick Bates and Tim Barnett—faced any discipline from the commissioner.

Gambling. Accepting bribes, failing to report a bribe offer, betting on NFL games, and associating with gamblers are identified a "conduct [that] may result in severe penalties, up to and including a fine and/or suspension from the NFL for life."

Despite the NFL's less than stellar record on dealing with players arrested for domestic violence, the league's director of player programs, Dr. Lem Burnham, was offered a seat on the National Advisory Council on the Violence Against Women Act. The council consists of prominent leaders (physicians, law enforcement officers, entertainers, scholars, and domestic violence specialists) from around the country, all of whom are appointed by Attorney General Janet Reno and Secretary of Health and Human Services Donna Shalala, who chair the commission.

The national committee meets a few times a year in an attempt to design policy strategies to improve law enforcement response to domestic violence and to reduce the frequency of spousal abuse in the country. The NFL's Burnham was offered a seat on the council as a result of the league's particular influence on young men in the United States.

The authors interviewed members of the council, including Bonnie Campbell, of the United States Justice Department; Norm Stamper, chief of police for the city of Seattle; and Vickii Coffey, a member of the board of directors for the Chicago Foundation for Women. All three wholly endorsed Burnham's presence on the council and praised his efforts.

Nonetheless, the committee members each expressed frustration with the league's unwillingness to confront the problem it faces within its own ranks.

"It is a credit to the NFL that they are represented on this advisory council," said Stamper. "It's also incumbent upon the leadership of the National Football League to do everything possible to communicate the message of prevention and be unequivocal in their response to situations where domestic violence has occurred. And I think the track record is spotty at best."

Similar to the complaints raised by Vermont Congressman Bernard Sanders, members of the advisory council voiced their dissatisfaction to Burnham over the NFL's attitude of denial. Chief Stamper, among others, directly raised this contradiction with Dr. Burnham at one of the council meetings. The authors asked Stamper how Burnham responded: "The substance of the response was that the NFL does take this problem seriously and that the problem is no more widespread within the sports arena. And that through United Way ads and contributions to the United Way, the NFL has made an enormous contribution to the cause of ending domestic violence."

Ironically, in the NFL's letter to Sanders which accused him of unfairly singling out players, NFL senior vice president Joe Brown wrote, "The NFL is already working with President Clinton, Attorney General Reno and other public leaders and business executives through the President's Advisory Council on Violence Against Women." What Brown did not say was that the council's consensus was that the league's ability to reduce domestic violence was undercut by recurring arrests of NFL players for wife beating.

"We can all benefit from celebrating successes and acknowledging contributions, but it's clearly still a problem and it's a big problem that needs to be addressed head on," Chief Stamper insisted. "Pride and loyalty to one's organization are understandable and admirable qualities. But I don't think we can let them stand in the way of doing the right thing—which is stepping up and intensifying our efforts to prevent that kind of behavior in the first place. That means communicating in advance that we're simply not going to tolerate it. And where it does happen, to move quickly with appropriate and necessary due process rights being respected to deal with it." The NFL is not doing either.

When Dr. Burnham was contacted by the authors, he declined comment.

"NFL management is trying to sell a product," said domestic violence judge Ed Newman. "They became, perhaps a little late in the game, more proactive for marketing purposes. They're not totally altruistic. It's not strictly because it's right. They're doing it, in part, because they want to sell a wholesome product. They want America's kids to see the players as role models."

Despite the NFL's insistence that it is addressing the problem through public service announcements and contributions, the national advisory committee has been unable to persuade the league to use its high-profile players to appear in public service announcements denouncing domestic violence. This puzzled some council members. "There is an enormous fear on the part of the professional sports associations to even, for example, do PSAs with one of their more popular athletes for fear that six months later he'll be arrested and they'll look foolish," said Bonnie Campbell in an interview conducted in her office at the Justice Department.

"They're very gun-shy. They're almost schizophrenic. They really want to help, but they don't know who the batterers are and they think it will come back to bite them."

What to Do

The advisory council members, along with other experts interviewed, agreed unanimously that punishment is an essential part of correcting and reducing domestic violence—something the NFL does not do. "I'm asked all the time, 'Why do men batter?' " said Campbell. "There's a very simple answer. They batter because they can and we let them. There are no consequences. Until men are stigmatized for battering, punished legally, and held accountable in their lives, they will continue to abuse because it gets them what they want. If there's a connection between athletes and violence it has to do with power and control—who's got it and who doesn't."

The experts interviewed by the authors agreed that players who abused women should be suspended and in some cases dismissed altogether. But there was not unanimity over whether a single incident should trigger disciplinary measures.

Regardless, the NFL has *never* suspended even one of the many players who have beaten their wives or girlfriends.

"What if a player used drugs?" asked Campbell. "He'd be fired, wouldn't he? If he gambled it wouldn't even be debated. I don't understand why hurting another person in the worst kind of betrayal can continue without consequence. That's wrong whether you are a pro football player, a doctor, or a lawyer at the Justice Department. It is wrong morally and legally."

"The NFL has to take the situation as it is," said Stamper. "Sugarcoat it, underplay it to make it look or smell better, I think, is a huge mistake. Present it with accuracy and clarity. What's the nature of the problem? Freeze-frame on that."

Campbell disputed the NFL's claim that due process prevents them from taking punitive measures against players who criminally abuse their wives and girlfriends. "The due process argument doesn't apply any more for battering than it does for drugs," she said. "For example, the FBI has taken the position that if you are a law enforcement officer and you beat your wife once, you're gone."

Is the FBI any less concerned with due process than the NFL?

Campbell, nonetheless, maintained that the league should maintain some level of flexibility in their disciplinary procedures. As for those players who demonstrate a repeated problem, however, experts agree that termination is the answer. When the case of Miami Dolphins wide receiver Lamar Thomas (see Chapter 8) was brought to the attention of Bonnie Campbell, she said: "That's inappropriate, clearly inappropriate. If I were developing a policy I wouldn't be ambivalent about it. I'd make players sign the same kind of statement regarding domestic violence that they sign with regard to drug use. At some point, if there are three or four allegations, you've got to ask yourself, 'What is really happening here?'"

The Lamar Thomas case was also brought to the attention of Judge Ed Newman. "For some of those who are domestic violence abusers, it's too late for reform," said Judge Newman, who pointed out that this was the exception rather than the rule in the NFL. "There are criminals who cannot be redeemed. There are batterers who can't be redeemed. The domestic violence batterer who is a chronic batterer and doesn't seem to respond to the treatment, it may be a three-strikes-and-you're-out type of deal. An argument can be made that that's what should happen in the NFL."

While recognizing that the due process rights of players arrested for domestic violence is a viable concern, the seriousness of this crime nonetheless mandates that the NFL significantly step up its response to players who batter. By doing so, there is a potential for the league to see an overall decrease in other crimes attributed to players. "Domestic violence really helps to create an atmosphere of crime in the home that spills out onto the streets and follows children to their schools," said Seattle police chief Stamper. "There are so many victims of that form of violence, which I see as the most insidious form of violence in our country."

Judge Newman echoed Stamper's view. "Domestic violence spawns generational effects, drug abuse, a multitude of other problems," Newman said. "It is one of the first causes for social evils. It is a cycle for violence. It is a systemic problem. It is possible to show it as a first cause and predictor for other problems—truancy, dropout rates, drug problems, criminal activity, a repeat cycle of violence."

However, experience has shown that the mighty dollar is what dictates the NFL's behavior. Without sufficient resolve and pressure from the public, who pay to watch players perform, criminal violence in the homes of America's most celebrated athletes will continue. "It's time for the American public to stick its collective face into the face of professional sports and say, 'It's time to stop this behavior,' " said Chief Stamper. "Here are people who are, whether they like it or not, in positions that are conceived of as role models. And every time a single player on a ball club engages in that kind of behavior it really sends a wrong message. The real question now is 'What are we going to do about it?' And I think the challenge, not just for the NFL, but to every quarter in our society, is to communicate that domestic violence is criminal."

11

The Elephant in the Room

The Race Card.

As Johnnie Cochran so dramatically proved, it can trump any DNA evidence, outpoint any statistics, or be used to bluff any jury. It is the card that can make businesses, politicians, researchers, and even journalists fold when it is pulled. So daunting are the race card's consequences that the mere threat of its use can make important subjects seemingly disappear from our collective radar screens.

Why, then, should it be a surprise when the NFL, faced with mounting criticism of its players' off-the-field conduct, reaches for the bottom of the deck and plays the race card?

Just ask Vermont Congressman Bernard Sanders (see previous chapter). Sanders, along with other leaders in Washington, called for the NFL to "step forward" and address the repeated incidents of domestic violence within the NFL's own ranks. NFL senior vice president Joe Brown rebuffed Congressman Sanders in an April 19, 1996, letter which read in part: "To single out athletes will unfavorably serve to perpetuate stereotypes—including as to ethnic and racial groups. . . ." Brown then warned that any attempt on the part of Sanders to introduce his resolution would be "open to criticism as discriminatory."

Like Sanders, the authors were given a subtle hint that the league would adopt a similar strategy to criticize our book. When the authors contacted the NFL and requested an interview with Commissioner Tagliabue in March of 1998, NFL spokesperson Greg Aiello declined. He then added, "You . . . are trying to sell a book and it's a book that is going to stereotype athletes as criminals, most of whom are black—let's face it."

The authors' attempt here is to "face it"—publicly—and attempt to provide some perspective.

In the course of researching this book, the authors read countless press reports of NFL players who had been charged with crimes. A cursory sampling of the photographs accompanying many of these reports leaves the impression that it is virtually always black players who are in trouble with the law. While press pictures and headlines are hardly a reliable basis for drawing such conclusions, that is often all that readers are left with. For all the reporting on crimes committed by athletes, there has been almost no attempt to explain the apparent discrepancy between the number of black and white professional athletes being charged with crimes, or whether black players are in fact arrested at higher rates than white players.

Why hasn't this subject been dealt with? There are numerous answers to that question. First off, race is arguably the most sensitive topic in this nation's public discourse. In an effort to avoid stereotyping, or to even be perceived as stereotyping, the race component of the athlete-crime issue is delicately sidestepped. The problem, of course, is that as long as professional football players and basketball players (the overwhelming majority of whom are black) are celebrities in American culture, their misdeeds will continue to dominate the headlines. Without some context to go along with the litany of reports showing black athletes in handcuffs, stereotypes will persist.

After compiling data on the racial composition of the criminals in the NFL, the authors consulted with a number of individuals who provided diverse perspectives and analysis. They include: Rev. Jesse Jackson; William Bennett; Harvard Law Professor Randall Kennedy, author of *Race, Crime, and the Law;* Minnesota Supreme Court Justice Alan Page, former Minnesota Viking and a member of the NFL's Hall of Fame; and former East St. Louis high school football coach Bob Shannon, who coached a number of players who are now in the NFL. The authors also supplied all of their statistics to Carnegie Mellon Professor Alfred Blumstein, the nation's most renowned expert on crime statistics analysis. His steering was particularly helpful. It should also be noted that Justice Page, due to his position as a sitting justice on a state supreme court, provided helpful perspective but is prohibited from expressing opinions for attribution.

Each of those interviewed by the authors warned of the risks associated with doing this kind of research. "There is a deep association of criminality and blackness in American culture," explained Randall Kennedy, pointing out the misconceptions that could be drawn from learning that a substantial number of the criminals in the NFL are black. "The demographics of criminality have historically been used against black people. And it has been the case that people have used the nether side of activities engaged in by black Americans to stigmatize black Americans as a group."

While expressing caution, none of those who were interviewed discouraged a thorough and truthful investigation into the topic, despite not knowing how the results might turn out. Why? Because, as each of them said, truth provides the best weapon against stereotyping. "The fact of the matter is when these press reports [of athletes committing crimes] come down month by month by month, people are not stupid," said Kennedy, who is black. "If you're reading the newspaper and you have the pictures of athletes involved, it is not as if people don't draw dots. It's not as if you have to bring it to people's attention that the substantial number of athletes involved in serious criminal affairs are athletes of color. People read and know about these things. The options are to run away from this issue and leave the subject open to prejudice and stereotyping or educate people and give them a well-rounded understanding of what is going on here.

"It is a disturbing subject," Kennedy continued. "But researchers should not be inhibited in investigating a subject because it seems some people are going to be made uncomfortable by it."

William Bennett echoed these sentiments, adding that athletes' visibility in society required a more honest examination of these questions. "You have to look at this with straight eyes," said Bennett. "True, NFL players are disproportionately black. But they are also disproportionately heroes. Any person big enough to be a hero is big enough to have the truth told about him. If they are going to be such omnipresent figures in the lives of young people, we have to ask these questions, no matter how unpleasant the answers."

To examine this issue from a statistical standpoint, it is first necessary to look at the racial composition of the NFL. Over the past three seasons (from 1996 to 1998) the percentage of players in the league who are black has ranged between 67 and 71 percent. Of the 509 players whose criminal histories were researched by the authors, 78 percent of them were black, 18 percent were white, 2 percent were of other races, and 1 percent of the players were unidentifiable in terms of racial composition due to incompleteness of the public record.

The research revealed that of the 109 players who were found to have a serious criminal history, 96 (or 88 percent) were black, 8 (7 percent) were white, 2 (nearly 2 percent) were of other races, and 3 were unknown. The tendency here is to want to focus exclusively on the glaring discrepancy between the percentage of black players who had a record and white players who had a record. Without considering other factors, this produces very misleading conclusions.

For example, while blacks represented 88 percent of the players who had been arrested, they also compromised 72 percent of the survey population. The authors turned their findings over to Professor Blumstein and asked him to compare arrest rates for black players in the NFL to black males in the general population. Based solely on racial comparisons (in other words, no account was taken here for income, education obtained, background, and so forth), Blumstein determined that blacks in the NFL are arrested at rates *lower* than black males in the general population. (See Appendix II for a more detailed explanation of how Blumstein compared the authors' arrest rates for NFL players to the national arrest rates for blacks and whites.)

More important, since 368 of the 509 players in the survey were black and only ninety-six of the black players were charged with a serious crime, that indicates that the vast majority of black players were found *not* to have a criminal record. Put another way, the majority of the law-abiding citizens in the league are black, a point of paramount importance that seldom if ever gets emphasized. "What's extraordinary is that there's an awful lot of men who came from dysfunctional backgrounds who are doing quite well and who have made a great deal out of their lives," observed William Bennett after reviewing the research. "And they are disproportionately black. That is a very positive thing."

The bottom line here is that there is no basis for framing the issue surrounding criminals in the NFL as a race issue. It is a crime issue. NFL players who are committing crimes are not being singled out because they are black, but rather simply because they are criminals. Since an overwhelming majority of the players in the league are black, they naturally make up a large percentage of the players who run afoul of the law. If the NFL were truly concerned about cutting down negative racial stereotyping in this area, it would simply rid itself of criminal players. This would not only cut down on the misleading images that get promoted through the media, but it would largely do away with the league's public relations problems associated with criminal conduct. Yet the league would rather ignore that teams are employing criminals, as long as they play well enough.

"Crime is not a function of race," pointed out Jesse Jackson. "Crime is the function of sociology and psychology, your environment, and your mind-set." While race does not cause people to commit crime, the absence of any real consequences does.

As mentioned in Chapter 1, conventional wisdom suggests that giving players who have been in trouble with the law an opportunity to obtain a degree and earn a very healthy living would diminish criminality. The authors' research showed, however, that of the 109 players with an arrest record, seventy-seven (70 percent) of them were arrested *after* joining the NFL. This appears to cut against the popular belief that sports participation reduces poor behavior, instills character, and promotes self-discipline. However, it must be remembered that sports at the professional level provides a license to act in ways otherwise viewed as socially unacceptable. A pro contract can act as an exemption clause, a free pass from responsibility for one's actions.

This change can largely be attributed to the professional sports leagues' willingness to employ criminals. In the quest for talent, they have lowered the bar. This is not to say that professional sports teams and leagues should simply punish and cast aside athletes who commit crimes. But the long-term result of near total absolution from responsibility for behavior that would not be tolerated in any other profession provides the root for this problem. "If people are committing crimes, who are they committing crimes against?" Professor Kennedy asked rhetorically. "Some of the most poignant cases have involved these players who are batterers. Immediately, there is this call for redemption—we've got to protect these young men. Well, what happened to the women? The guy, a thousand arms embrace him. The woman is sort of left hanging out there. She's the villain after she's been wacked around a couple of times."

The willingness on the part of NFL teams to repeatedly embrace criminally violent athletes raises this question: Are the second chances an act of genuine concern for the welfare of the troubled player?

"By and large, we are seeing the end result of a long line of exploitation," explained Jesse Jackson, who played college football. "Men being used who come out of very desperate straits, having extraordinary, exploitable, commercial talent. They are put on a pedestal in high school, removed from the earth and its responsibilities. Then they are recruited by the top colleges. Students who score 1200 on the SAT and make straight As can't get in, yet some of the athletes get in with lower scores and study less difficult subject matter because they are actually working [for the universities]. These guys have been exploited from the time it was obvious they could jump higher and run faster. Athletes of stature don't walk on the ground and are allowed to play by different rules. Once their use is gone, they are no longer protected. But while they are playing ball, much of their behavior is cushioned. They are insulated from regular rules, attending classes, adhering to regular socializing processes.

"Those who are the most commercially exploitable are taught to live with the least amount of social responsibility," Jackson said. "But when they are no longer playing, these players often crash. There is a 75 percent divorce rate. Guys who made all kinds of money can't get a job. Drugs and liquor become anesthesia for their pain and some get caught selling it."

As Rev. Jackson pointed out, these after-career problems are not unique to black players. Nor is the crime problem. There are, however, reasonable explanations for why black players being drafted by NFL teams are, in some cases, particularly at risk for ending up in the headlines for the wrong reasons. "I see an unhealthy trend with some players," said legendary high school football coach Bob Shannon, who coached his predominantly black East St. Louis team to six Illinois state championships. "There are guys who are not African-American who get into these problems, but for the most part there's a trend that a lot of African-American players are getting caught up in. There's a mentality where guys are brought up to disrespect law and order. When players of this mentality go through the recruiting process they learn that they can get away with things that others can't get away with. By the time they make it to the NFL they feel very special. Just because these players suddenly find themselves with a lot of money doesn't mean they will start respecting the law. Some of them have already crossed the line of criminal conduct before receiving that big contract. They've had a taste of doing wrong and getting away with it. Now it is twice as hard for them when people, like old friends, put pressure on them to engage in unlawful activity."

Shannon has produced more than his share of NFL players. His accomplishments have even been chronicled in *Sports Illustrated* and captured in a full-length book. "Environment plays a tremendous role," Shannon told the authors, explaining the roots of many ballplayers' criminal tendencies. "When kids come out of an environment of poverty, gangs, and a lot of disrespect for the law, they learn a lot about 'getting over.' As early as elementary school they start coming in contact with petty crime and criminal thinking. Then they start getting recruited hard by gang members. They see people who are doing illegal things and seem to be thriving.

"It's not that all inner city kids are bad," Shannon continued. "But there are certain types of pressures on them that are not as widespread on other kids. There's pressure on all kids, but inner city kids see adults who don't have respect for the law and who have been living that criminal life for a long time. The African-American athletes are affected by this more because a lot of them come out of these bad situations.

"Kids who grow up in middle-class backgrounds are more likely to learn the value of work," Shannon said. "They see both parents getting up each day and going off to work. And they learn that the things they have are a result of working. On the other hand, kids from the ghetto look around and see people who have things as a result of stealing or selling dope or some other method. When you have a man out there selling drugs and he's standing by the fanciest car in the neighborhood, kids pick up on that."

"Framing is incredibly important," pointed out Randall Kennedy. "Things can only be framed after one has gathered a lot of information. This can't simply be framed as a race issue off the bat without doing a lot of investigation. A lot of times what appears to be a race issue really isn't. There are other variables which explain the situation much more than race. Our eyes go to race because we are very sensitive toward it. But there are other things going on that are actually the explanation. Race is not the explanation. It is a dependent variable as opposed to the independent animating variable."

Rev. Jackson suggested that the NFL is hardly in a position to raise claims of racism, given its poor treatment of blacks during the league's history. "There is a disproportionate number of blacks on the field," Jackson said, "but the NFL properties display at Super Bowl time looks like a seventeenth-century textile show. There are these patterns of exclusion within the NFL. All the owners are white. Though blacks have offered to put up money to purchase teams, they can't leverage money and stature to get in. If you look at the patterns of exclusion, who the owners are and who the banks lend to, that's the pattern.

"You have all these blacks on the field generating crowds and entertainment. Blacks have moved in horizontally, but they can't move up vertically. Blacks have gone from picking cotton balls to picking footballs, basketballs, and baseballs. What was bad about picking cotton was that you could not go beyond working at the raw material base. You could not turn cotton into textiles and go into the marketplace. Here, in pro sports, blacks are limited. They can't go beyond the field vertically and get into the marketplace.

"There are patterns of exclusion in ownership, capital, and licenses for NFL properties. Here we are 400 years later still proving the obvious, that we can coach a football team, that we can play quarterback. Still having to prove the self-evident—now that's racist."

12

Immunity

On February 27, 1998, television soap operas were interrupted in the New England area by breaking news of a real-life soap opera unfolding north of the border. New England Patriots star running back Dave Meggett had been arrested earlier that morning in a posh Toronto hotel and charged, along with former Patriots practice squad player Steve Brannon, with sexually assaulting a prostitute. Meggett, the NFL's all-time leading punt returner, was also charged with robbing the woman of $400 after allegedly slapping her about the face. Strapped to a stretcher, the victim was wheeled out of the hotel and transported by ambulance to an area hospital. Meggett and Brannon left the hotel handcuffed in the back of a police car.

Meggett's was but one among a two-week flurry of off-season arrests involving NFL players:

• On February 16, Jets kicker John Hall was arrested in Florida for possession of marijuana (charge is pending).

• On February 17, Packers running back Travis Jervey was arrested for possession of marijuana (charges were dropped).

• On February 25, Redskins wide receiver Leslie Shepherd was arrested for assaulting a man at a bar (acquitted at trial on June 2, 1998).

• On March 1, Jets lineman Matt Finkes was arrested in Arizona and charged with drunk driving after crashing his car (charge is pending).

• On March 3, Bengals running back Corey Dillon was arrested for drunk driving in Seattle (pleaded guilty to a reduced charge and served one day in jail).

The charges against Meggett were the most serious of the lot, and the most difficult to come to grips with by fans. An NFL player caught with weed? Sure. Players drinking and smashing up their cars? It happens. Guys mixing it up in a bar after a few too many brews? No surprise there. But a prostitute who says she was raped in an NFL star's hotel room? The public is far less willing to believe such charges. And why would a millionaire rob anyone, much less a prostitute, of $400?

Welcome to the erotic nightlife of celebrity athletes, where the narrow gap between sexual indulgence and sex crimes offers a murky view of who's telling the truth—the woman who says she was violated, or the player who says she wanted it.

Shortly after Meggett's arrest, his accuser, a thirty-three-year-old Toronto woman who made no effort to conceal her occupation as both a dancer at a Toronto gentleman's club and as a high-priced call girl, offered her side of the incident. In a published report, she revealed that she had known Brannon for two years, meeting him for the first time in a Toronto strip club. On March 26, 1998, hours before the alleged rape, the woman said she received a phone call from

Meggett, whom she claimed to have never met previously, asking her to meet him and Brannon in Meggett's $460-per-night suite at the Royal York Hotel.

When she arrived at the hotel, she said that Brannon met her in the lobby and escorted her up to Meggett's room. Alone in the room, the woman and Brannon had protected sex. Meggett then entered the bedroom unannounced, sat down on the bed beside them and reportedly said, " 'It's party time.' He was counting [a big wad of money] out loud," the woman said.

According to the woman, Meggett put on a condom and joined his friend and former teammate in having intercourse with her. She suddenly demanded that both of them stop, however, when their condoms unexpectedly broke.

"I told him [Meggett] to put on [another] condom, and he didn't," she said. "Anybody that knows me, knows I'm really into safe sex. Steve got in front of me and held up my arms. Meggett was in back of me. Meggett said the Patriots test him for AIDS all the time and I wouldn't catch anything."

She eventually untangled herself from the men, went into the bathroom, and rinsed herself off. "I got dressed and when I came out, Meggett was going through my fur coat and demanding I give him back the money," she said. "I started yelling at him that I wasn't giving the money back, and he started hitting me. I told Meggett, 'If you are willing to beat me for it, you must need it more than me.' "

Meggett and Brandon, through their attorneys, insisted that any sex that took place that night was consensual. Meanwhile, Meggett's lawyer, Alan Gold, according to press reports, hired a private investigator "to scour Toronto's night life . . . in an effort to discredit the woman's sexual assault claims."

As bad as the allegations against Meggett sounded, athletes have little to worry about when they are arrested for sex crimes. Of the 217 felony sexual assault complaints against college and professional athletes that were reported to police between 1986 and 1995, only sixty-six ever reached the trial stage. And of the sixty-six players who stood trial, 85 percent were acquitted. Conversely, Bureau of Justice statistics confirm that based on a 1990 study, 54 percent of the arrests for rape in the United States resulted in a conviction. The sordid circumstances surrounding the Meggett case illustrate an increasingly familiar scenario that makes convictions hard to come by when professional athletes are charged with rape: an alleged victim tells authorities she was raped by a professional ballplayer; the accused player admits to having sexual relations with the accuser, but denies the criminal charges; and well-paid defense attorneys remind the public that while it may be nontraditional for revered athletes to engage in group sex or in trysts with strippers and groupies, it is, however, not criminal.

The seamy nature of these cases initially tarnishes the player's image in the popular press. In court, however, lurid tales of sexual impropriety often hurt the accuser far more than the accused athlete, particularly if the accuser is a known call girl, nude dancer, or sports groupie. Under these circumstances, jurors don't necessarily believe the athlete to be more credible, but simply conclude the woman's occupation and her conduct leading up to the alleged incident raise too much doubt to find the player guilty. Consider the following:

In March of 1998, Rams offensive lineman Ryan Tucker pleaded no contest to aggravated assault and received a suspended sentence of 180 days in jail. *(Tarrant County, Texas, Corrections Center photo)*

Patrick Bates, the Atlanta Falcons defensive back who was cut from the team in 1997 one week after authorities charged him with brutally assaulting his girlfriend and endangering a child. *(Photo courtesy of the Atlanta Falcons)*

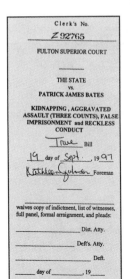

Clerk's No.

Z 92765

FULTON SUPERIOR COURT

THE STATE
vs.
PATRICK JAMES BATES

KIDNAPPING , AGGRAVATED ASSAULT (THREE COUNTS), FALSE IMPRISONMENT and RECKLESS CONDUCT

True Bill

19 day of Sept. , 19 97

Kathleen Johnson Foreman

waives copy of indictment, list of witnesses, full panel, formal arraignment, and pleads:

_____ Dist. Atty.

_____ Deft's. Atty.

_____ Deft.

_____ day of _____, 19____

A copy of the indictment returned by a grand jury against Patrick Bates in September of 1997. On March 23, 1998, Patrick Bates pleaded guilty to a felony charge of criminal damage to property and second degree battery. Just over a month later, he signed a contract with the Oakland Raiders. *(Fulton County, Georgia, Superior Court)*

Cornelius Bennett, the Atlanta Falcons All-Pro linebacker who was charged by New York authorities with rape, sodomy, sexual abuse, and false imprisonment in May of 1997. *(Photo courtesy of the Atlanta Falcons)*

Cornelius Bennett, flanked by defense attorney James M. Shaw, entering a Buffalo, New York, courtroom. He was sentenced to serve 60 days in jail after pleading guilty to a reduced charge of sexual misconduct. *(Buffalo News)*

Bengals running back Corey Dillon, the AFC's 1997 Rookie of the Year. Before joining the NFL, Dillon had eleven criminal cases brought against him in his home state of Washington. After his rookie season, he was again arrested in Washington. *(Photo courtesy of the Cincinnati Bengals)*

```
MORRIS, BYRON LEKEE
01/12/98        09:40
   19980118
```

Baltimore Ravens running back Bam Morris after his off-season arrest for illegal possession of drugs. *(Rockwall County Sheriff's Department photo)*

The Ravens' leading rusher, Morris was released by the team after he was sentenced to 120 days in prison in Texas for violating his probation. *(Photo courtesy of the Baltimore Ravens)*

Ravens owner Art Modell. After Bam Morris was jailed in Texas for failing to keep appointments with his probation officer, Modell submitted an affidavit to the prosecutor stating: "Given the complex nature of Mr. Morris's position on the club, it was vital that Mr. Morris not miss any time from work. . . ." *(Photo courtesy of the Baltimore Ravens)*

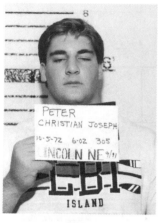

University of Nebraska standout defensive lineman Christian Peter. He was drafted by the New England Patriots in 1996 and then promptly released when owner Bob Kraft learned of his run-ins with the law in Nebraska. *(Lincoln, Nebraska, Police Department photo)*

Patriots owner Bob Kraft, who has steered away from employing players with criminal histories. *(Photo courtesy of the New England Patriots)*

Prior to joining the Rams, defensive end James Harris twice pleaded guilty to assaults against women and was sentenced to a ten-day jail term in Minnesota. After joining the Rams, federal authorities indicted him and accused him of providing money to drug dealers in East St. Louis. A federal judge acquitted Harris. *(Photos courtesy of the St. Louis Rams)*

Miami Dolphins wide receiver Lamar Thomas, who played under Dolphins head coach Jimmy Johnson at the University of Miami. *(Photo courtesy of the Miami Dolphins)*

Lamar Thomas was arrested and convicted for assaulting his pregnant girlfriend. *(Metro Dade, Florida, Police Department photo)*

A copy of the criminal complaint filed by the State of Florida against Lamar Thomas. *(Broward County, Florida, Court)*

IN THE CIRCUIT COURT OF THE SEVENTEENTH JUDICIAL CIRCUIT
IN AND FOR BROWARD COUNTY, STATE OF FLORIDA

THE STATE OF FLORIDA   INFORMATION FOR

vs.

LAMAR THOMAS   I. AGGRAVATED BATTERY ON PREGNANT FEMALE

       II. AGGRAVATED BATTERY ON PREGNANT FEMALE

IN THE NAME AND BY THE AUTHORITY OF THE STATE OF FLORIDA:

MICHAEL J. SATZ, State Attorney of the Seventeenth Judicial Circuit of Florida, as Prosecuting Attorney for the State of Florida in the County of Broward, by and through his undersigned Assistant State Attorney, charges that LAMAR THOMAS on the 4TH day of JULY, A.D. 1996, in the County and State aforesaid, did unlawfully and intentionally touch or strike Ebony Cooksey against her will and at the time of said touching or striking Lamar Thomas knew or should have known that said Ebony Cooksey was pregnant, contrary to F.S. 784.045(1)(b) (L7),

COUNT II

AND MICHAEL J. SATZ, State Attorney of the Seventeenth Judicial Circuit of Florida, as Prosecuting Attorney for the State of Florida in the County of Broward, by and through his undersigned Assistant State Attorney, charges that LAMAR THOMAS on the 4TH day of JULY, A.D. 1996, in the County and State aforesaid, did unlawfully and intentionally touch or strike Ebony Cooksey against her will and at the time of said touching or striking Lamar Thomas knew or should have known that said Ebony Cooksey was pregnant, contrary to F.S. 784.045(1)(b) (L7),

Dolphins wide receiver Charles Jordan, a former member of the Bloods who was held on murder charges that were later dropped before joining the NFL. *(Photos courtesy of the Miami Dolphins)*

HARGRAVE, CARL PHILLIP
Date Booked   07/04/1997
Arresting Agency   EDEN PRAIRIE

Running back Lawrence Phillips, after his arrest in Lincoln, Nebraska, for assaulting his ex-girlfriend. *(Lincoln, Nebraska, Police Department photo)*

Minnesota Vikings assistant coach Carl Hargrave was arrested on charges of drunk driving, obstructing the legal process, disorderly conduct, and refusing to take a breathalyzer test. He later pleaded guilty to refusing to submit to chemical testing. *(Eden Prairie, Minnesota, Police Department photo)*

(Left to right) Vikings head coach Dennis Green, assistant coaches Richard Solomon and Carl Hargrave, and team president and CEO Roger Headrick. The Vikings coaching staff was embroiled in controversy following sexual harassment accusations.
(Photos courtesy of the Minnesota Vikings)

HENDERSON, KEITH PERNELL
Date Booked   12/31/1995
Arresting Agency   BLOOMINGTON

Former Minnesota Vikings running back Keith Henderson was convicted of sexually assaulting three women in a nine-month span.
(Eden Prairie, Minnesota, Police Department photo)

Former Bengals defensive back Lewis Billups (#24) served time in a federal prison after making threats against NBA player Rex Chapman and his sister Jenny Chapman. Billups also pleaded guilty after being indicted for sexually assaulting a Florida woman while another man videotaped the incident.
(Photo courtesy of the Cincinnati Bengals)

Former Rams cornerback Darryl Henley (seen here carrying the ball) was convicted for soliciting the murder of a federal judge and a Rams cheerleader who testified against him. Henley is currently serving 41 years in Marion Federal Prison in Illinois.
(Photo courtesy of the St. Louis Rams)

• On October 3, 1990, a Seattle woman who was a known sports groupie had sex with Cincinnati Bengals player Lynn James in his hotel room. She later sued nineteen of James's teammates in federal court, claiming she was gang-raped by as many as a dozen players while teammates rooted each other on. No criminal charges were ever brought against the players, yet ten of them contributed to a $30,000 payoff to keep the woman from going forward with her claims. "It wasn't brutality or something that could be classified as criminal," said one of the accused players after the jury in the civil trial found the players not liable. "It was in fun, a human act. When are we allowed to drop the role model? What I mean by that is that a single guy doesn't have the pleasure or same ability a married guy has. A married guy can go in the privacy of his home and whatever happens happens. But a single guy's gotta get it from somewhere."

• In April of 1991, a twenty-three-year-old Austin, Texas, woman accused three Houston Oilers (Mike Rozier, Cris Dishman, and Richard Johnson) of sexually assaulting her in a hotel after the players reportedly met her in a club earlier that evening. According to the accuser's own admission, she was intoxicated at the time she left the club. Johnson, while admitting that he had consensual sex with the accuser, conceded to authorities that "she was asleep during intercourse." A Travis County grand jury listened to the evidence, including testimony from the players, and declined to indict.

• In August of 1995, La Crosse, Wisconsin, authorities received a complaint from a woman who said she had been sexually assaulted by members of the New Orleans Saints during training camp. The alleged victim had accompanied one of the players to his dorm room and had sex with him.

She told authorities that other players then entered the room unannounced and forced themselves on her. The players' version, in part, is described in the following excerpt from an Investigation Summary written by the prosecuting attorney's office: "Player 1 . . . and Player 2 did lie down and took their clothes off. . . . He [Player 1] stated that he and Player 2 did perform sexual intercourse with her and that she also had oral sex with him. He stated that at one point when she was having oral sex with Player 2 that he had sexual intercourse with her from behind. . . . When Player 9 entered the room . . . he took his clothes off and then attempted to put a condom on. . . . Player 1 stated that he specifically remembers seeing Player 5 standing in the doorway because he made the comment that he couldn't even get into the room with all the guys in there."

Despite the alleged victim's wishes to go through with criminal charges, prosecutors declined to indict the players. "I believe the credibility of the woman who reported the assaults would be insufficient to convince a jury beyond a reasonable doubt that the sexual contact she had with numerous players was not consensual," said prosecutor Ron Kind. The woman, it turned out, was an exotic dancer.

In cases of acquaintance rape, which so often boil down to a "he said-she said" swearing contest, credibility is paramount. And in jurors' eyes, groupies, strippers, and prostitutes who willingly go to celebrated athletes' bedrooms get little sympathy. Criminally accused athletes, as a result, actually benefit from describing the affair as a random sexual liaison. Seemingly, the more indiscriminate the sexual behavior that players are willing to admit to, the less likely it is that they will be convicted, much less indicted for a sex crime.

In short, convictions are generally tough to come by in any date rape case. But they are particularly rare when the accused is a celebrated athlete. Juries have their doubts about consent and force, even in cases of alleged gang rape where the accuser may have been drunk, asleep, or mentally impaired at the time of the incident. In the Bengals case mentioned above, the accuser claimed *and players admitted* that more than a dozen teammates rooted on players as they took turns having sexual contact with her. "I was trying to hide my eyes, ears, and nose to it because it's not very pleasant," said Judge Walter McGovern, who presided over the Bengals' civil trial. Prior to trial, McGovern and his law clerk were presented with over twenty hours of videotaped depositions detailing the alleged rapes. Without expressing an opinion as to whether or not the players' conduct was criminal, McGovern said in an exclusive interview, "I'm sure that it [the players' conduct] would really turn off 99 percent of the people in this country."

With so much riding on how jurors perceive the accuser, the public's familiarity with groupies and women who willingly have sex with athletes provides a potent weapon for defense attorneys. The more notorious rape cases involving professional athletes in the past decade have involved groupies or prostitutes. As a result, some jurors (and it only takes one for a not guilty verdict) warm up quickly to defense attorneys' portrayal of any accuser of an athlete as a groupie-type. This has a chilling effect on the willingness of other women who are sexually assaulted by players to come forward and press charges. "Women who indulge athletes in sex have got to start participating in some of the responsibility for athletes getting away with sexual assault," said Lori Peterson, a Minneapolis attorney who has represented five women in separate civil cases involving NFL players. "By acting like it is an honor to be bedded by a football player, these women are perpetuating the stereotype and endangering other women."

So what happens in cases where the alleged rape victim is neither a groupie, exotic dancer, or prostitute? Do accusers who are mere social acquaintances, live-in girlfriends, teenagers, or even minors fair any better in court? To explore these questions, the authors examined numerous rape cases, some of which never made it to the indictment stage and have been previously unreported by the press. Relying heavily on police reports and court documents, the authors also went back and interviewed key figures in each case chronicled below. The circumstances surrounding these cases illustrate why professional athletes often seem immune to prosecution for rape.

Together, Indianapolis Colts defensive tackle Tony McCoy, six feet and 282 pounds, and New Orleans Saints defensive tackle Darren Mickell, six foot four and 291 pounds, anchored the University of Florida's defensive line from 1989 through 1992. In the spring of 1992, both players were drafted into the NFL, McCoy by the Colts and Mickell by the Chiefs. Both quickly earned starting positions and developed into premier pass rushers. In 1996, Mickell was traded from Kansas City to New Orleans.

According to police reports on file at the University of Florida's campus police department, McCoy's and Mickell's odyssey to NFL stardom was checkered with complaints of sexual assault. Despite pages of police documents detailing alleged assaults involving both players, none of this ever came to light. Here's why.

On October 5, 1995, three years after both players had left Florida, the university's police department received a telephone call from Carmen Nichols.* A former student, Nichols reported that she had been gang-raped in the football players' dormitory back in 1991. According to Nichols's extremely detailed and lengthy police complaint, back on June 28, 1991, she was in her apartment when her phone rang at approximately 2:00 A.M. Nichols told police that she hung up the receiver when the male voice on the other end refused to identify himself. Minutes later, a former boyfriend whom Nichols had been intimately involved with telephoned. The boyfriend, a Florida football player, asked Nichols to meet him in the lobby of Yon Hall.

When Nichols arrived at the entrance to the boyfriend's dorm minutes later, she encountered Darren Mickell, who told her that he was the one who had called just prior to her boyfriend and refused to identify himself. Unnerved, Nichols backed away from Mickell and started back toward her apartment. She noted in her police statement that she was aware of Mickell's "reputation," but did not elaborate. A criminal background check on Mickell revealed that while on a football scholarship he was charged with resisting police officers three times. In 1992 he pleaded no contest to a felony charge of grand larceny and served two days in jail.

As Nichols walked away from Yon Hall, her boyfriend emerged from the dorm and persuaded her to go up to his room. She agreed. But to her dismay, the boyfriend then let Mickell in his room as well.

Nichols told the police that within minutes, another member of the football team and Tony McCoy entered the room.

According to the police report, Nichols, on more than one occasion, asked her boyfriend to make Mickell leave the apartment. Nichols told police that Mickell refused and instead started fondling her breasts and leading her toward the bedroom. At this point, the police report notes, Nichols "told them [the players] that she wanted to go home."

In response, her boyfriend "told her 'she knew what was up, and don't play games,'" according to the report. All four players started pawing at Nichols. McCoy and the fourth player, according to Nichols, then had sexual intercourse with her, each looking on as the other took his turn.

In her statement, Nichols said that neither McCoy nor the fourth player used physical force prior to intercourse. The police report notes, "She was too scared to say no."

After taking Nichols's telephoned-in report, the Florida campus police were left with an alleged four-year-old incident involving suspects who had all since moved out of state. Most troubling was the accuser's admission that she had not said no to McCoy and the other player. Hardly a provable case, the police nonetheless turned the matter over to the State Attorney's Office for review. Why? Because Nichols was not the first woman to file a formal police report singling out McCoy and Mickell in conjunction with a sexual assault.

According to other University of Florida police reports obtained by the authors, in the summer of 1991, weeks after the time period during which Nichols claimed she was assaulted, Gretchen Daniels* met with Officer Angel Allen and reported a scenario remarkably similar to the one described by Nichols. In a 1991 police report, Daniels said she too was assaulted at Yon Hall after being invited to the room of Nichols's former boyfriend. Like Nichols, Daniels also knew him socially and felt comfortable going to his room at his invitation. Also like Nichols, Daniels told the police that she was surprised when she arrived at Yon Hall expecting to meet the player and was instead greeted by Darren Mickell.

Daniels told police that a short time later, while she and the player were in bed together, Mickell and McCoy and another male athlete barged in. The three players then "took turns having sexual intercourse with Daniels," according to the police report. Additionally, the report notes, "Daniels felt helpless to resist as she was naked in a room with several football players. . . ." In the course of taking turns climbing on and off Daniels, the players, as they did with Nichols, repeatedly remarked "that [Daniels] would not have come to the room if she was not expecting to have sex with all the athletes."

In her 1991 report, Daniels said she realized she had been "set up" by the players. According to the report, Daniels told police that she believed the experience was "a common scam among this particular group of athletes." The report also takes note of a concern that "many other females were too afraid and ashamed to report the gang rapes occurring in Yon Hall."

Attempts to interview Darren Mickell for this book were unsuccessful. Tony McCoy claimed he had no knowledge of the police reports against him until they were brought to his attention by the authors. "I never knew those reports were filed," McCoy claimed in an exclusive interview. "To this day, they never came up. I don't even want to dignify them." McCoy did, however, confirm that he was friends and teammates with the other players named in the police reports. "Mickell and [the other player] were good friends, but I didn't make it a habit of hanging around them and doing the things that they did," said McCoy. "We didn't hang around the same crowd. We are from two different sides of the street."

McCoy's agent, David Levine, skeptical toward the reports, asked rhetorically why a woman would bother filing such a complaint if she had no intention of pressing charges. He also suggested that it was "hard to believe" that authorities would not pursue the charges upon receiving a complaint of the nature described in the police reports.

Perhaps. But it is not uncommon for police to take formal statements from citizens and file a report while stopping short of opening an investigation when the person declines to swear out a formal complaint.

Daniels said she was too scared to press charges.

And Nichols claimed she was too afraid to say no to the players.

But afraid of what?

In her 1991 report, Daniels provides a clue. She told police that she feared McCoy "because she was aware of the recent sexual battery charges against McCoy by his girlfriend." Previously, McCoy had been indicted in a nine-count felony sexual assault case. The charges against him included kidnapping (one count), sexual battery by use of threat of a deadly weapon (two counts), aggravated battery (three counts), aggravated assault (one count), and battery (two counts). Daniels knew about the incident because it took place on campus, with some of the sensational details unfolding in broad daylight in front of numerous witnesses.

According to police reports, on November 21, 1989, at just after one o'clock in the afternoon, U.S. postal carrier Joe Simpson was delivering mail on campus when he stumbled across a completely naked woman cowering behind a newspaper box. Startled by his discovery, Simpson's attention was nonetheless immediately diverted away from the nude woman when a large man began shouting at the woman from an apartment across the street.

"Becky,* come here," the man from across the street demanded as he stepped out of the apartment to come toward the woman and Simpson.

Simpson quickly removed his shirt and handed it to the woman to put on.

"He's got a knife," Becky screamed as she sprang from behind the newspaper box and ran hysterically down the street wearing only Simpson's U.S. Mail shirt.

Minutes later, police were on the scene and Simpson recounted his experience to investigators. Becky, the woman discovered by Simpson, was McCoy's girlfriend.

Despite living in Yon Hall with the other football players, McCoy also had his own apartment. He rarely slept there, but he let Becky live there on a full-time basis. According to Becky, when McCoy showed up at the apartment on November 19, 1989, and his male neighbor was inside watching television with Becky, he was angry.

Two brothers had taken Becky out for dinner on the nineteenth, and then returned to her and McCoy's place to watch television. One left prior to McCoy's arrival. The other left when McCoy showed up.

"What is this guy doing sitting in my house and in my chair?" McCoy yelled at Becky, according to police reports. He then accused her of having sexual relations with the man. Ultimately, he told Becky to get out of the apartment. As she packed her bags, however, McCoy entered the bedroom and demanded that she take just one set of clothes and return to get the rest of her things at a later date. Although he confiscated her key, McCoy told her that she could contact him and he would open the apartment so she could recover the rest of her things another time, according to the police report.

Heading for the door with her one set of clothes, Becky was suddenly stopped by McCoy. He told her to "get undressed, go to bed, and get some sleep." According to the police report, when Becky indicated that she needed to call her mother first, "McCoy told her she was not going to see or talk to her mother that night." He took her purse, searched through it for her address book, and began flipping through the pages looking for names and numbers that were unfamiliar to him. Then he threw it at her.

That night McCoy decided not to return to the dorm. Becky told authorities that he had intercourse with her before going to sleep and again in the morning. At noontime, he got out of bed and left the apartment, telling Becky that he was going to pay a visit to the apartment of the guy who was watching television with her the night before. Becky reported that she hurriedly got dressed and followed McCoy to the man's neighboring apartment. Her arrival angered McCoy, who escorted her outside and back toward his apartment.

Initially reluctant to return with him back to his apartment, Becky gave in when McCoy lifted her off the ground and started carrying her. Once inside, "McCoy demanded that she take her clothes off," the report indicates. Becky told investigators she complied out of fear "because he had previously been violent with her." McCoy insisted that she get back on the bed. After he started kissing her, he exited the bedroom and went into the kitchen.

The following excerpt from the police report details what happened after McCoy returned from the kitchen and climbed into bed. "After McCoy got back in the bed [Becky] felt what she thought was fingernails scratching her neck. She said when she looked down she saw McCoy holding what she identified as a steak knife that had a serrated edge. McCoy was using the blade of the knife to make cuts on Becky's body. When she yelled out he told her he would kill her."

McCoy then grabbed Becky's right breast, took the tip of the knife, and cut her chest, according to the police report. Repeating the threat to kill her if she yelled, McCoy "asked her how she would like to lose her eye. He then took the knife and moved it around her eyes, face and ears," the report states.

Officer Jackie Kerr examined Becky shortly after the attack and documented the following observations: "The most visible of the cuts were observed by this investigator on Becky's chest just above her right breast and close to the center of the sternum. This appeared to be a puncture type wound. The wound was approximately a quarter inch in diameter. Above the breasts this investigator observed numerous small lacerations. These were made when McCoy used the sharp edge of the knife to inflict cuts. On the left breast near the nipple, there is what appears to be a large bite mark. This investigator observed a laceration on Becky's left leg, that appeared to be approximately one half inch long. There were lacerations on her left hand, including a laceration on the inside of the thumb and one on the palm. These were approximately one half inch long."

Becky told Kerr that while McCoy was cutting her with the knife, he asked her if she had ever been raped. According to Kerr's report, "he took the edge of the knife and cut away her bra and also one side of her underpants." The report also notes that McCoy struck Becky in the face and spit on her.

Kerr's report then describes the following: "He took the handle of the knife and placed it inside her vagina, rubbing the knife in circular motions. He got up on her chest and had her arms pinned to the bed with his knees. McCoy forced his penis into her mouth telling her to perform oral sex on him. After she had done this he told her she was a 'chicken head.' McCoy put his hands around her throat and started to choke her. . . ."

According to Kerr's report, McCoy finished by taking a pillow and placing it over her face. When she faked having passed out, he slapped her in the face before walking away from the bed area and over toward the window. Becky reported that at that instant she ran for the door and dashed out into the street naked. Kerr's report notes, "[Becky] said the reason she felt she was able to escape from McCoy was the fact that he did not think she would run out the door nude."

"None of that stuff happened," McCoy emphatically stated in an interview with the authors. "I do admit to there being an argument and some pushing and shoving. I do admit there was a strong relationship between Becky and I. She is someone who I cared about tremendously. I really loved her as a person. And I didn't treat her right. A lot of men don't treat women right, especially when they're young. But the rape and the knife, none of that stuff ever took place."

According to McCoy, a lot of the information in the police reports was "fabricated, stuff that did not happen." When asked by the authors, McCoy acknowledged that

Becky was mentally stable when she told her account to the police. He also added that in his three-year relationship with Becky, he had never known her to falsely accuse him or any other individual. Nor was she known for making up outlandish stories.

What, then, was her motivation to lie? "We had an argument," McCoy explained without hesitation. "I got this other girl pregnant and Becky was asking me to leave this girl. I told Becky, 'No, I'm going to marry this girl,' which I later did. This is the thing that really pushed Becky over the edge. I was involved with a lot of women at the time. She knew I was fooling around, but she always had this ideal that I would be with her. I thought I loved her, but I never showed it because I was always fooling around with other women. That would make anyone who is stable unstable."

Why would she run into the street naked? "She never ran into the street naked," McCoy said. "We were arguing. She pushed me and I pushed her. I went and sat down in the chair. She looked at me and said, 'You'll never know how much I love you.' And she walked out. I was thinking that she wanted me to run after her. Well, I didn't. And my apartment was tucked back away from the road, meaning you could step outside and no one would see you unless someone just happened to be walking by. It was just my luck that when she stepped out, lo and behold, a neighbor was walking by, saw her, and pulled her into her apartment.

"When this lady saw her, Becky came up with this story. Becky was embarrassed and she got herself into something too deep, where she had to continue to cover up. My mother always used to say, 'You tell one lie, and you have to tell another and it just never stops until you tell the truth.' And eventually the truth came out, we had an argument and there was nothing more than that."

But what about the postal worker who told police that he removed his shirt and gave it to Becky after discovering her completely nude and cowering behind a newspaper box? "I'm saying she was not naked," McCoy said. "She did have her panties on, but no bra. And she didn't run, she walked out."

Mailman Joe Simpson was not the only witness who reported seeing Becky nude and hiding behind a newspaper box. Cris Iddings, who lived across the street from McCoy, and her friend Sylvia Campedelli called 911 after noticing Becky hiding without any clothes on. As a result of Iddings's call, police were on the scene in minutes and discovered Becky wearing Simpson's shirt and otherwise unclothed.

Officers took Becky to Shands Hospital and she was examined by Dr. David Minton. A rape kit was administered to Becky by R.N. Sharon Coullis, which was then turned over to investigator Nick Vellis. Finally, rape victim advocate Loretta Golden met privately with Becky.

LaWanda Highsmith, a close friend of Becky's, showed up at the emergency room and informed investigators that she was also acquainted with McCoy. In her statement to police, Highsmith said, "She was present on one occasion when Tony McCoy and his ex-wife were involved in a domestic dispute." According to the police report, "During the dispute Ms. Highsmith observed McCoy hit [his ex-wife] twice, as hard as he could." Highsmith claimed that since McCoy's divorce from his wife, his violent outbursts had become progressively worse.

Following the long ordeal at the hospital, Becky was released into the care of Highsmith, who took her home. Back at McCoy's apartment, campus police arrested McCoy and seized evidence from inside. They discovered a brown-handled steak knife matching the description given by Becky. It was lying in a pan of dirty dishwater. Officers also found a pillow on McCoy's bed with slash marks on it. "It appeared to have fresh stab type cuts in it," the report notes.

When asked by investigators how Becky sustained cuts on her chest, "McCoy said that as breakfast was cooking he and Becky played with knives pretending to slash and stab at each other. He said she may have been cut accidentally, but doesn't remember her being wounded," according to the report.

When asked how the slash marks ended up on the pillow found on his bed, "McCoy said it was an old pillow given to him by his mother. He said the 'cuts' were old tears," according to the report.

When asked why Becky would run from the apartment nude in broad daylight, "He said he could not explain why she ran out." According to the police report, "McCoy thought she might have become angry over her jealousy regarding another female he dated, whom he identified [as McCoy's ex-wife]."

McCoy was booked and jailed on November 21, 1989. As a result of the serious nature of the charges against him, McCoy was suspended from the football team and expelled from the university. However, on March 19, 1990, all the charges against McCoy were suddenly dropped. Becky, after some time had passed, decided to no longer cooperate with prosecutors. "It's not uncommon for victims to not want to go forward in domestic cases," said Officer Nick Vellis, who recovered the knife allegedly used by McCoy on Becky. "But in my career with the University of Florida Police Department, I've never seen another case where a knife was used."

State Attorney John Carlin, since retired, was in charge of the McCoy prosecution and was particularly distraught over Becky's decision. "We felt we had a very strong case against Mr. McCoy," Carlin said in an interview for this book. "I was upset when the case was not able to go forward. At the time, I thought we had a strong case. But without the victim, there was no way to go forward."

According to McCoy's criminal lawyer, Huntley Johnson, he knew before the prosecutors found out that Becky wasn't going to go forward. "I spoke to her in my office and she told me that she was going to recant," Huntley said in an interview for this book. "I said, 'Fine. Let's set up a deposition.' "

When Johnson deposed her under oath, Carlin was present. By the end of the questioning, Johnson knew McCoy was in the clear. "She was going to make a terrible witness," Johnson said candidly in an interview with the authors. "She went in the tank. She was not going to testify [at trial]. Without her, the case was mighty, mighty tough to prove."

Yet there was circumstantial evidence. A police officer witnessed and documented knife wounds on Becky's chest; a wooden-handled knife, matching the one described by Becky, was seized from McCoy's apartment; a pillow with slash marks on it was recovered by police from McCoy's bed; and Becky was seen by multiple witnesses running down the street naked in broad daylight. Carlin insisted, however, that without Becky's willingness to testify against

McCoy, the prospects of prevailing at trial were suspect at best. "By law, we could have subpoenaed the victim to appear," Carlin explained. "But it is a very, very rare occasion when you subpoena a victim to testify when they are reluctant to do so. It is a hairy situation to call someone to the stand when you're not sure what they're going to say. They could blow the case right out of the water."

Johnson, himself a former state prosecutor, agreed with Carlin's decision to drop the case, offering the following personal experience as an illustration of why: "As a young prosecutor, I had a woman who had thirty scars on her back where this guy hit her thirty times with a coat hanger. She was a reluctant witness. I subpoenaed her and made her go to trial. She got on the stand, cried, and said it was an accident. The jury convicted the guy of the least charge they could and the judge gave him three months' jail time. The point is that with a reluctant victim you don't have a hell of a lot."

Despite dropping the case against McCoy, did Carlin believe the allegations laid out in the graphic report? "As a prosecutor, anytime you have a case that you file charges on, you have got to file the charges in the belief that you have probable cause to believe the individual did the crime and that you can prove it beyond a reasonable doubt," Carlin said. "Otherwise, you wouldn't file those charges. This case was dropped not because of any new evidence. We dropped the case because the victim did not wish to testify. The allegations that were made were particularly brutal. Whatever happened that day, the woman was scared enough to run out of the apartment naked."

And Johnson's beliefs about the acts attributed to his client? "I remember the report as being brutal," said Johnson, stating that he never had to answer the question as to whether the report was accurate because the trial never took place. "But I was coming from the other end of the spectrum, which was to represent Mr. McCoy's interests the best I could. I didn't question the state's decision to drop the case. I just went on to the next case. I was just glad that one was over with. I wasn't worried about why they did it. I hate to sound cold about it, but I'm there to defend Tony McCoy."

McCoy, now married and an ordained minister who preaches regularly in the Indianapolis area, was reinstated to the University of Florida following the state's decision to drop the charges against him. After censuring him for committing "disorderly conduct" in connection with the incident, a school judicial panel accepted McCoy's application for reinstatement. He played his senior season and went on to be drafted by Indianapolis, where he says he is actively involved in working with abused women. McCoy said that his We As One ministry in Indianapolis buys and refurbishes drug houses in the inner city and then uses them to provide housing to abused women.

"I have no regrets," McCoy told the authors. "When you're young, you make mistakes. You do stuff foolishly. You learn from it. And you go on. I feel like God has been blessing me ever since. That was a point in my life where, truthfully speaking, I thought that I was someone who deserved special things and special treatment. What kid doesn't coming out of an enviroment like I did and into the college atmosphere and becoming an All-American? You begin to think that your odor doesn't stink.

"That incident was a good wake-up for me. I never ever

admitted to rape. And I never will admit to rape. I never admitted to any of those things that happened in that whole scenario of acts.

"A lot of kids don't get a second chance," McCoy mused. "I got a second chance. I'm thankful for it. I often look back and just thank God for where he brought me from."

Back in 1991 when Gretchen Daniels reported to police that she had been assaulted by McCoy and Mickell, she referred to McCoy's alleged sexual assault on Becky in her decision not to press charges. Shortly after officers took Carmen Nichols's 1995 telephoned-in report, they discovered that she too had filed a more timely complaint against McCoy and Mickell back in 1991. After going to the campus infirmary for medical treatment and reporting the matter to her residence hall advisor, Nichols filed a formal police complaint with campus police officer Angel Allen in the summer of 1991. But at that time, Nichols told Allen that she did not want to press charges. Investigator Allen complied with Nichols's wishes, labeled her 1991 report "confidential," and filed it away.

On December 21, 1995, two months after recontacting the Florida campus police and asking that charges be pressed, Nichols was notified that Assistant State Attorney Jeanne Singer would not be indicting McCoy, Mickell, and the others. It was not, however, because their cases weren't worthy of prosecuting. The statute of limitations had expired, barring prosecutors from seeking an indictment. The final page of the lengthy case file on McCoy and Mickell reads, "This case is closed, no criminal charges will be filed."

No one will ever know the truth.

* * *

McCoy, years removed from his days at the University of Florida, is about to hang up the telephone at the conclusion of his long interview with the authors. Then he pauses. "Let me just share this," he said pointedly. "That was a part of my life when I was a young man who was just not very mature at the time. This whole incident caused me a lot of pain. It's a part of my life that's over and I'm done with. I was exonerated of the whole thing. I feel I've forgiven myself and I've forgiven Becky. And I asked her to forgive me, not for the things I was accused of, but for the disorderly conduct—for not treating her as a woman should be treated. I'm over it. I know God has forgiven me and I'm moving on with my life."

The Benefit of the Doubt

Even if Nichols and Daniels had decided to press charges back in 1991, they would have confronted this sobering reality: the players would have probably been acquitted, if charged at all. Unless the accuser has sustained serious physical injuries, juries usually give the benefit of the doubt to the athlete.

Take the case of Freddie Bradley, who was drafted by the San Diego Chargers in 1996.

Before the Chargers drafted Bradley out of California's little-known Sonoma State College in 1996, he was a running back for the University of Arkansas. He ended up at Sonoma only after Arkansas stripped him of his football scholarship in 1992. Why would Arkansas get rid of a guy who had the goods to run in the NFL? Bradley was indicted for raping a thirteen-year-old girl in the student-athlete dorm on the Fayetteville campus.

On the morning of April 22, 1992, Bradley and teammate

Derrick Martin picked up two girls, ages thirteen and fourteen, at the Woodland Junior High School and brought them back to their dormitory. The girls, who went willingly to the players' room, later testified that Bradley and Martin put on condoms and had sexual intercourse with them. Under Arkansas's statutory rape law, it is illegal to have sex with a child under the age of fourteen. Since the thirteen-year-old was by law too young to give consent, Bradley was, by definition, guilty of statutory rape if he merely had sex with the girl, consensual or otherwise.

The thirteen-year-old, who had turned fourteen by the time the trial took place, took the stand and testified that she did have sex with Bradley. Police recovered condoms from Bradley's room. Yet, Bradley testified that he did not have sex with his accuser. On January 26, 1993, a Washington County jury acquitted both players.

University of Arkansas Chief of Police Larry Slamons, sensing from the start that this was going to be a high-profile case in the community, personally took charge of the investigation and concluded that sex definitely took place between Bradley and the child. "That didn't make any difference to the jury, who said, 'They're doing it voluntarily,'" Chief Slamons said in an exclusive interview. "The jury ignored that particular part of the law."

Assistant District Attorney Terry Jones, who prosecuted Bradley and Martin, explained why the jury let the players off. "Bradley and Martin were two very handsome, cleancut, soft-spoken, nice kids except for what they were doing," Jones explained. "There's one theory about those kind of cases: that the women [on juries] tend to blame the victims a lot. The trouble is that these guys [athletes] are smarter than the average bear. They're good-looking kids. They come to court and they're cleaned up and they look good and make great defendants.

"It is very difficult when you have willing females, who go out of their way to make dates with or arrange liaisons with athletes to go up in their bedrooms, to not have the blame placed on the girls for a considerable amount of what happens to them. They're not regarded as innocents anymore. And it's very tough to convince a jury that they either were not victimizing the athletes or that they were not willing participants in the sexual activity that ensues."

If thirteen- and fourteen-year-olds can be seen as more blameworthy than adult athletes in a statutory rape case, the odds of getting a jury to convict only get worse when the accuser is an adult. "My frustration with these cases is that I'd like to get a good one, one of these days," mused Jones, who has prosecuted other University of Arkansas athletes for sex crimes. "I'd like to have one with substantial evidence and credible witnesses."

After playing two seasons with the San Diego Chargers, Bradley was released by the team after a career-threatening knee injury. He underwent successful surgery and, according to his agent, Timothy Shanahan, Bradley was hoping to sign on with a team before the start of the 1998 season. Bradley declined to be interviewed for this book.

13

Rapists Never Retire

"I had a teammate whose motto was 'If she ain't freakin', we ain't speakin,' which meant: I don't even want to talk to you if you're not talking about going back to the hotel," former NFL quarterback Don McPherson said in an exclusive interview.

After quarterbacking for both the Philadelphia Eagles and the Houston Oilers in the late 1980s, McPherson was hired by the Center for the Study of Sport in Society at Northeastern University in Boston. There he directed Mentors in Violence Prevention (MVP), a program that uses male athletes to train college- and high-school-age young men in how to reduce abusive treatment of women.

McPherson said that NFL players often encounter groupies during their careers, and as a result sometimes have difficulty discerning which women are coming on to them for sex and which ones aren't. "If she's coming on strong and knows something about the team that's one thing," McPherson said, in explaining the drill that players run through their mind when meeting women for the first time. "Or she could be just a big fan who happens to think that you're a nice person. But some players won't think that because they're dogs. A dog is just like the animal, it indiscriminately will hump anything that slows down long enough for you to back up to it. I shouldn't say this, but when you're someone who has a lot of money and commands a lot of respect, you usually don't have to do anything. You can, one way or the other, find your own."

Evidence has shown that NFL players, like other pro athletes, may get away with taking sexual liberties during their playing days. But what happens to those NFL players whose sexual aggression, whether criminal or consensual, goes unchecked throughout their NFL careers? In other words, how do players like those referred to by McPherson as "dogs" cope when they are no longer able to find sex?

After examining ten cases of ex-NFL players charged with a sex crime, the authors chose two players, running back Keith Henderson (San Francisco 1989–92, Minnesota 1992–93) and cornerback Lewis Billups (Cincinnati 1986–91, Green Bay 1992) for illustration here. In addition to interviewing law enforcement authorities and players, the authors relied heavily on court documents and police reports for this chapter.

As the evidence will show, both Henderson and Billups were notorious for being sexually active and both faced allegations of abuse by women during their careers. Neither player, however, was ever convicted for any sex crime while playing in the NFL. The immunity afforded professional athletes is nice, while it lasts. Retirement—at least for these two players—brought on a different story altogether. Both committed rape within a month of leaving the NFL, and both continued on a spree of attacks on women that landed both Henderson and Billups in prison.

* * *

In early 1993, Sally Michaels* was waitressing at Puzzles, a Minneapolis bar located in the Mall of America, when she first met six-foot-one, 240-pound Keith Henderson. A fullback on the Vikings, Henderson frequented the bar often and enjoyed a reputation as "friendly" among the waitresses and bartenders. On September 26, 1993, Henderson, who had been released by the Vikings four weeks earlier, asked Michaels for a ride home after her shift. She hesitated but ultimately agreed after receiving assurances from her colleagues.

At 12:30 A.M. the pair left Puzzles and soon arrived at Henderson's apartment, which he shared with a male roommate. While Michaels sat talking briefly with Henderson in her car parked in front of his apartment complex, security guards asked the two to either park or leave. When Henderson invited Michaels inside so they could continue their conversation, she agreed, later telling police that she did so out of "politeness."

Once inside, Henderson introduced Michaels to his roommate, Kevin Johnson, before briefly retreating to a room in the back of the apartment. Moments later Henderson called for Michaels to come back where he was. "Why?" she asked.

"Just come in here," Henderson said in a friendly tone.

Michaels was surprised to reach the end of the hallway and discover that Henderson had been calling to her from the bathroom. His shirt was unbuttoned, and his facial expression was changed. Not sure what to say, Michaels stood speechless. Henderson suddenly grabbed her by the hips, propped her up on the counter, shut the bathroom door, and flipped off the light. "This is weird," Michaels said nervously.

As Henderson started groping her breasts, Michaels's hand fumbled in the dark for the light switch. By the time she found it, Henderson was pulling her underwear down. "No," she said, flipping on the switch. "I really have to go now."

Henderson ignored her pleas, while dropping his underwear. When Michaels refused Henderson's directive to place her hand on his penis, he forced her hand down to his crotch. With Michaels trying desperately to break free, he quickly spun her around and began forcing her legs apart from behind.

"No, no," she begged, her panties now being tugged down and Henderson's massive hands clamped tightly on her arms. Standing up, her face and chest pressed up against the bathroom wall, Michaels sobbed quietly as Henderson forcibly penetrated her vagina from behind. Despite Michaels's tears, Henderson remained inside her until he ejaculated. He then withdrew quickly and pulled up his pants.

Before pulling up her underwear, Michaels wiped the semen off the inside of her legs. Seemingly oblivious to the physical pain he caused, Henderson then followed Michaels out to her car and said that he would call the following day. "He acted as if nothing had happened," Michaels later told investigators.

Initially, she did not go to the hospital or report the incident to the police. Instead, she chose only to confide in a few trusted friends. That all changed when Michaels learned that she was pregnant.

Not wanting to believe the worst, she tried to convince herself that she was not carrying Keith Henderson's child. After all, she had sexual intercourse with her boyfriend eight days before being raped by Henderson. Her boyfriend could be the father. There was one problem, however: prior to the single sexual encounter with her boyfriend, Michaels had been a virgin. In other words, there was only a fifty-fifty chance that her boyfriend, rather than Henderson, had impregnated her.

Michaels finally told her boyfriend, who then underwent blood tests, which confirmed that he was not the father. On March 4, 1994, Michaels, by then six months' pregnant, faced the horrible truth and reported Henderson to the Eden Prairie police.

Detective Jim Lindgren was assigned the task of locating and questioning Henderson. According to police reports, when Lindgren showed up at the running back's last known address—apartment no. 5 at 1601 East 80th Street in Bloomington—he encountered a man who said that Henderson had previously moved out because he was wanted by the law.

Lindgren was unaware that Henderson was under investigation by the Hennepin County prosecutor's office for another rape that he committed on October 6, 1993, just one week after he had raped Michaels.

According to police reports and investigation summaries obtained by the authors through a public records request, on November 1, 1993, Sergeant John Billington of the Minneapolis Police Department's Sex Crimes Unit was sitting in his office when seventeen-year-old Mandy Sims* walked in and reported that she had been raped one month earlier. Sims was one of a number of teenage girls who had been hired to appear as extras in the filming of the movie *Little Big League*, which was being shot at the Metrodome. On

October 4, while on the set, Sims was approached by a man who introduced himself as Keith Henderson, an NFL running back. He had actually been cut by the Vikings a month earlier and was trying to catch on with another team. In need of work in the meantime, Henderson took a job on the movie set as an extra.

For three consecutive days, Henderson engaged Sims and her friend in friendly conversation. After filming concluded on October 6, Henderson offered to drive the two teens from the movie set to a nearby parking garage a couple blocks away where all movie employees were asked to park their vehicles during filming each day. Sims climbed into the front seat of Henderson's white, two-door sports car, while her friend got in the back.

When they reached the garage, Henderson directed Sims's friend to go up and retrieve the girls' vehicle from the third level because he wanted to talk privately with Sims. As soon as she was out of sight, Henderson leaned over and kissed Sims. "Take out my dick," he then instructed her. Stunned and embarrassed, Sims refused. Henderson then undid his pants, exposed himself, and said, "Kiss it."

"No," Sims repeated as she quickly opened the door and jumped out of the car. Before she could reach the door to the parking garage stairwell, Henderson caught up to her. "What's wrong," he demanded, his penis still exposed.

"I'm not like that," said Sims.

"Yeah, sure," Henderson said mockingly, as he cornered her in the stairwell. Unable to escape, Sims felt Henderson force his hands underneath her underwear. "Just let me touch it," he said.

"No," she pleaded, pushing in vain against his thick chest.

Henderson's attack came to an abrupt halt when he heard

Sims's friend drive up in front of the stairwell. Sims told the sex crimes detectives that Henderson's fingers were inside her vagina for approximately ten seconds, during which time his penis remained exposed. She also told them that she noticed a video surveillance camera was mounted in the top corner of the stairwell.

After taking Sims's statement, Sergeant Billington contacted the production office for Castle Rock Films. The movie company had no address or home telephone number on file for Henderson, only a pager number. Billington later dialed 1-800-324-3333 and entered Henderson's PIN No. 94740. When Henderson returned the page, Billington identified himself and said that he was investigating allegations of sexual impropriety made against Henderson by a woman. With Billington unwilling to give more detail over the telephone, on November 30, Henderson went to the Minneapolis Police Department to learn who was accusing him. He did not bring an attorney.

The following excerpts are taken from Sergeant Billington's summary of his interview with Keith Henderson:

"I asked Henderson to tell us why he wouldn't do anything like this [commit a sexual assault], and he said because he has a lot of women.

"I asked Henderson if he ever had any sexual contact . . . whatsoever with Sims and he said no.

"I then explained to Henderson that I wasn't sure if he was aware of this, but there was a camera in the hallway of the parking ramp where he was with Sims. I told him that we had a copy of that tape, and that it was being enhanced at the FBI offices in Washington, D.C., and that the tape would be coming back very soon. . . . I then asked Henderson if there would be any reason why he would be on that tape in the hallway.

"Henderson said it could be him.

"I told Henderson I looked at the tape, and I said that the big guy in the tape sure looked like him, and that it almost looked as though his penis was out.

"Henderson said that his penis was out, but said that his hand was not inside her pants, but just near her belly button."

Billington, a seasoned investigator who had handled approximately 400 rape cases during his career, then appealed to Henderson's NFL-size ego. He talked about the way women pursue professional athletes for sexual purposes, and how it must get difficult to weed out the ones looking for sex and the ones who were just being friendly. Billington then asked Henderson if mixed signals may have been behind the incident with Sims.

"Something like that," said Henderson.

"I then asked Henderson how long he had his hands in Sims's pants, and he admitted to having his fingers in her vagina for about 10 seconds. I asked Henderson how many times Sims told him no, and he said twice."

Unaware that he had just admitted to committing a felony sexual assault, Henderson then agreed to give a more formal statement while the police ran a tape recorder. The following portion of the transcript picks up at the point in the interview where Sergeant Billington is asking Henderson what took place after he and Sims exited the car:

Q: What happened then?
A: Well, I opened the door [to the parking garage stairwell], she walked in, and I walked in behind her. I think I

reached over to kiss her, and by then I think I may have took my penis out and she wanted to touch it, or whatever.

Q: So you took your penis out of your pants?

A: Yes.

Q: What happened then?

A: Um, I reached over to touch her, around her stomach and I don't know if she pushed me or what . . . I was just basically trying to get her close to me.

Q: But she did push you away, didn't she?

A: Yes.

Q: What was she saying to you when she was pushing you away?

A: Well, she was sayin' no, and laughin' at the same time, so I didn't really, I guess mixed emotions.

Q: So are you saying that she said no to you, but you didn't think she meant no?

A: Yes.

Q: Did you put your hand down her pants?

A: Yes.

Q: Did you stick your fingers into her vagina?

A: Well, the edge of it.

Q: Before, you told me that you put your fingers in her vagina for about 10 seconds, is that about right?

A: Yes.

Q: What happened then?

A: Well, then she said no again, then I realized she meant no, so I stopped. . . . When she said it the second time, like, she wasn't really smilin' like she was the first time, so I stopped.

On February 9, 1994, the Hennepin County prosecuting attorney swore out a warrant for the arrest of Keith Pernell

Henderson for committing criminal sexual conduct in the third degree against a juvenile, a felony carrying a fifteen-year prison sentence. On May 10, 1994, a second criminal complaint was filed by the Hennepin County prosecuting attorney, this one charging Henderson for criminal sexual conduct in the first degree for the assault on Sally Michaels. This crime carried a potential thirty-year prison term.

One week later, before Henderson was in custody, on May 19 Bloomington police received a 911 emergency call reporting a rape. Officer Michael Taylor was dispatched to a Mobil gas station located at 7920 France Avenue, where the call had been placed from a cellular phone. When Officer Taylor arrived, he found Dawn Brown* and her brother, who had placed the 911 call. The brother informed Officer Taylor that his sister had called him from a pay phone at the Mobil station minutes earlier, saying she needed help. He told Officer Taylor that when he reached the Mobil station he found his sister in a state of hysteria, and she told him that she had just been raped.

Shortly after Officer Taylor arrived at the scene, Brown was taken to nearby Fairview Southdale Hospital where a sexual assault exam was performed. Brown later told Bloomington police that her attacker's name was Keith Henderson. She described him as a former Vikings football player. And she said that she often ran into him at the Cattle Company, a popular bar located across the parking lot from the Mobil station where he and other Vikings players were regulars.

According to police reports, Henderson got into a verbal altercation with a man who was dancing with Brown. When Brown left the bar to call her brother for a ride home, Henderson followed her outside. Angry and demanding to know where she was going, Henderson abruptly grabbed Brown and dragged her into the parking lot behind the bar. He then spun her around so that she was facing the back of the building, removed her pants, and raped her from behind. Brown told authorities that "she had to hold onto the brick wall with her hands to prevent her head from being smashed against the wall."

"Please stop," Brown cried, according to her police statement.

Saying nothing, Henderson continued the assault until he ejaculated inside her. "I'll call you tomorrow," he then told Brown, echoing what he said to Sally Michaels after raping her from behind.

The report almost sounded too brazen to be true. However, the Bloomington police quickly discovered the two outstanding arrest warrants issued against Henderson in the other rape cases. And on May 26, the Hennepin County prosecutor added a third charge against Henderson, this one for criminal sexual conduct in the third degree. Later that day, the Hennepin County Sheriff's Department finally arrested and booked Henderson. On the booking sheet, Henderson's occupation was listed as "football player." Under employer, it read "unemployed." His bond was set at $235,000.

On February 6, 1995, Henderson entered pleas of guilty in all three cases. As part of the agreement, the state agreed to reduce each charge to a fourth-degree criminal sexual conduct. Henderson was sentenced on April 10, 1995, to six months in jail, placed on probation for ten years, ordered to attend sex offender treatment, and required to register as a convicted sex offender in the state of Minnesota. All three victims were present in court at the sentencing hearing.

*   *   *

So how did Keith Henderson descend to the point where women were seen purely as sexual prey? Henderson's own criminal defense attorney offered his view in an interview with the authors. "My take on Keith," said Robert Miller, who has defended a number of accused sex offenders, "is that he started out as a superstar in high school, then he went to college as an All-American. He was somewhat of a hero all the way through. As a result, you lose perspective in the normal social setting with women because they come up to you all the time. They seek these athletes out. After a while, the players change and act differently toward women. I think it's difficult in Keith's position to react with women as the average man would."

"Professional athletes are people who have done a lot to deny their true feelings because to be a pro athlete you have to deny physical pain, emotional pain, and overcome adversity," explained quarterback McPherson. "There are a lot of things that you are in denial over. When it comes to women and sex, some players may be at a point where they say, 'Well, she probably doesn't want to, but I'm so good she's going to love this.' Because that is what you tell yourself. You lie to yourself about how good you are in what you do on the field. You have to. Because the minute you doubt yourself, you're done as a player. You have to pump yourself up so that you can't be beat, and then you go in with confidence. When you talk about sex as casual sex, as a recreation or as conquest, why would your attitude be any different when you approach it in that way? It is very congruent with how players live in so many other ways."

The authors found no record of Henderson ever being convicted of a sex crime as a player. Yet, in examining the police files in the Henderson cases in Minnesota, the authors discovered an inconspicuous, one-page affidavit dated May 6, 1994. It was sworn out to the Bloomington police by a woman whose name was expunged from the record. In her affidavit, the woman stated that in December 1992 she had been "forced by Henderson to perform oral sex and then he forced intercourse on her." The woman, a Minnesota native, was living out of state when she learned of the pending criminal allegations against Henderson. She agreed to fly to Minnesota and tell her experience to the police in hopes of assisting in the prosecution. In order to protect her privacy, the police removed her name from the affidavit.

Marilyn Scofield* agreed to be interviewed for this book on condition that her identity be protected.

An airline stewardess who was engaged to be married at the time of the interview, Scofield said she talked to the authors despite her concern that she might be stereotyped because she worked at Hooters when the alleged rape occurred. It was during her brief four-month employment at Hooters that she met Keith Henderson. "I met a lot of the players due to my job," said Scofield. "Hooters had an arrangement with the Vikings. We went to a lot of the football games for promotional purposes. And the players used to come into Hooters all the time. Keith, in particular, came in a lot."

One evening when Scofield was not scheduled to work, she went with her friend, another Hooters waitress, to visit a Vikings player at his apartment. It was the first time Scofield had ever accompanied her friend to the player's apartment. She was unaware that other Vikings players lived in the complex, including Keith Henderson, whose apartment was just across the hall. While Scofield's girlfriend and the Vikings player who they were visiting went to sit in the apartment complex's hot tub, Scofield stayed behind in the player's apartment and took a nap. To her surprise, almost immediately after dozing off, Henderson forced his way into the apartment.

"I think he saw my girlfriend and the guy who she was with leaving the apartment to go down to the hot tub," said Scofield. "I don't know if he saw me go in or what. He must have. I don't know how else he would have known I was in there."

Caught off guard, Scofield nonetheless recognized Henderson right away, having waited on him numerous times. Before she could sit up, he immediately started talking about sex. "He used a lot of foul language, and I told him that I didn't want to have sex with him," Scofield recalled. She then retreated to the bathroom. What Scofield described next had an eerie resemblance to what Sally Michaels experienced in Henderson's bathroom.

"He assaulted me in the bathroom and was ripping off my clothes and then pushed me into the bedroom," said Scofield. "He was on top of me, forcing himself on me. I totally fought him the whole way. I was kicking and screaming. I kept telling him, 'No. You're not going to have sex with me. Stop.' "

As Henderson was about to penetrate Scofield, her friend and the player who she was with returned from the hot tub. When Henderson heard their voices, he quickly jumped off Scofield and buttoned up his pants. When his teammate and Scofield's girlfriend entered the room, Henderson looked down at Scofield, who was still on the bed, and said, "Thanks baby. I hope it was as good for you as it was for me."

"He tried to make it look like we had just had consensual sex," said Scofield.

The next day, Scofield encountered an unexpected reprimand when she reported to work. "My manager came up to me the day after I was assaulted by Keith Henderson and told me, 'If you don't give the players what they want, you're going to be fired,'" said Scofield. "Keith had gone to my manager at Hooters and complained that I was rude to him. Keith was totally livid and he really came down hard on my boss."

As a result of the treatment received from her boss, Scofield quit her job and hired an attorney who specialized in sexual harassment. "Hooters was making my job miserable because Keith Henderson complained about me," said Scofield. "Hooters is a restaurant. Admittedly, in a place like that you expect a little harassment from the customers. I could handle that. But you don't expect harassment from your employer."

Scofield's lawyer confirmed that she received an undisclosed amount of money in an out-of-court settlement with the company.

After leaving Hooters, Scofield ran into Henderson at the Cattle Company, the same club where he would later sexually assault Dawn Brown. "I saw him at the club, but I didn't say anything to him," said Scofield. "He was mad just because I was there. He was still furious from the night that I wouldn't consent to have sex with him."

When Scofield left with a male acquaintance, Henderson followed her out into the Cattle Company parking lot. As Scofield was climbing into the passenger's side of her friend's Bronco, Henderson brandished a knife and slashed her across the arm. Although the blade did not pierce her skin, it slashed a large hole in her thick leather jacket. "He threatened to kill me," recalled Scofield. "He lifted me up and was shaking me against the Bronco. He was calling me all these names like 'white bitch.' He was screaming at me.

He really wanted to hurt me. Luckily, it was a busy place and people started coming toward the vehicle when they heard him yelling. I just don't think he wanted to literally punch me out in front of all those people."

As soon as Henderson let go of her, Scofield scurried into the Bronco and the driver sped off. "I didn't realize until after we had left that Keith had cut my coat with his knife."

Scofield reported neither the sexual attack nor the knife attack to the authorities. One primary reason was that she did not want her family to find out, particularly her parents, who lived in Minneapolis. "I was actually going to press charges," said Scofield. "But I didn't want to go through with it. At the time I just wanted to leave Minnesota and get away. There was a lot of bad memories."

However, when Scofield was notified by her civil attorney from the Hooters case that Henderson was wanted for raping a teenager, she felt compelled to fly to Minneapolis and cooperate with authorities. "I did go back to Minnesota and make a police statement in the case of the teenage girl who was assaulted," Scofield confirmed to the authors. Less than a week after reporting her experience to investigators, Henderson was apprehended.

"A lot of the players were always out to get laid," said Scofield. "But Keith was just more forceful than most. He wouldn't take no for an answer. He just thought that because he was a professional football player, that every girl that he wanted to have sex with, should have sex with him."

"Rape is the toughest crime for victims, without question," said Sergeant Billington, who has since left the sex crimes unit and now oversees the training of police cadets for the Minneapolis Police Department. "In a homicide, the victim is dead. In a rape, the victim has to go over and over and over this stuff. And some of them never come out." This is hardly the concern of coaches and general managers when a player is arrested for rape.

Players, as long as they are cutting it on the field, are permitted to slouch through their careers, their deviant lifestyles excused by the old cliché that NFL players live life in the fast lane. Then they retire and crash full speed into the laws and restraints that govern the rest of society.

For Lewis Billups, the term "fast lane," however, had a more literal meaning. On April 9, 1994, eighteen months after retiring and six days after being released from federal prison, Lewis Billups was killed in a horrific car accident. Racing down Florida's Interstate 4 at speeds in excess of 100 miles per hour, Billups lost control of his 1987 Corvette convertible, destroying over fifty feet of metal guardrail and slamming into a concrete barrier. The passenger in Billups's car was killed on impact. Billups's body was discovered by highway patrolmen on the roadside at approximately 1:00 A.M. after being thrown from the vehicle. He was pronounced dead at Orlando Regional Medical Center hours later.

In the eighteen-month period following his retirement and leading up to his death, Billups was reported to authorities thirteen times for assaulting women, convicted once for raping a woman in Florida, and imprisoned by federal authorities in Georgia for stalking another woman.

For the numerous women who were the victims of his violence, Billups's violent death was viewed as a blessing. Unlike Keith Henderson, who was shamelessly crass, Billups was a stealthy predator who coupled physical violence and threats with his sexual attacks. Known during his playing days as a gritty cornerback who harassed wide receivers, Billups was notorious among his teammates for using intimidation to get what he wanted from women—sex. "He felt a certain dominance [over women]," ex-Bengals wide receiver Tim McGee told the authors. "He felt he had power over them. He had them in control. I think that had a lot to do with confidence. It was probably an ego thing. He felt he could control them, sexually and physically."

McGee and Billups were both drafted by the Bengals in 1986. While going on to establish himself as one of the Bengals' all-time leading receivers, McGee also became one of Billups's closest friends. He was one of only two Bengals players who made arrangements to attend Billups's funeral.

"The thing about it was that Lewis was the sweetest person in the world to my wife," McGee said, recalling Billups's chameleon-like treatment of women. "He was the sweetest person in the world to other players' wives too. But he was an asshole to the women he dated. When he got girls behind doors, for some reason he either hit 'em or he wanted his way sexually. He was a spoiled brat."

Indeed. While playing for the Bengals, Billups was arrested numerous times for abusing women and was sued in federal court for raping a woman. Never convicted, however, his career went uninterrupted despite his off-the-field violence. Tracy Fair, a Cincinnati woman who was Billups's girlfriend through part of his career in Cincinnati, agreed to discuss her abuse with ESPN only because Billups was killed. "I was inches away from dying," Fair said in a 1994 interview. "He beat me for three and a half hours and probably three of it was to my head. I had six plastic surgeries, six on my nose and one on my ear, just that I suffered from blows to my face. Then he cut my hair off."

Fair filed police complaints on more than one occasion,

but never pressed charges. "I knew if I went through with it, he would kill me," she told ESPN. "He also told me that he would pay somebody to finish my face off. People don't understand the fear that battered women live in and they think, 'Well, she dropped the charges. She's a liar. It didn't happen. He's a big football player and she's slandering his name.' I was a nobody out of Cincinnati coming after this big professional football player."

McGee was familiar with the attacks suffered by Fair. "He really messed up Tracy's mind," McGee confirmed to the authors. "She's a sweet girl, but he really messed with her mind." And Fair was not the only girl familiar to McGee as a victim of Billups's violence. Jenny Chapman, the sister of NBA star Rex Chapman, endured repeated abuse at Billups's hands. With Billups's career winding down in 1991, Jenny Chapman finally pressed charges after Billups threatened to end Rex's NBA career by breaking his legs in retaliation for Jenny breaking off her relationship with him.

"He hit me close-fisted," Chapman told ESPN. She too was only willing to discuss publicly the situation on account of Billups's death. "He slapped me. He choked me . . . to the point where I'd just pass out and wake up the next morning and have to deal with it all over again."

According to McGee, Billups's physical violence toward women was connected to his warped sense of sexual prowess. He used physical violence to gain sexual control. "That's what he wanted to do with Jenny," McGee said. "He wanted to control her mind, her body, everything."

The FBI wiretapped Jenny's phone and began monitoring Billups's phone calls to her while he was in his last year in the NFL. The following is a partial transcript from an FBI-recorded call between Billups and Chapman:

J.C.: You gonna have somebody else do your dirty work or you gonna do it yourself?

L.B.: I don't ever get my hands dirty, Jenny.

J.C.: Yeah, I know, because, see, a real man would.

L.B.: No. A real man who got power wouldn't.

J.C.: How can you sit here and think that I would want to be with you when you threaten people that I love? How can you think that I would even want to even be associated with someone like you?

L.B.: Because I'm a hard mother [expletive] and I'm gonna prove it to you. I promise you that on my mother's life.

"I think it was his transition coming into football, coming into money so quickly," Chapman said, trying to explain Billups's violent tendencies toward her. "Never having that great amount [of money] just to do whatever you wanted to do and then all of a sudden it brings you power and it brings you all this fame just to do whatever you want whenever you want. He was used to getting what he wanted. If I was not going to give that to him, then he would become violent."

McGee, who was sympathetic toward Chapman, agreed. "Being an athlete, you get notoriety, wealth, and power," McGee explained to the authors. "Lewis was a person who used his. He used his to the fullest. I mean he had wealth. He drove a Lamborghini. He drove a Corvette. He had this very plush, gorgeous home in Orlando. But that wasn't enough for him. He had to use his power of controlling to get somebody. 'Hey, I'm Lewis Billups and you know I have all this stuff.' And then once he got 'em over to his house, he wanted to control them."

*   *   *

So what does a guy like Billups, who used his fame to get access to and exploit women, do when all of that dries up? As confirmed by a stack of police reports and court records, the authors found that after retirement Billups preyed on women in clubs and bars, portraying himself as an active NFL player and seducing them into social encounters that ended in brutal sexual attacks.

After the Bengals released Billups following the 1991 season, he was signed by the Packers. However, one month into the 1992 season, Green Bay replaced Billups in the lineup with rookie first-round draft choice Terrell Buckley. After being let go by Green Bay, Billups was left without a source of income. The timing could not have been worse. Billups had to hire a criminal lawyer to defend him in the midst of the ongoing federal probe being conducted in the Jenny Chapman case. Billups also had to hire a civil defense lawyer to represent him in Seattle where he had been sued for rape. Meanwhile, creditors were hounding him for debts that were run up while he was living the high life of an active player. The following is a letter Billups wrote to American Express weeks after the Packers let him go:

"I, Lewis Billups, cannot pay American Express Centurion Bank. The reason is, that on or about the day of October 7, 1992, I was fired from the Green Bay Packers. I am now in the process of trying to get on with another team. I have no other means of employment or cash flow. At this point in time, I have no money in the bank. I am trying to sell my house and car to get some cash, but until that happens, I have no money. Thank you and please understand."

Shortly after writing this letter, on November 30, 1992, Billups convinced Wendy Williams,* whom he met at an upscale Orlando club, that he was still playing in the NFL. Unlike some women who go to clubs in search of gaining a sexual relationship with famous athletes, Williams knew little about football. She was, however, undergoing some marital problems at the time she met Billups and his friend.

Playing the part of the rich, famous athlete, Billups eventually convinced Williams to come join him at his $800,000 Orlando mansion for lunch. "It was something interesting," Seminole County prosecuting attorney Stewart Stone, who would later prosecute both Billups and his friend, explained to the authors in an interview. "She was intrigued and excited about the opportunity to go with two young, wealthy men, one of whom was a professional football player. She got in over her head."

Shortly after Williams arrived at Billups's home, he slipped a depressant into her beverage. Once it took effect, he raped her while his friend secretly videotaped the attack. Williams, unaware that her assault was filmed, chose not to report the incident to police. She feared that Billups's celebrity would guarantee a media circus. But days later, Billups and his friend showed up at her house in broad daylight and presented her with a videocassette depicting the entire ordeal. Billups then threatened to deliver a copy to her husband's office unless Williams came up with $20,000.

Billups and his friend repeated their threat numerous times during that week. Finally, Williams telephoned the police moments after the two men showed up in her driveway a second time. Moments later, police apprehended Billups and his friend and seized a videotape from the back seat of their car. "The tape depicted sexual contact," confirmed prosecuting attorney Stewart Stone to the authors. "It appeared that she was under the influence, but not obviously. There was no sign of overt force, but it was not necessary to prove overt force because Billups was charged as raping someone who was mentally impaired." Billups's plan was to drug Williams so that she appeared to be consenting, thus making the video all the more valuable for extorting money.

The following day, Billups's arrest on rape charges was reported in the *Orlando Sentinel*. As a result, six more Orlando area women came forward and reported being similarly seduced, raped, and videotaped. "There was no question in my mind that Billups was guilty," said Stone. "Billups and [his friend] definitely had a thing going."

As investigators soon discovered, there was more, much more:

• Just weeks earlier, on December 3, 1992, Billups had been arrested for drunk driving. Police had been called to respond to a dispute outside an Orlando area bar, where Billups was berating Patty Abdelmessih and spitting on her. Abdelmessih had provoked Billups's wrath when she tried to prevent him from forcing another woman into his car. Abdelmessih discovered the woman in the women's bathroom, moaning and sweating profusely after Billups had been buying her drinks all evening. Referring to the sick woman, Billups's male companion said, 'We didn't mean to dose her.' Police arrested Billups after he refused to respond to their questions and attempted to drive away.

• In November of 1992, a woman had contacted police and alleged Billups had assaulted her during a tour of his mansion. In her complaint, the woman reported being stripped, raped, robbed of the $50 in her purse, and kicked out of the house. Her clothes were thrown out after her. No arrest had been made because she declined to press charges.

• In July of 1992, an Orlando woman had obtained a restraining order against Billups after reporting that he had been hostile and abusive toward her and had threatened to physically harm her.

• In a neighboring county, sheriff's officials confirmed that Billups had been involved in at least three additional incidents at several nightclubs, all of which required police intervention.

Before Seminole County authorities wrapped up their investigation into Billups, he was convicted and sentenced to a year in federal prison in Georgia for the threatening phone calls made to Jenny Chapman. While incarcerated, Billups agreed to plead guilty to the charges filed in Orlando in connection with the Williams case. Although Billups was imprisoned, the prosecutors in Florida were disadvantaged due to Williams's decision not to testify against him if the case went to trial. "It was extremely difficult," said prosecutor Stewart Stone. "Williams feared Billups."

It all became academic, however, when Billups died in the car accident less than one week after walking out of federal prison.

"Even though he's dead, I'm still scared of him," Chapman said in her interview with ESPN. "I think about the prospect of him being alive and it's too much. I'm scared of the memories. I'm scared of what could have happened if he were alive. I don't think I could have had peace in my mind had it ended any other way."

14

The Gambler

"I wish," Art Schlichter said, raising his voice over the shouting in the background and the static on the phone, "that I could have just been addicted to drugs or alcohol. Because if drugs were my problem, who knows . . ." At that moment, a prerecorded message drowned out the end of Schlichter's sentence. The message informed the listener that "this call is from an inmate at an Indiana correctional facility."

Such is Art Schlichter's luck. He was ready to boast that given the state of quarterbacking in the NFL today, he might still be drawing a paycheck from the league. But before he could finish, he was once again reminded that he's in a place where arm strength doesn't matter, where his story means almost nothing.

But what a story it is. Once one of the most promising college quarterbacks in America—a player so complete that the Baltimore Colts traded away starter Bert Jones to draft him with the fourth pick of the first round in 1982—Schlichter today sits in the same Pendleton, Indiana, lockup that once housed Mike Tyson.

Schlichter is guilty of the only sin that the NFL has decided it can't tolerate—gambling.

"You have to admit it is hard to believe that people who have killed, people who have raped, and people who have sold drugs are still in the league," said one longtime agent who once played against Schlichter, "but a guy who gambles, no, there's no place for that in the NFL. I don't condone gambling, but it isn't the worst sin being committed out there."

The NFL's stance has always been that gambling eats away at "the integrity of the game." But, Schlichter wondered aloud one evening, "does that mean beating your wife, raping a woman, or beating people senseless has nothing to do with integrity? How can the league, in a way, say one problem like gambling is worse than those others?"

Yet if the NFL was looking for a poster boy for the evils of gambling, Art Schlichter provided the perfect picture. If any one man had it all, it was Art Schlichter. High school All-America. Most prized recruit of the legendary Woody Hayes. Four-year starter at one of the nation's most famous football-playing schools, Ohio State. Two-time Big Ten Most Valuable Player. Highest finish ever by a sophomore in the Heisman balloting. Drafted into the NFL ahead of Marcus Allen and Jim McMahon. Heir apparent to the mantle worn by Earl Morall and Johnny Unitas. Considered the next great quarterback in a league that adores its quarterbacks.

He could run and throw. He was polite and articulate. He was good-looking and single. He had never touched a drop of alcohol, never tried drugs. He hadn't even lit a cigarette.

But there was one factor NFL prognosticators like the Cowboys' Tex Schramm didn't consider when rating

Schlichter a "can't miss" prospect—an addiction that would one day cost him everything.

It began when he was in junior high school with a nickel bet on a card game with his grandfather. As a college freshman, the thrill climbed to another level when a buddy took him to the race track with information about a "fixed" race—one he would bet on and win. "That was an incredible walk on the wild side," he said in an interview from prison. "It gave me my first real thrill of doing something wild." Schlichter and his buddy, though, were so sure they would get caught by police that they didn't cash the ticket from the fixed race.

Schlichter's love for gambling seemed more legitimate when, as a junior at Ohio State, one of his coaches started meeting him at a local horse track where they discussed not football, but a little "action."

For a man who loved competition, nothing short of a long post route to a wide receiver could present him with the rush of gambling. He felt an incredible thrill when he watched his coach/betting partner "wheel a horse," betting $72 and winning $3,000. "I figured if it was all right for him, it was all right for me," he said. "And that was exciting seeing all that money."

From then on, Schlichter didn't just bet, he made outrageous, exotic bets that he believed would provide him outrageous payoffs. Those bets, though, always came with outrageous odds. Art Schlichter refused to accept the dictum: when something seems too good to be true, it often is.

"As an athlete, I had never lost, no matter what sport," he said. "Gambling was the first thing that ever kicked my butt. I refused to believe I couldn't win." Art Schlichter could beat a defensive back. He couldn't beat the odds at the track.

Schlichter's appearances at the track became more regular. And as the popular and effervescent quarterback of the Buckeyes, he had no shortage of friends there. "Everyone was always giving me tips. If there was inside information, they wanted me to have it. People were trying to help me win, and I was still losing. I had saved money since I was five years old winning 4-H contests, and now I was losing it all.

"During the winter of my junior year at Ohio State I tore my ankle up pretty bad playing basketball, so I started spending a lot more time at home while I was in rehab. I was betting with some bookies, betting sports. I lost, in just a few weeks, about $5,000 to $6,000. That was a lot of money. The bookie called my dad. He told him, 'Your son better pay his gambling debts off.' My dad approached me about it and I said, 'Dad, I'm in trouble, I need some money. I've got to pay this guy.' I didn't even know the bookie because I was betting through someone else. My dad came up, he had the cash in his hand, got down in front of me, and just shook me. He went nuts. He said, 'You are screwing your whole life up. You are ruining everything you hope to have with this gambling. If you don't stop now, you're going to ruin it all and end up in jail someday.' My mother had had a mastectomy for breast cancer. He handed me the cash and said, 'This is your mom's insurance money. You are taking a piece of your mom and giving it to some guy because of betting.' I cried my eyes out. I have no idea why that didn't stop me. I went right out and started doing it again. I wanted to go out and win the money back so I could pay my father back.

"I guess maybe gambling was my way of trying to kill pain. I was in a lot of pain, physically and emotionally. The pressure was real great being the All-American quarterback. I wasn't real comfortable with who I was. Every time I gambled, I was away from that pressure. I never could really be myself. I always had to be on my best behavior as the big quarterback. I did everything I was supposed to do. Gambling was like my little dirty deed. My little way of rebellion against having to be that way all the time. When you're a quarterback at a major university, the pressure is tremendous. Not only to win, but win convincingly. I was supposed to be Ohio State's second two-time Heisman Trophy winner. That didn't work out my junior year. So the pressure of that mounted because people started asking why. It made me feel like a failure. The more I felt sorry for myself, the worse my gambling got. Looking back, I had everything anyone could ask for. I had no right to feel sorry for myself."

By the time he arrived in the NFL, Schlichter was hooked. If it moved, Art would bet on it. He always drew the line on betting on his own league. While playing college football, that sport was off limits. When he played for the Buckeyes basketball team, he wouldn't bet college basketball. He brought that standard with him to the NFL. "It was my form of denial," he said. "I knew I wasn't addicted if I wasn't betting on my league."

But during his rookie season with the Colts, the absolute worst thing that could have happened to Schlichter did—NFL players went on strike. He was young, suddenly wealthy, addicted to gambling, *and sitting idle.*

He filled his afternoons and evenings by going to the track. He started betting heavily with bookies. In the seven weeks of the strike, he lost every penny of his $350,000 signing bonus and his entire $140,000 salary. He started borrowing from banks, friends, boosters. He started selling his memorabilia—jerseys, game balls, even the Big Ten MVP trophy. Like the addict he was, he always believed that the next bet would cover all his losses. "I was always chasing the money that I lost," he said. "Chasing it and losing more."

Through it all, Schlichter was living a dual life. He told bankers and friends that he was borrowing the money for "investments" in land. While everyone knew he liked to bet, no one—not even his family—had any clue about the depths of his problems. That made the shock of what happened over the next year all the greater.

As the losses mounted, the bets to cover those losses had to become more outrageous. He started betting parlays—three team parlays, four-team parlays, you name it. The odds were like playing the lottery. He crossed his own line and started betting NFL games, laying down money on as many as ten games. "I was in so deep I was willing to bet anything," Art said. "But I still thought I was okay because I wouldn't bet on Colts games. That became my new standard.

"Here I was, in team meetings, in quarterback meetings, and my mind was on what I bet and lost the night before and how I was going to borrow money to gamble again. If you look at my notes from those meetings, they were terrible. My mind wasn't there. And as I lost concentration, I lost the ability to keep up with the team. As I lost that ability, I lost confidence. I was caught in a downward spiral from before the time I was drafted. I had the skills. I had the arm. Howie Long, when he was with the Raiders, said I was the best scrambling quarterback he'd ever seen. But I had no confidence. I was thinking of myself as a loser.

"The guys on the Colts used to think I was the greatest womanizer of all time because I was always on the phone.

One time, Mike Pagel, the backup, took all my stuff out of my locker and put it in a locker next to the telephone as a joke. But I wasn't calling women. I was calling bookies."

During one week in February 1983, Schlichter went wild trying to win "his" money back. On seven consecutive nights, he bet three-team parlays on NBA games. Each night he wagered between $65,000 and $75,000. Each night, he lost nearly every bet. In one week, Art Schlichter went into debt more than $350,000 to bookies. Over his two years in the NFL, he lost more than $700,000.

His betting out of control and with bookies threatening his life, Schlichter finally told a friend about his predicament. The friend advised him to go to the FBI. He did, and with the help of agents in Columbus, Ohio, Schlichter worked a sting on the bookies. As Schlichter sat and listened from a parking lot across the street from the Columbus airport, agents wearing microphones moved in on the bookies.

A day later, a lawyer for the bookies called the press and the storybook career of Art Schlichter was in tatters. He agreed to go to counseling for his addiction and, while Art was still in treatment, NFL Commissioner Pete Rozelle announced that the league was banning Schlichter from the game—but he could apply for reinstatement in one year. Rozelle's timing might have been good for league public relations, but it was the worst thing that could have happened to Schlichter's prospects for rehabilitation.

In his announcement, Rozelle referred to Schlichter as a "bad apple." In a subsequent interview with Howard Cosell, the commissioner told the nation that Schlichter was, in his opinion, the only NFL player involved in gambling and that a harsh penalty was being levied to dissuade others from starting. "The players know that it strikes at the integrity of the game, and I don't think there's gambling in the National Football League," Rozelle said boldly.

"That was so untrue," Schlichter said. "Gambling among players is the NFL's dirty little secret. Players gamble, and the NFL knows it. More than half of the players I played with on the Colts were gambling. After I moved to Las Vegas, I watched many NFL players come in and lose thousands in casinos. I flew back to Indianapolis a couple of years back with a leading player from the Colts, who had spent part of his off-week in Vegas gambling. The NFL has to know about this."

The Cleveland *Plain Dealer*, in an investigative story released just two weeks after Schlichter's gambling became public, confirmed Art's claims. The paper reported that the gambling habits of no fewer than a dozen other NFL players had been discovered by NFL security during its Schlichter investigation. Though follow-up stories confirmed the *Plain Dealer*'s accusation, no other NFL player was identified or suspended as a result. To this day, Schlichter is the last player suspended from the league for gambling.

Additionally, Schlichter's point about the involvement of NFL owners in the business of gambling played itself out on a grand scale in late 1997. It was then that one of the league's most high-profile owners, Edward DeBartolo, Jr., handed over control of the five-time Super Bowl champion San Francisco 49ers while under federal investigation for fraud in a Louisiana riverboat gambling project. The federal investigation stemmed from DeBartolo's successful attempt to secure a license for a riverboat casino in Bossier City, Louisiana, site of one of three thoroughbred racetracks the DeBartolo family already owns.

Yet if it had not been for the alleged criminal activity, De-

Bartolo's pursuit of a license to operate a casino would have drawn no sanction from the NFL, which must have known about his gambling-related business ventures. The league has no policy, as major league baseball does, prohibiting its owners from involvement in gambling entities.

Former Commissioner Rozelle summed up the league's apathy toward the subject in a 1983 interview about the gambling troubles of former Philadelphia Eagles owner Leonard Tose, who reportedly lost millions at the tables in Vegas and Atlantic City. Said Rozelle: "I would be a hell of a lot more concerned if I knew that [a player] had bet at the casinos. An owner doesn't control the outcome of a game. . . . Anyone close to football knows that an owner doesn't interfere with the coaches or players. He's not going to send in plays, except in infrequent situations."

After sitting out one year, Schlichter came back to the Colts in 1984 and started at quarterback for the team's last five games. He was living on a $2,000-per-month budget, using the rest of his salary to pay off gambling debts. It looked like he might be over the hump when, after being named the Colts' first-string quarterback at the start of the 1985 season, the NFL discovered that he had left game tickets for a friend who was a well-known gambler. The Colts cut Schlichter early in the 1995 season. No other teams called.

The next year Schlichter gave the NFL one more run but was cut by the Buffalo Bills, who replaced him on their roster with Jim Kelly. His last NFL pass, appropriately, was intercepted and returned for a touchdown. In the fall of 1987, he signed a contract with the Cincinnati Bengals but was denied reinstatement to the NFL by Rozelle. His NFL career over and all his money gone, Schlichter filed for bankruptcy in 1988. He played half a season with the Canadian Football League's Ottawa Rough Riders that year, but wasn't even good enough for that league anymore.

Schlichter slumped back into his habit of outlandish betting while playing three years in the Arena Football League. He earned $100,000 a year while leading the Detroit Drive to the league championship in 1990 and was named the league's Most Valuable Player. Yet he was always broke. Then, in 1994, he made possibly his most fatal mistake—he moved to Las Vegas, where he became a popular drive-time sports talk show host and an even greater loser at the gambling tables. To cover those bets, his borrowing had turned to bad check writing. His promises had turned to theft.

He hit rock bottom in the fall of 1994 when his wife took their two children and moved back to Indiana. In one last desperate attempt to dig himself out, Schlichter went to the sports book and bet a three-team parlay. He took $2,000 of the $2,300 he had in his pocket and bet on Michigan to cover the spread, Virginia Tech to beat Boston College, and Louisiana State to beat a heavily favored Auburn team. If all three hit, Schlichter would have won $32,000. As the day progressed, the first two teams won. Schlichter sat in his apartment watching as LSU took a 23-9 lead into the final eleven minutes of its game. A friend called, excited that Schlichter finally was going to win. The friend said he was coming over. But it all unraveled for both LSU and Schlichter. LSU threw five interceptions in the final eleven minutes. Three of them were returned for touchdowns. LSU lost, 30-26.

"When my friend walked in, I was self-destructing," Schlichter said. "I was pounding my face until it started to bleed. I was crying. If ever there was a day I would have committed suicide, that was it. That's when I knew it was over for me. I think about that day every day."

In November 1994, he was charged by federal officials with mail fraud. In the indictment, officials detailed more than $500,000 in bad checks that Schlichter had drafted. He was so good that the list of those Schlichter talked into cashing his bad checks includes nearly every big-name casino in Las Vegas. All the while, Art, his wife, and children were living in a small apartment on the edge of poverty.

Schlichter went on to serve time in federal and state prisons throughout the Midwest. He was released for a short while, but once again stole and cashed a check for cash to gamble. He signed a plea agreement in 1996 and was sentenced to as many as sixteen years in prison. The earliest Art Schlichter could walk out of prison a free man is in the year 2000.

In 1997, working with addiction expert Valerie Lorenz in Baltimore, Schlichter was prescribed the drug Serzone, which helps control compulsive behavior. "Art's mind, before he was put on medication, used to just shoot in all directions," Lorenz said in an interview with the authors. "He couldn't focus. Couldn't concentrate. Couldn't finish with anything. Couldn't carry through with things. And that was the result of his biochemistry. Art's psychiatrist put him on Serzone and he was also in very intensive psychotherapy."

Lorenz said it should come as no surprise that a top-flight athlete like Art Schlichter developed a gambling problem. "Gamblers, first of all, are very competitive," she said. "They're very good with numbers. They do tend to have a very strong athletic history and they're above average in intelligence. Of course Art and many of your pro athletes meet that description."

The NFL hired Lorenz, who is recognized nationally as one of the top five experts on compulsive gambling, to meet with its rookie class during the summer of 1997 and alert them to the addictive nature of gambling. During the session in Chicago, she polled the future pros about their gambling habits. The results? "Higher than anticipated," Lorenz told the authors.

"The initial questions were some psychological factors. Like: Would you describe yourself as a loner? Certainly compulsive gamblers are loners. Then we also took a number of gambling-specific questions. What do you gamble on? What's the largest amount you ever won or lost? How frequently do you gamble? Do you chase your losses? Questions like that. Do you think you have a problem? Has anyone else ever told you you have a problem? And then summed up with, 'If you think you have a problem, where would you turn for help?' Because if we get a sense that they will turn to their coach or their manager or to their team doctor or something, then that's something that can be developed. But then we also asked the question, 'Who would you not turn to?' It was almost unanimous that they would not turn to anyone within the NFL. From our standpoint, that is of incredible importance to the NFL because it certainly tells what the relationship is. These high-priced and highly publicized players—they don't get a sense that if they're in any kind of difficulty with a psychiatric illness that they can get support from their company."

Lorenz shipped the results to the NFL. Ten months later, nothing was being done. "We have never been able to connect with the NFL to follow up as to what the NFL is going to do about it. Certainly there are any number—a surprisingly high percentage—of rookies who are at risk. Not even all the rookies answered, which is kind of suspect."

Lorenz agreed with Schlichter that the NFL's position on gambling is "hypocritical. It's shortsighted. I think it's a rather naive policy. It also makes the assumption that every compulsive gambler is going to throw a game. And of course, that's the fear of the NFL management—that an addicted gambler will throw a game. I think that's more television hype than reality. Does anybody not think that a drug-addicted athlete might do the same thing—throw a game—to pay off his drug dealer? The irony of it is, in supporting athletes who have a drug addiction, they're giving them supervision and random testing or even regular testing and getting them into treatment programs for use of a substance that's basically illegal. Whereas, most of the athletes that we deal with go to a legal gambling establishment—like Art went to horse races. So, to come down harder on athletes because they resort to legal gambling, which is highly touted and often supported by professional sports in one way or another—and then not follow through with giving someone some mental health treatment and education within their own ranks, to me, just doesn't make any economic sense. You can take an athlete, he can be charged with sexual abuse against a woman and you get slapped on the wrist. He may get fined. But somebody like an Art Schlichter, who is treatable, who has never physically injured someone—who has respect for humans—they just totally turn their backs on people like him."

Trim, healthy, and thirty-eight, Art Schlichter might be correct in believing he could be playing in the NFL today—if it weren't for his addiction. "It is incredible that this could happen to someone who had all that I had going for me,"

Schlichter said. "I'm talking with you in prison. *Prison!* It shows you the power of the addiction, the power of gambling. I don't want sympathy. I just want people to understand what this disease—and it is a disease—does to people. It ate me alive. It chewed me up and spit me out. How many guys out there are ready to kill themselves because of gambling? A lot more than you can imagine.

"All the conning that I did, I didn't do all this so I could have fancy cars, big houses, mink coats, or eat at expensive restaurants. I did it to feed an addiction. I could have bought 100 Mercedes with the money I've blown.

"I would never argue that the NFL was wrong for banning me," Schlichter said. "But the NFL needs gambling to survive. Without gambling, how many people really care about St. Louis vs. Seattle? Who, other than gamblers, cares about the NFL injury reports? If the league is so set against gambling, why do they fine teams that don't release those injury reports on time? The league says one thing, but its actions say another.

"And their argument that gambling allows the wrong people to get their hooks into you isn't the end of the story. Athletes with drug habits are just as susceptible. Athletes with gang backgrounds are just as likely to be pulled down by the outside. Gambling, especially to an addict like me, is bad. But I find it hard to believe I was the worst guy in the last twenty years of the NFL, that I deserved a ban when so many others—"

Schlichter was cut off again. The recorded voice began: "This call is from an inmate . . ."

15

Rude Awakenings

When Detroit Lions defensive lineman Reggie Rogers awoke in the emergency room at Pontiac Osteopathic Hospital in the early morning hours of Thursday, October 20, 1988, he was unable to move. Tubes were running in and out of his body. The room seemed out of focus and he did not know how he got there. Doctors informed him that he sustained a fractured neck and multiple injuries in an automobile accident shortly after midnight. Weeks into his second season, Rogers's career seemed finished.

That was the least of his problems. Toxicology tests revealed that Rogers was legally drunk at the time of his accident. All three occupants of the vehicle he collided with were dead. As soon as Rogers was well enough to be discharged from the hospital, the Oakland County district attorney planned to formally charge him with three counts of involuntary manslaughter with a motor vehicle. In Michigan, the offense was punishable by fifteen years in prison.

Before the accident, Rogers was out drinking with teammate Devon Mitchell at Big Art's Paradise Lounge in Pontiac. At 1:30, the two players left together in separate vehicles. At 1:50, three young men in a 1987 Dodge Omni entered the intersection of University Drive and Wide Track Drive. Immediately struck on the passenger side by Rogers's 1988 Jeep Cherokee, the Omni burst into flames. There were no skid marks at the accident scene. Mitchell, who was ten car lengths ahead of Rogers, returned to the intersection after hearing the crash.

The victims, all teenagers, were visiting the Pontiac area to attend the funeral of a relative. Kelly Ess, age eighteen, died at the scene. His brother Dale, age seventeen, died an hour later at Pontiac General Hospital. Their cousin Kenneth Willett, nineteen, was kept on a life-support system for nearly twelve hours before being declared dead the following afternoon. Beer cans were discovered in both vehicles. The Oakland County medical examiner later testified that the two passengers in the Omni had a higher blood alcohol level than Rogers, and the driver was probably legally drunk as well.

An All-America defensive star at the University of Washington, Rogers was the Lions' first-round draft choice in 1987, the seventh overall pick in the draft. At six foot six, 285 pounds, he possessed tremendous speed and quickness. "I'm not saying drafting Reggie Rogers has made us the best team in the NFL, but it helps," said then-Lions defensive coordinator Wayne Fontes on draft day.

While Rogers's defensive skills left pro scouts salivating, his personal life was coming apart at the seams. On June 27, 1986, two months before his senior campaign at Washington began, Reggie's older brother, Don, the starting free safety on the Cleveland Browns, died of a cocaine overdose. The circumstances around Don's death triggered a series of events that left Reggie on a crash course to self-destruction. Staying in a hotel only minutes from where Don overdosed, Reggie spoke to his brother by telephone just hours before emergency room doctors declared him dead. "I'll see you in the morning," was the last thing Reggie said to his brother before hanging up. "The next time I saw him he was dead. I had a major problem with 'What if I would have went home? Maybe I could have stopped him.' "

Rogers, guilty and grieving, turned increasingly to the bottle. Within weeks of Don's passing, alcohol abuse brought Reggie into contact with the law for the first time. He was arrested for driving under the influence in Seattle. Before finishing his senior year, he would be arrested again, this time for assault.

Teams that had pegged Rogers as a first-round pick grew leery of him after his brother's cocaine-induced death. Some clubs invested substantial money and time checking into his background searching for evidence of drug abuse. One club admitted going as far as to hire a private investigator to follow him around Seattle.

Although no evidence of drug abuse was found, Rogers's alcohol-related problems scared teams off. "Let's say it was enough to convince us we shouldn't draft him," Green Bay Packers head of scouting Tom Braatz told a Wisconsin newspaper after extensively researching Rogers.

After Rogers's fatal drunk driving accident, Lions officials downplayed their prior knowledge of Rogers's alcohol abuse. "I've never heard of hiring a private investigator and I don't believe it is true," Lions coach Darryl Rogers told a Detroit reporter in response to the Packers' admission.

Regardless of whether the Lions fully appreciated the depth of Rogers's problems prior to drafting him, the coaching staff was nonetheless made aware of the situation long before the fatal crash. In a clear-as-day plea for help, Rogers went to the coaches before the start of the regular season and confessed to severely abusing alcohol. "I went in," Rogers said, "and told them, 'I'm having a major problem with my brother's death. I'm drinking a hell of a lot. And I'm basically totally out of control. I need some help dealing with my brother's death.' I was letting them know that this was bigger than football."

The Lions' response to his admission convinced Rogers that in the NFL nothing is bigger than football—especially when you are the number one draft choice.

Rogers was admitted to a Detroit-area rehab center where he underwent emotional counseling for thirty days. He was released in time for the Lions' annual Thanksgiving Day game. Despite receiving no treatment for his alcoholism during his thirty-day admittance, the Lions' coaching staff never raised the issue with him again. "They forgot about it," Rogers told the authors. "They didn't want to know."

According to Rogers, the two coaches most familiar with his problems were head coach Darryl Rogers and assistant Wayne Fontes. As the defensive coordinator, Fontes worked directly with the big lineman. Weeks after being present when Rogers confessed to abusing alcohol, Fontes was himself arrested and charged with two counts of drunk driving.

Like a dark omen, Fontes crashed his automobile while driving drunk after leaving a bar on October 21, 1987. Three hundred and sixty four nights later, police in the same county would respond to Rogers's accident scene.

When Oakland County sheriff's deputies discovered Fontes's car in a ditch not far from his Rochester Hills home, the coach was nowhere to be found. He had walked to a nearby convenience store and placed a call from a pay phone to his wife requesting that she come pick him up. As fate would have it, ex-Lion Ken Fantetti—a linebacker who was coached by Fontes—was present when Fontes entered the convenience store. "He didn't look like himself," Fantetti later testified at Fontes's preliminary hearing. "[Fontes made] an off-the-wall comment that who knows what else they might find [in the car]."

Investigators at the crash scene soon discovered Fontes driving his wife's vehicle out of the nearby convenience store parking lot and pulled him over. Telling police he drank two or three vodkas on the rocks at a nearby bar, Fontes failed various roadside sobriety tests and a breath-alcohol analysis test.

In the process of towing Fontes's vehicle from the ditch, police discovered a vial of cocaine on the floor after opening the driver's side door. When confronted about the cocaine, Fontes insisted that his twenty-one-year-old son was the driver. But the 1986 Mercury was registered to the Lions organization and lent to Fontes for his personal use. More importantly, Fontes's wife told authorities at the accident scene that their son was in Florida. After repeatedly asking the police, "Do you know who I am?" Fontes revised his story, saying that someone else was the driver.

The authorities added a cocaine possession charge to the two DUI charges, leaving the leading candidate to succeed Rogers as the Lions' head coach in jeopardy of facing four years in prison if convicted on the felony drug offense.

Fontes's attorneys fought vigorously to have the cocaine charges dismissed. Two weeks after the arrest, a Rochester Hills district judge ruled that the police conducted an illegal search of the car, saying they should have obtained a warrant first. Unable to introduce the cocaine into evidence, prosecutors dropped the felony charge. On December 21

Fontes pleaded guilty to one count of drunk driving and was sentenced to eighteen months' probation. Less than a year later, the Lions promoted him to head coach.

"Certainly, anyone who consumes alcohol is subject to making mistakes," said Lions GM Russ Thomas after the promotion. "But I don't think he's the kind of guy who has problems with that sort of thing. I look at him based on what he's done for us on the field."

Fontes too downplayed the seriousness of his substance-abuse-related arrest. "The organization stood behind me," Fontes told the Detroit press on the day his promotion was announced. "They believed in me. I was innocent of all that BS, so that's behind me."

However, the Lions did not stand behind Rogers, who at the time of Fontes's joyous press conference was lying in serious condition in the hospital recovering from an operation on two broken vertebrae in his neck. During his entire six-month hospital stay, no Lions official visited Rogers. "They turned their back on me," Rogers said. "They wouldn't even return phone calls made by me and my family from the hospital."

At the end of the season, Fontes left Rogers unprotected. Recovering from neck surgery and awaiting trial, Rogers was not picked up. The Lions then let him go altogether, kissing off a first-round draft choice and setting their sights on Barry Sanders, whom they took in the 1989 draft.

Meanwhile, on January 16, 1990, a jury found Rogers guilty on three counts of negligent homicide and he spent the next sixteen months incarcerated in a Michigan state penitentiary. "When I was at the University of Washington, it was like a family there and coaches were like your dad," said Rogers. "That's where I made the mistake in trying to tie that to the NFL. Because they don't give a damn. I had a rude awakening."

The tragic consequences of Rogers's drinking were extraordinary, but his conduct leading up to them was terribly routine among NFL players. According to the authors' research, drunk driving was second only to domestic violence as the crime NFL players were most likely to be arrested for. And the league's most celebrated players are by no means immune to alcohol abuse. Consider one four-month stretch during 1997 which resulted in the arrests of: Redskins All-Pro running back Terry Allen (charged after driving 133 miles per hour while attempting to elude police), the NFL's 1996 Defensive Player of the Year, Bruce Smith (found slumped over the wheel of his car at an intersection at 6:21 in the morning, the motor still running), and the NFL's 1997 Defensive Player of the Year, Dana Stubblefield (observed speeding down the median strip by the California Highway Patrol), were all arrested for driving under the influence.

Alcohol abuse can also have the most unpredictable, even deadly ramifications. In December 1993, their team in the midst of an eight-game winning streak, Houston Oilers players and coaches were stunned by the suicide of starting defensive tackle Jeff Alm. Killed after inserting a shotgun into his mouth and pulling the trigger, Alm's death was largely viewed as an example of the dangers that can accompany gun ownership. "That's the bad thing about having a gun handy sometimes," said then-Oilers defensive coordinator Buddy Ryan. "Because . . . all at once you make a decision that you wouldn't have, probably, if you had thought about it a little longer."

True enough. But alcohol, much more than guns, was the culprit behind Alm's death. On December 14, Alm lost control of his 1993 Cadillac Eldorado while trying to negotiate a curve on an exit ramp off Interstate 610 in Houston. In the crash, passenger Sean Lynch, Alm's best friend since childhood, was thrown from the car. His body went over a guardrail and plunged twenty feet down an embankment, landing underneath the overpass. His friend lying motionless and failing to respond to his pleas, Alm placed a frantic 911 call from his cell phone.

"I have a buddy dying!" he yelled at the operator.

The operator's attempts to communicate with Alm then went unanswered.

"Sean, are you all right?" the operator could hear Alm screaming.

"Hello, hello."

The 911 operator then heard three gunshots. Drunk and guilt-ridden over the sight of his best friend's lifeless body lying beneath him on a service road, Alm retrieved a shotgun from his car and fired three shots into the air. He then sat down on the ground, stuck the barrel in his mouth, and blew his head off. Autopsies on both bodies confirmed both men were drunk at the time of the accident. Alm's blood alcohol content level was three times the legal limit for drivers in Texas.

League-wide, reaction to Alm's manner of death was one of profound shock. Nowhere in his background or personality, it was widely reported, was there any hint that he possessed the potential to kill himself. But alcohol alters personality, arrests free will, produces risky decisions and sometimes fatal results. Alcohol is a factor in 30 percent of the suicides, 50 percent of the homicides, and 30 percent of the accidental deaths in the United States. It played a major role in the accidental shooting death of Charles Blades by his cousin, Seahawks wide receiver Brian Blades. And other NFL players killed in auto fatalities while legally drunk include Miami Dolphins running back David Overstreet (1984), Los Angeles Raiders defensive back Stacey Toran (1989), and Atlanta Falcons tight end Brad Beckman (1990).

Despite recurring high-profile tragedies, frequent player arrests for driving drunk, and stepped-up provisions in the collective bargaining agreement allowing the commissioner to discipline players for abusing alcohol, the tide of alcohol abuse in the league shows no sign of dropping.

December 27, 1997

His big-screen television tuned to the Denver Broncos–Jacksonville Jaguars playoff game, ex–Seattle Seahawks defensive lineman Mike Frier positions his wheelchair between the sofa and the soft-back chair. His feet, inside of large, loosely tied high-top sneakers, rest motionless on the chair's metal footpads. Underneath green cutoff shorts, his once powerful legs, now a reflection of deteriorated muscle mass, twitch on occasion. With hands too feeble to operate the remote control, Frier directs his father, Ulysses, an ex-Marine who now lives with his son and cares for him twenty-four hours a day, to lower the volume.

Once a six-foot-five, 300-pound run-stopper, Frier watches a lot more football then he ever did when he played the game. Rendered a quadriplegic weeks after signing with the Seahawks, there is little else he can do. On December 1, 1994, then-twenty-five-year-old Frier joined Seahawks All-Pro running back Chris Warren and rookie running back Lamar Smith for his first "boys' night out" since coming over from the Cincinnati Bengals. For Frier, it ended up being his last night out when an intoxicated Smith drove his car into a utility pole.

"The experience is hard to deal with," Frier reflected two years after the fact. "One day you're working out, doing all the things you do. Now it's just taken away from me."

Four weeks after signing with the Seahawks, Frier finally decided to go out with the boys for a night of drinking. "Where's the hangout spot?" Frier asked Warren after practice.

"Couple guys be hangin' out at Shark's," Warren told him.

Shark's, the bar formally known as the Kirkland Shark Klub, is located near the Seahawks' practice facility. Frier began the evening of December 1 at the club with four of his teammates drinking and playing pool. After drinking eleven fourteen-ounce glasses of beer and two twelve-ounce bottles of beer, Warren, Frier, and Smith left Shark's at 8:00. Warren would later tell authorities that he and Smith split the eleven glasses of beer.

Planning to get drunk before going out, Frier prearranged for his girlfriend to pick him up at Shark's to insure his safe arrival home. "I never wanted to get a DWI and end up on ESPN or in USA Today," Frier said. "So I always made sure someone else was driving."

However, when Smith and Warren unexpectedly decided to go to a different bar after spending only an hour and a half at Shark's, Frier went along. Shortly after 8:00, the three arrived at T.G.I. Friday's where they ordered a round of double Crown Royal whiskey drinks. Smith downed two double Crown Royals and one single, the equivalent of six and one quarter ounces of straight alcohol. The tab, which police later requested, confirms that no food was ordered.

From T.G.I. Friday's they drove to a convenience store and purchased a twelve-pack of beer and two cigars. En route to Warren's house, Smith took a detour to the Seahawks' nearby practice facility to pick up Warren's keys.

Driving in a light rain, Smith cruised at nearly twice the posted speed limit. With Warren in the passenger's seat and Frier reclined across the back seat, rap music pulsated from a 200-pound oversized speaker in the rear dash of Smith's car. Witnesses in cars passed by Smith would later tell police of being able to hear the music inside their cars, despite their windows being up and rain falling outside.

His newly born daughter and girlfriend back at their small apartment, Frier's first night out was momentarily perfect—brews, smokes, tunes, and speed.

At 8:40 Smith attempted to pass a car in a no-passing zone, and lost control of his Oldsmobile Bravada. Unable to regain control, he crashed head-on into a utility pole with such force that the rear of the car went airborn, rotated to the right, and smashed into a nearby tree. Smith's shatterproof windshield busted completely out. Flames from atop the utility pole illuminated the wooded area, the damaged electrical boxes ultimately exploding three times while witnesses and emergency personnel began responding to the crash site.

Warren broke two ribs and Smith sustained injuries requiring hospital treatment, but both climbed out of the car on their own. Frier, with a fractured spine, was crushed underneath the 200-pound speaker, which landed on him.

"I didn't want to show weakness," Frier's father said, explaining the stiff upper lip he had to show Mike when he first walked into Mike's room at Overlake Hospital after the accident. "I knew I needed to be strong for him. We made eye contact. He recognized me."

Exposed to his share of senseless violence during his military career, Ulysses Frier faced his son's forever-changed condition with dignity. "You say, 'Well, I hid in the jungle with these two guys and I got the worst of it,'" reasoned Ulysses, comparing soldiers in Vietnam to football teammates. "If Mike had been in the front seat, things would have been different. But you don't want to question what the Lord does."

The first witnesses to arrive at the accident scene said they could hear Frier screaming from inside the car after his teammates had climbed out. His spine severed, Frier lay trapped and bleeding in the crumpled car. By the time paramedics transported him to the hospital, his life was in the balance. "I was close to death," Frier recalled. "On a ventilator. I couldn't breathe on my own. They were just trying to keep me alive."

"S--t," Smith said to Warren, the two of them looking at the wreckage as police and firefighters sped to the scene. Within minutes the two were separately answering questions from investigators. Smith, his breath reeking of alcohol and his eyes bloodshot and watery, confirmed to Officer Greg Hicks, who ticketed him weeks earlier for speeding, that Warren, not he, was the driver. Smith provided a more than one-page statement to that effect, then repeated the claim to a firefighter at the scene and a nurse at the hospital where he was later examined. But when officers placed handcuffs on Warren at the hospital, Smith interjected, "No man, no. I was the driver. I'm the driver." Smith was indicted on a felony charge of vehicular assault on January 26, 1995.

While Smith continued to practice and play with the team, therapists finally attempted to introduce Frier to rehabilitation exercises. Having regained some motion in his arms, Frier was first asked to raise his arms while one-pound plates rested in his hands. "I'd been lifting weights for ten years," he said. "Big old forty-five-pound plates. Suddenly I could not lift my arms up with one-pound plates." Once able to bench-press 450 pounds, one-pound rings now proved too much.

The image of a once-mighty NFL lineman confined to a wheelchair generated a great deal of dialogue in the media regarding alcohol abuse among Seahawks players. "A lot of us are getting tired of alcohol abuse among the Seahawks," wrote *Seattle Times* columnist Steve Kelley. "We're sick of reading in the newspaper about another DWI, or a tragic car wreck that didn't need to happen."

Months before Smith crashed his car, paralyzing Frier, Seahawks defensive back Patrick Hunter was sentenced to jail in Seattle after committing his second drunk driving offense since joining the team.

Then just fifteen days after the accident, Seahawks defensive back Orlando Watters, who was caught driving without a license, registration, or proof of insurance, was arrested for drunk driving in Seattle. Police also discovered marijuana and a knife in his vehicle. Seahawks head coach Tom Flores dismissed the seriousness of Watters's arrest. "All I can say is that he messed up," said Flores, who played Watters the following Sunday. "We will handle it in-house."

Downplaying the severity of the problem, then circling the wagons is a typical response to players' alcohol-related arrests. But if arrests are any gauge of the scope of the driving-under-the-influence problem within the NFL, the players are not merely slipping up and getting caught the first time they drive drunk. According to the National Highway Traffic Safety Commission, the average drunk driver operates his car between 200 and 2,000 times before being caught once.

Amidst heightened awareness of Seahawks players' drunk driving problems, newly hired head coach Dennis Erickson was arrested for driving under the influence on April 15, just two months before Frier's June 21, 1995, release from the hospital. A motorist on Washington's Interstate 5 called 911 from his cellular phone and reported that a 1995 BMW was being driven erratically. A Washington state patrolman then observed Erickson force three drivers to swerve or brake hard in order to avoid being hit. A breathalyzer test revealed that his blood alcohol level was more than twice the legal limit in Washington.

While disturbing, the arrest of Seattle's head coach is not unusual. From the mid-1980s to 1997, Seattle-area police arrested at least thirty Seahawks players and coaches for driving under the influence. The Seattle law firm Cowan, Hayne & Fox, which limits its practice to DUI defense, has represented approximately twenty-five Seahawks players and coaches charged with driving drunk during that period. "My impression is that professional athletes, particularly football players, drink substantially more than the rest of the population," said Douglas Cowan, the firm's founding lawyer, who has personally represented thirteen Seahawks coaches and players, among them receiver Brian Blades, defensive back Patrick Hunter, and All-Pro lineman Bob "Fig" Newton.

A former assistant district attorney in Seattle who began representing drunk driving offenders in 1978, Cowan has handled over 2,000 drunk driving cases in his thirty-year legal career. He has made a practice of talking to every one of his clients about the extent of their alcohol use. In arriving at his impression that NFL players abuse alcohol at higher rates than the general population, Cowan suggested that the mind-set required to play in the NFL can have a direct correlation to some players' abusive drinking habits. More specifically, he identified four factors that are associated with alcohol use and abuse among NFL players.

Reckless Abandon. According to Cowan, one out of four players he represented were diagnosed alcoholics. The rest he described as alcohol abusers who would drink socially, sometimes to excess. Cowan insisted that the problems he observed were not unique to the Seahawks. "Professional football players have to be people who can invoke a tremendous amount of emotion to do what they do," he said. "They have to be somewhat fearless. That requires a personality that does not fear consequences to the same extent that other people do. Not many people will throw themselves at 300-pound bodies running as fast as they can. You've got to have a certain amount of reckless abandonment in your personality to do that sort of thing. Because of that they live life to the fullest, pressing the edge at all times. This includes their social activities as well as their professional activities. NFL players don't think much about consequences, or they could not do what they do."

Manhood and Drinking. Even the casual observer recognizes the association between beer drinking and manhood that is promoted during televised football games. Cowan referred to it as "the testosterone factor." Masculinity, beer, and football go together. "There is an image of masculinity that many of them feel they have to project," said Cowan. "You talk about a man's man. Pro football players epitomize that. They are very masculine, very aggressive. There is an image factor that goes into that—'Real men drink. And real men drink as much as they want to.' There's an element to that that differentiates them from the general population. There's an image aspect."

Denial. "Football players are the paragon of health," said Cowan. And as a result, they are particularly resistant to admitting weakness. Cowan pointed to the questions that a player abusing alcohol will frequently ask. "How could I be an alcoholic and continue to achieve on such a high physical level? If I was an alcoholic I would be weak, wouldn't be able to get up in the morning, wouldn't be sober for my games, wouldn't have the strength that I do, I'd be dissipated, etc."

The NFL's Promotion of Alcohol. On February 14, 1997, new provisions went into effect under the National Football League Policy and Program for Substances of Abuse. While recognizing that "alcoholic beverages are legal substances," the policy prohibits the abuse of alcohol, declaring that "such conduct is detrimental to the integrity of the public confidence in the NFL and professional football."

Yet, as Cowan pointed out, there is an "extraordinary" amount of alcohol sold at NFL stadiums, not to mention the massive promotion of alcohol consumption on television during the broadcast of NFL games. "It's not just a mixed message," Cowan pointed out. "It is hypocritical as hell.

You think of football, you think of beer. They have the Bud Bowl on Super Bowl Sunday every year."

"Alcohol abuse is out of control in the NFL," said Frier. "If alcohol is there, it's going to be abused by the players. Simple as that. I had a friend when I played for the Bengals, Reggie Rembert—he had to take piss tests two or three times every week. But he was still out there taking chances." Rembert was arrested three times for driving under the influence while playing for the Bengals and ultimately sentenced to a year in jail.

"If you've got an alcoholic, there's only one way to stop them from driving drunk," said Cowan. "That is to stop them from drinking. Period. You can take away their cars, family, jobs, anything. But until you sober them up, they're not going to stop driving drunk."

Many teams do not understand this concept. After cutting Rembert following his third DUI arrest, the Bengals drafted the University of Miami's outstanding defensive back Tremain Mack in 1997. Prior to the draft, Mack had been arrested six times, three of those for driving under the influence. "He's in terrible shape," said Frier, familiar with Mack's situation through his friends still on the Bengals squad. "He's lucky to be in the NFL. Cincinnati would cut him if he was a regular rookie free agent making no money. But they try and help out their top players, and try to hide problems."

Mack was arrested on October 25 for driving eighty-two miles per hour while under the influence. He was sentenced to thirty days in jail. "We hire people as players," said Bengals president and general manager Mike Brown following Mack's admission to the Clermont County Jail. "You have to realize that these are human beings who are not perfect and some of them will at times run up against a wall." Brown, though, could only hope that a "person" with Mack's record of DUI would not run *into* a wall.

As was the case with Rembert, the Bengals stated they would give Mack more chances after undergoing counseling. "We hope we can help him but if we can't, if he fails two more times, then he's out, done," said Brown. "That's the way it works."

Despite being an advocate for treatment and rehabilitation, Cowan concluded that NFL teams don't always act in players' best interest. "There should be a line of accountability," he said. "The greatest enablers in the world are the NFL, or have been historically. At some point in time you have to say, 'We're not going to put up with this anymore. We're not going to continue to support you in your path to self-destruction.' That's part of recovery. If they did that with some players, maybe some players would get the point and take care of themselves and then have a chance to reenter the league."

While awaiting the outcome of Lamar Smith's pending retrial on vehicular assault charges, the Seahawks signed Broncos wide receiver Mike Pritchard on June 19, 1996. Pritchard had been arrested for vehicular assault and drunk driving after he hit two pedestrians on October 29, 1995. He later pleaded guilty to two misdemeanor charges and was put on eighteen months' probation and ordered to attend an alcohol rehabilitation program.

Meanwhile, Lamar Smith and Mike Frier agreed to an out-of-court settlement in August of 1997, where Smith would pay at least $1 million to Frier.

On January 9, 1998, after over three years of legal wrangling that included a trial that ended in a hung jury and an appeal to the Washington Supreme Court, Smith pleaded guilty to vehicular assault and was sentenced to four months in prison. When entering his plea, Smith admitted to making "a horrible mistake."

Smith's mistake was not learned from, however, not even by teammate Chris Warren, who barely escaped the accident intact. On April 4, 1997, Warren was again at Sharky's in Kirkland drinking with teammates. And again he climbed into the passenger's side of a car being driven by a drunk teammate who drove away from the bar at excessive speeds.

This time it was fellow running back Mack Strong. Strong sped out of the parking lot and ran a stop sign at approximately twenty miles per hour. An officer then observed Strong's car straddling the lane divider and veering into the lane of oncoming traffic. After driving one block on the right-hand shoulder and then swaying back to the center lane and nearly missing an island, Strong was pulled over and arrested.

An open bottle of beer was found in the car and Strong was unable to perform simple sobriety tests such as accurately repeating the alphabet or standing on one foot for more than two seconds. After being booked at the police station, Strong was released into the custody of Chris Warren. On September 30, 1997, Strong pleaded guilty to a reduced charge of negligent driving. He was fined and received a suspended ninety-day jail sentence. Warren escaped again without life-threatening injury.

"My God," said Cowan when he learned of Warren riding in Strong's car after his experience in the Smith case. "Amazing. That is amazing. It sure as hell makes me shake my head."

Tragedy as a behavior-changing tool has a very short shelf life, especially in the NFL. "I'm just another casualty," Frier said. "Life goes on. To tell you the truth, if this happened to someone else, I wouldn't be hangin' out drinkin' all the time. But it wouldn't stop me from drinkin' because a guy's career was cut short."

In March of 1998, Smith was furloughed from a Seattle jail so he could fly to New Orleans to sign a four-year, $7.1 million contract with the Saints. "All I can say is, 'There but for the grace of God go I,'" said Saints head coach Mike Ditka, referring to Smith's conviction. "We've all done it. We've used bad judgment with alcohol and a vehicle. Most people who do it get away with it. Some people get caught."

16

The Convict

August, 1997

John Shaw, President
St. Louis Rams
St. Louis, Mo.

Dear John,

I know you're shocked to hear from me, but you shouldn't be. You told me the same thing when you visited me in Los Angeles Metropolitan Detention Center. I've always viewed your character with good admiration, even though I always felt I was underpaid, like every other athlete I've played with! I don't know how you've done it for so many years, battling agents who represent clients, who all believe their clients are much better than they are, to make figures work. I'm sure ten, twelve years ago you never dreamed of having to pay a non-quarterback athlete ten, fifteen million bucks in a single contract period, and some are actually much higher than that.

The reason I'm writing to you is for one reason only. I want you to know how thankful I am that you supported me during some extremely stressful times in 93 on through 95. Never once did you question my guilt or innocence. You always tried to put the fire out or contain it as best you could. Your loyalty should never be questioned, however, I'm sure your critics have found ways to tarnish that, too. I hope the St. Louis community realizes they've got a winner there with you. I've often pondered why you'd take such a liking to me and I never came up with any acceptable reasons. With this latest drama in my life you probably can't figure that one out either, but regardless of any of my circumstances, I salute you on behalf of myself and my wife and my beautiful daughter, and I apologize for any unwanted grief I have caused you in your support of me as a person, not as an athlete, a defendant or an inmate. I'm proud to have been someone you believed in.

But as I was reading the sports page I came across an article which saddened me. Allegedly a back up defensive tackle for the Rams faces conspiracy charges for crack cocaine or something or other.

John, has anyone heeded the tragedy I experienced? Do the guys realize that a wrong decision can ruin their lives and send their families in great pain. We as athletes have got to realize that we are not above the law, in fact we are at greater risk because of the negative exposures. It kills me to know that athletes haven't learned from my ridicule. These guys must think they're invincible, invincible from trouble and/or harm. They must not know I was a starter for four and a half out of the six years, graduated 3.1 GPA, never tested positive for any form of drug abuse, not even liquor. I come from excellent parents and family, never been arrested prior to the charges. But look what happened to me. My immediate down fall was allowing a circle of guys to get too close to me knowing full well their interests were different from mine. That mistake was the beginning of what would ultimately become the worse nightmare of my life.

I really wanted to write to Lawrence Phillips before the '96 season got under way to give him some support. I suppose I basically wanted to introduce myself to him to bring actual reality of a fallen athlete into his realm of thinking. I do regret not writing that letter because maybe a few words of encouragement from me could have saved him from some unwanted press. But then again maybe not. It's just hard having to watch other athletes succumb to negative temptations that often end up biting them in the ass like it did to me.

Good luck this season. I'll always consider myself a diehard Ram.

Thank you much,

Darryl Henley
Inmate #01915-112
Marion—United States Prison

If ever NFL Films were to create its own version of the critically acclaimed 1972 anti-crime movie *Scared Straight,* Darryl Henley would be a natural for the starring role. He wouldn't play the role of host in the movie, which Peter Falk (of television's *Columbo* fame) handled so ably. Falk, you see, was an outsider, walking juvenile delinquents through a real-life maximum security prison in an effort to scare them into walking on the other side of the justice system.

No, Henley, once one of the NFL's most feared defensive backs, would play the part of the insider, the hardened inmate who was the real star of the show. For Henley, like that inmate, is hoping that by telling his horror story he might keep others from taking the same path.

In the first and only interview the six-year pro granted

since his 1997 sentencing to forty-one years in America's toughest prison, Henley didn't want to talk about his crimes. He didn't want to talk about his prison mate, Mafia boss John Gotti. And he didn't want to talk about the many books he now has time to read.

He did want to talk about the NFL, about players breaking the law, and about where it can all end up if someone doesn't step up and scare some players straight.

A second-round pick out of UCLA in 1989, Henley was everybody's All-American. In most drafts, Henley's coverage skills would have made him the toast of his position, but he happened to enter the NFL the same year as a gold-drenched, brash young man named Deion Sanders.

While Sanders was making an immediate impact on and off the field in Atlanta, Henley was drawing praise for his round-the-clock practice and study habits with the Los Angeles Rams. In 1989, Henley's rookie season, the Rams played their way into the NFC championship game, the last time the franchise has been to the playoffs and the last time the team posted a winning season. Though Henley's playing time was limited, winning soothed his ego. The next year, Henley earned the starting spot, but the team began a five-year spiral under coaches John Robinson and Chuck Knox that turned playing for the team into a "miserable experience."

As a starter in his third and fourth years with the Rams, Henley led the team in passes broken up in both 1991 and 1992 and finished fourth on the team in tackles both years. Yet the Rams ended those seasons 3-13 and 6-10.

With each frustrating loss, Henley's attention turned further and further from the field. "At a certain point, I hated going to the [Anaheim] stadium," Henley said. "I hated getting in my car and going to practice. I hated it. Everyone started pointing fingers. People said, 'Well the coach was this . . .' That wasn't it. That wasn't it at all. It wasn't management. It wasn't John Shaw. It wasn't John Robinson. It wasn't Chuck Knox. It wasn't those guys. It was the dudes on the team. They didn't have the desire and the commitment. They didn't have the attitude to win. They weren't staying around practice, working out. You get beat by deep balls, you should be staying after practice, showing up on Tuesday on a day off. Nobody was doing that. My rookie year, when I was screwing up, on Tuesday mornings, on my day off, they had me up there with the coaching staff. I was up there and I loved it. They had my ass working out, going over mistakes that I made to the point where I started doing it on my own. And then in '91 and '92, we didn't have that anymore. Those dudes were getting killed. Crunched. Offensive and defensive. But at the end of every practice, the discussion was 'What are we doing afterward?' After a while it starts to have a real effect on you. A real effect. To the point where I lost my love for football. I allowed myself to become bored with something that I had always wanted to do all my life. How can you get bored with money, women, football, cameras, TV? How can you get bored with that? It's everybody's dream. How can you get bored with that?

"And when I got bored, when I lost the love for the game, I started listening to people I never listened to before. That was my mistake. I started looking for something else to excite me. And that always leads to trouble."

* * *

As bad as life for Henley was on the field, it didn't begin to unravel off it until July 1993, when FBI agents pulled an attractive nineteen-year-old waitress named Tracy Ann Donaho from a line of passengers arriving at Atlanta's Hartsfield International Airport. Donaho, who had drawn attention by purchasing her ticket to Atlanta with cash, was asked about a suitcase labeled as hers. Unbeknownst to her, agents had discovered twelve kilos of cocaine in the case, a load that would fetch $250,000 on the street. Donaho said the suitcase belonged to a friend and she couldn't open it because she didn't have the key. Agents kept the case, but let her leave. Several hours later, when she and Henley returned to the airport to retrieve it, police swept in and arrested her. As Donaho was being placed in handcuffs, Henley "expressed shock," according to police, and made a point of telling them he was a professional football player who spoke out against drug use. The result: Donaho was taken to jail, Henley got in his car and drove home.

Within hours, Darryl Henley's life was in freefall. Donaho, a Rams cheerleader, kept quiet the first day after police arrested her. But she would eventually say it was Henley who had arranged for her to carry the suitcase, telling her it contained cash to be delivered to a friend. She said Henley, whom she had dated, paid her $1,000 to deliver one suitcase to a friend in Memphis, then more to shepherd the case to Atlanta a month later. In exchange for reducing charges against her, Donaho agreed to become a government witness against Henley. Investigators chose not to arrest Henley, but did begin a full-blown inquiry into his life.

When he learned that Donaho had fingered him, Henley immediately called coach Chuck Knox, who gathered the team's brass for an impromptu meeting. "They said we had to put together a team," Henley said. "I needed a lawyer, an investigator, experts, the whole O.J. thing. And they said we had to keep this quiet."

The federal government, peeling through his life like the skins of an onion, lawyers calculating his every off-the-field move, and coaches waiting for their quiet deal to break, Henley surprised everyone in the Rams organization by coming out at the start of the 1993 season and posting near All-Pro numbers through the first five games. Then the secret became public and by December he was indicted, named as the kingpin in a national cocaine trafficking ring. He was charged with conspiracy to deliver narcotics along with four others, including his uncle and a childhood friend.

No one knew what should happen next. The NFL wanted to suspend Henley based on the sheer seriousness of the charge. Henley's lawyers argued against suspension, claiming that to cut Henley would be a presumption of his guilt. The Rams were left in the middle. But when the controversy became a distraction for an already distracted team, Henley voluntarily took a leave of absence. "I wasn't forced to take the leave," he said. "In fact the Rams paid me my full salary [$600,000] that year, that was the deal. It was just better for everyone that I step away."

The next summer, his trial delayed until January 1995, the Rams announced they were bringing Henley back for the 1994 season. A deal between Henley, the Rams, and the court allowed Henley to travel with the team after posting a $1 million bond and agreeing to pay the cost of a court officer to accompany him on road trips. Despite those restrictions, Henley again amazed coaches and critics by leading the team in interceptions. During a November game with Denver, he recorded a career-high eleven solo tackles as the Rams held

John Elway to forty yards passing in the first half. For his play, Henley was given the defensive game ball. Though the Denver game was one of the best in his career, Henley consistently played so well that coaches openly marveled at his concentration, his ability to block out the distractions and be the team's rock in the defensive backfield.

Henley and the Rams ignored questions about the propriety of paying an accused major drug trafficker to play in the National Football League. This was definitely not a United Way commercial waiting to happen. The Rams, some said, were selling their soul. If so, the team, which finished 4-12, got little for the sale.

In late January, Henley's new team—a band of lawyers and investigators led by future CNN television legal anchor Roger Cossack—opened his defense in federal court.

During the trial, the government detailed an elaborate scheme to move drugs nationwide. Cossack attempted to reduce the case to one of a conspiracy to sully the name of a professional football player.

"I was always surrounded by groups of people," Henley said. "And those people were always telling me not to worry, 'Okay, man, we're going to get out of this.' Everybody tells you, 'Man, just watch, just wait, it'll be over soon.'"

Henley, who was rarely beaten as a defensive back, believed all those hangers-on. Confident to the point of appearing cocky, Henley stood when the jury foreman prepared to announce the verdict eight weeks later. To his surprise, the foreman's response was only one word, not two. "As I heard the word—guilty—my knees buckled," Henley said. He was immediately sent to the federal detention facility in Los Angeles to await sentencing.

Though Henley's attorneys announced an appeal immediately after the conviction, the Rams finally acknowledged they may lose the service of one of their best defensive players. A week after the guilty verdict, the Rams signed Anthony Parker to replace Henley in the lineup.

Then came a twist so bizarre even the hardened cynics were left scratching their heads. According to prosecutors, while in the federal jail, Henley befriended a guard who provided Henley with a cellular phone. Using that phone, Henley arranged for a $1 million heroin shipment to be sent to Detroit and for cocaine to be moved around Southern California. With the profit he earned from those transactions, Henley offered to pay for the murder of Donaho and U.S. District Judge Gary Taylor, who had presided in the case and would be determining his sentence.

What Henley didn't know was that federal marshals were on to his scheme. An inmate whom Henley had asked to help plan the murders turned out to be a jailhouse informant. The voice on the other end of Henley's cell phone when he ordered the judge's murder belonged to a federal undercover agent. The conversations, he would later learn, were all being recorded.

Within days, Henley and a whole new group of defendants were brought before a new federal judge, charged not only with drug trafficking, but with attempted murder. This time, those charged included Henley's brother Eric, along with Henley's girlfriend and the mother of his child. The whole family, it seemed, was going down with Darryl. Henley's own parents, in fact, lost their home in foreclosure after they spent $100,000—including $83,000 from their retirement funds—on their sons' legal defense funds.

Before the murder-for-hire case could go to trial, Henley

and his brother both pleaded guilty to trafficking charges and to Henley's part in plotting the murders.

In one day, March 10, 1997, Henley appeared in back-to-back hearings where federal judges ordered him to spend the next forty-one years of his life in prison—not just any prison, but the United States prison in Marion, Illinois, one of two "super-maximum-security" prisons in the United States. Where once Henley had proudly proclaimed his inclusion in one of America's most select fraternities—the 1,600 players in the NFL—he now was in even more select company: only 700 inmates in America are housed in the nation's two super-max federal prisons.

"You screwed up your life, didn't you?" U.S. District Judge Manuel Real asked before announcing a twenty-one-year sentence for drug trafficking. Head bowed, Henley said nothing until his attorney whispered in his ear.

"Yes," the once flamboyant athlete said after the prompt.

Down the hall in the federal courthouse, Judge James M. Ideman added another twenty years for the murder plot. "It is obvious he's even more dangerous in custody than out of custody," Ideman said. "Any speeches [to Henley] would be a waste of time. If ever there's a guy that deserves to be in Marion, it is you."

In April 1997, marshals escorted Henley past the twenty-foot-high fences of razor-sharp concertina wire and down the iron-gated halls of America's toughest prison. His social time—once spent with politicians and world-class athletes—now would be shared with the likes of John Gotti, mass murderers, and those convicted of blowing up the World Trade Center. His closet of flashy suits would be replaced by a bright red prison jump suit and white flannel long johns for the cold days. The Rolex watch gave way to shiny silver handcuffs. His entourage now consisted of two guards, nightsticks in hand, who stay with him step for step every time he leaves his cell. Where once he looked up to see thousands of fans yelling his name, now the same view included towers and snipers.

"Walking into Marion was only the second time in my life— the other was when the jury said I was guilty—that I could barely walk," Henley said a year later. "My knees shook. This was real.

"Why do most people want to play professional football? Money. Fame. Women. Cars. Houses. But there are only so many cars you can buy," Henley said, searching for the beginnings of his end. "There are only so many women that you can have a night. There is only so much money can buy. Really. I had everything you could want and I still wasn't happy. I don't know if this is part of the message because it's really directed at the athletes—the guys who want to become athletes. Everyone likes to say 'Football is not my life.' That's not true. To many players, it is their life. It shouldn't be your life, but it is. You should have some other interest—family, to turn to when things aren't working out on the field. I didn't have those interests. That's what made me the perfect guy to get caught up in these situations. When you allow yourself to become bored, you start looking at other ways to pique your interest. Sometimes you find some things that are totally, totally different from anything that you have ever experienced or done. You're on a plane and you are gung ho, you're enjoying what you do. You're enjoying life. Someone comes to you and they slide up under you and they give you a sales pitch and it's not too strong, but you can see the mystique and danger and you know you should say, 'No, I'm cool. Thanks anyway.' Maybe it's a friend. An old friend. We're just talking and kicking back. A sales pitch. An approach. You're comfortable now, with your lifestyle. You go to the left, I go to the right.

"But when you're not comfortable with yourself, the sales pitch works. And it works immediately when you don't turn and run. The minute you say, 'What was that? Say that again?' he's got you.

"My problems were with me. It was within me. It didn't have anything to do with anybody else. It was Darryl Henley. I lost interest in football and started listening to other opportunities, dangerous and mysterious opportunities.

"From there, from just listening, things snowballed. Next thing, I was in with people I knew I shouldn't be in with. Then when things started coming down around me, I was willing to do whatever might get me out of that situation, even crazy stuff, stuff I can't believe today I even thought about. That's when bad went to worse. Suddenly, all I wanted was to be back on the football field. But I was too caught up in saving my ass to get there.

"The problem is that everyone believes it can't happen to them, they'll never get caught. And they look at the guys like me who get caught and assume it must be because I had a background that was worse than theirs, or wasn't as smart as they are, or something. But to say that, you've got to know who I am.

"All I ask is that before people sit in judgment of me, they need to understand that I'm not some undereducated black guy who came from the ghetto and was banging and shooting people in junior high school. I'm not a 'failure of the system' or a 'product of a bad environment.' Every member of my family, as of November of '97, has a college degree. My father migrated to Los Angeles from the South. He worked his butt off for Western Union. He packed my brother and I, packed us both on his back while he delivered packages because we couldn't afford baby-sitters and all that. He worked hard enough to allow us to move to the suburbs and that took everything he had. They spent everything they ever had to get us out of that environment. My father volunteered at [the local public] Duarte High School—he was a proctor there. He saw what was going on. He didn't want it for us and he moved us away. He enrolled us in a private Catholic school—a great school. Damien High School. We did well there. My older brother, Thomas, became the first black athlete to get a scholarship out of there. He went to Stanford University and started on the football team as a freshman. My younger brother went to Rice on scholarship. We all graduated. Every one of us graduated.

"We didn't have crack in our family. Never had handcuffs on. Never been in jail. Never had a problem. I didn't drink my first beer until I graduated from high school. Never had anything like that. It wasn't attractive to me. Never smoked a joint. I remember when I was leaving college some friends and I got together and went to the mountains—it was a girl, she invited me, and her friends and that type of thing. Me and one of my teammates were there and I just did the drug testing thing for the NFL Combine. I knew that the draft was coming up and then you've got to report for mini-camp. I was upstairs and I knew they were smoking dope downstairs and I panicked. I'm like, 'Ya'll wet some towels and put it all under the door.' I was like, 'Secondhand smoke. I ain't trying to get none of that stuff.' That was my attitude. That was my response."

With twenty-three hours a day alone in a six-foot by nine-foot cell, Henley has a lot of time to think through how his fall from grace began. As a result, he gets fighting mad when he reads about another athlete headed down the same path that landed him in Marion.

"I couldn't believe it when I saw that another Ram was being investigated for drugs. Remember, I'm just recognizing who I am, and it's not all pretty. And then I saw that. It made me so angry I just had to write John [Shaw]. I didn't even know James Harris. Didn't know anything about James Harris, but I was so angry that his name even came up—especially with the Rams. [See Chapter 7.] Everything was too close to home. Just his name, the Rams, I couldn't believe it. My first reaction was that maybe I should talk to this dude, tell him what he needs to do. But I was so angry that I couldn't do it. I was angry because I kept thinking: 'Am I just wasted, that this has happened here? Is this just a waste? People don't even recognize what the hell is going on? This ain't no joke. This is real.' This is not attractive. This is far different than what you could ever imagine.

"If you flirt with danger, it will find you," Henley said, sitting in the cramped interview room at Marion. "You want the message? That's it. If I can get caught up with the bad guys, with all that I had going for me, there better not be anyone out there who believes it can't happen to them. We're all vulnerable, just not all of us get caught."

17

Game Plan

Darryl Henley knows how it starts. The onetime star cornerback of the Los Angeles Rams knows how the slippery slope of abhorrent yet accepted behavior by athletes begins. He also knows how it can end. For him, it ended in the nation's toughest prison, where he sits confined in a six-foot-by-nine-foot cell twenty-three hours a day.

"We know, as athletes, when 'it' begins," Henley said, using his forefingers to punctuate his sentence. "It is when you know you are good enough to get away with stuff—and make no mistake, the better you are, the more you get away with. When you get to a certain level you get away with more. It starts out small. Come late to a meeting in college and you don't get in trouble. The other guys do. You get chastised, that's it.

"So you don't do it again for two months. You get chastised again. They say, 'You won't play on Saturday.' You're going to play and you know it. I heard one guy say his coach told him, 'I don't care what the hell you do during the week, long as you're there for that game on Saturday.' His job is based on Saturday's performance. He knows it. You know it too.

"It goes from a missed meeting to a Friday night frat party. You get in a fight because you're drunk. Then the coaches want to know what happened. You tell them and the institution covers it up for you. No big deal. So it goes from that to a drunk driving charge. You're not high, just drunk. Guys don't get pulled over because they're on coke. It's just drunk driving. 'We were having a good time, coach, and you know . . .' Well now you're not living on campus anymore, you're off campus. You can't walk to your dorm, you tell him. There's no such thing as drunk walking, so of course you're going to get caught drunk driving. He understands. He was there once. It's accepted behavior as long as you don't hurt anybody.

"Maybe it never gets that far because the dude who pulls you over is from the campus police. 'I've been here for several years,' he tells you. 'I know your coaches down there. I'll handle this.' He says, 'Look, I'm going to make sure you get home.' He doesn't say, 'Give me tickets and I'll take care of this.' It doesn't happen like that. That's propaganda. He squashes it. It gets dropped, or reduced to a misdemeanor. If you get the misdemeanor, well now you have to do fifteen hours of community service. First you think, 'Fifteen hours of community service!' Well, according to the coaches, you're already doing community service because most athletes who are somebody—the school has them going to talk to people. So you're there for three hours and you get marked down for ten. You get marked down for everything. The lunch and the drive and after the drive and by the time you make one trip, fifteen hours are gone. That's how that stuff works.

"Then what happens? You catch a touchdown against the big rival. All of a sudden you're a hero. Now you're talking to your girlfriend, maybe one of your girlfriends, and she says, 'Why were you with that girl?' 'Shut up!' Pop. You slap her. You smack her. Now I'm out of control. You figure it's okay because you're dating. I put my hands on her? That's the problem. What happens from there? Now it's not just yourself you're hurting anymore. You're dealing with other people. You assaulted a female. She's eighteen years old, nineteen years old. She's not used to violence and you smack her. Whether she reports it or not, look what's happening. You know you're going to get away with it. The coach asks, 'Did you smack her?' 'Yeah. I lost control.' 'The last time you had fifteen hours of community service. Now you got a hundred.' What does the player say? 'Do I still get to play?' The coach knows he's got it made. 'Because it's February, you're suspended for the spring. But be ready for the fall.' That's what happens.

"The next time, the next crime is worse. The pattern—if you don't put the fear of God in them the first time—will continue and never end. At least not until you end up dead or in jail. You see, each time, the coach tells you he's giving you a second chance. He might even tell you you have to 'earn' a second chance. But how many times do they let you get away with it, before it's not a second chance anymore? It is just expected.

"So you take a guy that has learned these lessons in college, you hand him $250,000 a year, maybe a million, and you wonder why you have criminals in the NFL? How can you even have a question? And then, trust me, it ain't getting fixed when they get in the league. If anything, they're even more forgiving. So it all continues and who is going to make it stop?"

Henley posed the question, paused, then shook his head slowly and asked it again.

"Who is going to make it stop?"

To some, no less than the future of the NFL hinges on finding an answer to that question.

"Ultimately there are fans, F-A-N-S, that support athletic leagues and teams and at some point I think you turn those fans off," said Pat Haden, a former Rams quarterback turned lawyer and broadcaster. "They stop going to games, they stop watching games, they stop listening to games, they stop buying products that are advertising the games. I think at some point you just get so sick and tired of it [the boorish behavior of athletes]. . . . There will come a time, when people aren't gonna show up or watch. The NFL's got to watch out."

"I don't think there's any question that when you lose Joe Blue Collar out there who buys the tickets, that you are going to eventually die," player agent Ralph Cindrich said. "It's still the values of that everyday man that fuels this league. If those fans become so sick and tired of it as to walk away from the game, I don't think there's any question the league will be hurting."

"The NFL is definitely on the road to a real disastrous problem if it continues in the direction it's going," Hall of Fame middle linebacker Lee Roy Jordan told the authors. "How many chances do you give a twenty-five- or thirty-year-old athlete who is making $150,000 to several million dollars a year? How many chances do they deserve before they take responsibility for themselves and live within the guidelines and the laws of the land?"

The NFL is accustomed to hearing suggestions that it

clean up its players' acts. From issues as diverse as domestic violence to drug use, some of America's most prominent leaders have suggested that the league step up and, through strong discipline, send a message to young people.

In nearly every case, the league has responded with silence or with a statement suggesting it is only a microcosm of society, that its problems are no greater than you'd find in any neighborhood.

House Speaker Newt Gingrich said in March 1998 that he would like to see all professional sports leagues demand that athletes who fail drug tests be suspended for life unless they turn over to authorities the name of the dealer that sold them their drugs. As powerful as the suggestion was, it was simply brushed aside by the NFL.

"The response of the NFL, like the other leagues, was really weak," Gingrich said in an interview for this book. "They issued some general comments that they're all free-standing businesses and they can't demand things like that from the commissioner's office. First of all, they need to remember we're describing behavior which violates the law. It is illegal to buy drugs. It is illegal to use drugs. So we could, technically, enforce these much more rigorously for people who engage in interstate commerce. There's not a single professional sport that is not, by definition, interstate commerce. So here you have leagues, many of which play in municipal stadiums with tax-free bonds building the facility they are involved in. They have all sorts of exemptions from antitrust in the case of some of the leagues. They make their living out of advertising which is tax deductible and tickets which are often bought as business expenses. Then having used the government to make sure they are as wealthy as possible, they try and say the government shouldn't stick its nose into our business.

"I'm just saying, as public institutions of public authority, that survive because of public purchase and public support, they also have a public responsibility," the Speaker said. "I was very disappointed. They had a chance to show leadership and they failed."

Gingrich was not the first leader in Washington to admonish the NFL to take a tougher stand against drugs. Back in 1989, then–U.S. Drug Czar William Bennett summoned the commissioners of each of the professional leagues to discuss how sports teams could demand that athletes be better role models.

"What I'm hoping for is a strong signal from this community that it understands its responsibilities," Bennett told the *Washington Post* in 1989. "What happens in these [pro] sports is a form of instruction and a national classroom. From those to whom much is given, much is expected."

If Bennett expected much from the NFL, he was disappointed. Little changed after the meeting Bennett convened in Washington.

The problem, as Darryl Henley said, is that there is an endless line of finger pointing. It is akin to the problems in education—high schools point to junior high schools, junior high schools point to elementary schools, elementary schools point at bad parents. In the end, kids who can't read keep pouring into the workforce, not sure who they should be pointing the finger at. Meanwhile, no one steps forward to solve the problem.

When it comes to the criminal conduct of our athletes, someone has to step up. Someone must send the message that Sunday's heroes can no longer be Tuesday's wife beaters or Wednesday's rapists.

There are at least four different "groups" that can send this message:

The Media. Media scrutiny of player backgrounds—not just at the professional, but also the college level—should equal that of the attention paid to backgrounds of other community leaders. Players should expect that scrutiny will accompany a scholarship or a job in the NFL, positions that, rightly or wrongly, demand that athletes act as role models. If the player knows that his actions may one day cause him and his family front-page embarrassment—and a loss of endorsement dollars—some might think twice before entering the ranks of the criminal.

Colleges. Colleges, where one might argue "chances" should be taken in an effort to straighten lives out, need to teach socialization skills to at-risk athletes. "Most of their lives, everything for these young men revolves around being football players, not people," said Steven Bucky, team psychologist for the San Diego Chargers. "They're not taught how to deal with relationships, with anger, with personal problems. Nobody has taken it upon themselves to develop within these football players the socialization skills that the rest of us learn. They just learn how to hit and run." Unfortunately those skills aren't being taught where they should be—at home—because too many parents spend their time fawning over young stars. So Bucky and others have proposed that colleges add this to their "real life curriculum."

NFL Teams. The league's thirty teams need to show more discipline. If teams were to hit players the only place where they seem to understand pain—the pocketbook—you may actually have a chance to stem the tide of abhorrent behav-

ior. Don't draft problem players. Leave a few of them unemployed and, soon enough, the point will come across. Cut
your criminals—most NFL contracts already include hereto-
fore largely ignored "character clauses" spelling out expected behavior—and then hope other teams can rise to the
same standard. Is that too much to ask? "No," New England
Patriots owner Bob Kraft said simply. "You just have to
have standards."

Though teams appeared to have made some strides in this
area during the 1998 draft, more than one draft insider believed that was a direct result of Lawrence Phillips's flop as
a Ram. "Had Phillips rushed for 1,500 yards each of these
last two years, Randy Moss would have been seen as less of
a risk and would have landed in the top five picks," agent
Jerome Stanley said.

The problem, as Darryl Henley described above, is that
coaches don't lose their jobs for what happens on Tuesdays.
So if teams like the New England Patriots choose to leave
talent in the draft in favor of character, they have to be
equally forgiving if their team loses a game or two. The history of the NFL doesn't show that teams are willing to do
that. The NBA found that same lack of discipline among its
teams, requiring that the league office insert itself in off-
court disciplinary decisions. "In terms of teams disciplining
players, teams always have their own private agenda, that's
why it was important for the commissioner to step in," NBA
deputy commissioner Russ Granik told the authors. "We
think fans don't want to see NBA players behave that way
and one of the responsibilities that comes with playing in the
NBA is that you conduct yourself in a certain way. We don't
think it's too much to ask that you don't engage in criminal

conduct. We think our fans are entitled to judge the NBA on the basis of the way it reacts to things."

The Commissioner. As Granik's boss, NBA commissioner David Stern, attempted during the 1997–98 season, NFL commissioner Paul Tagliabue must step in and set high standards. During the March 1998 owners meetings, Tagliabue made public a policy he had quietly begun distributing to teams sometime during the fall of 1997. The policy allows the commissioner to start meting out discipline for off-field behavior. For reasons that went unexplained, Tagliabue let the policy gather dust while players like Cornelius Bennett (see Chapter 2) continue drawing NFL paychecks. At the spring 1998 meetings—seven days after declining the authors' invitation to comment on the league's policy toward the criminal conduct of its players—Tagliabue announced that he was prepared to actually start using his power.

The league's new policy, scheduled to go into effect in July 1998, will finally begin treating all criminal convictions just as they do violations of the league's drug policy. NFL players convicted after the policy's effective date could face game suspensions, fines, or both. The policy will not affect teams' ability to draft and employ players whose criminal pasts are as long as their broad jump—as long as the arrests and convictions occur before joining the league.

While the policy is an obvious step forward, but it is several years and hundreds of victims too late.

Tagliabue's decision was a dramatic departure from the previous position the commissioner's office has taken—"There's no rule that says if you've been charged in a crime you can't play in the NFL," league spokesman Greg Aiello said after Seahawks wide receiver Brian Blades was arrested in 1995 for the shooting death of his cousin Charles Blades.

"We're not a law enforcement agency so when we go beyond what society has done to punish a person, that opens legal questions."

Tagliabue knows that while a hard-line stance on crime makes for good press—his announcement made page one of *USA Today,* after all—this is also an economic issue for the NFL. Ample evidence exists that free agency, constantly relocating franchises, astronomical player salaries and corresponding television contracts have distanced the relationship hard-core fans have with their teams and their heroes. If the commissioner doesn't draw a line—any line—on unacceptable behavior off the field, fans will continue to lose their connection. "A lack of respect for the law by highly paid athletes is a sore point with the fans," Harold Henderson, the NFL's executive vice president for labor relations, acknowledged after Tagliabue's announcement.

Opinions vary on where the commissioner's new policy should draw the line—should conviction for certain felonies trigger harsher penalties than convictions for others—but in interviews for this book, the authors found near unanimity in the belief that there needs to be a line of some kind. The following is a sampling of some of the views expressed to the authors:

"It would be nice to see the league—the NFL—work with the NFL Players Association and enact a zero tolerance policy for any sort of drug and alcohol abuse, and serious criminal offenses," Hall of Fame receiver Steve Largent, now a U.S. congressman, said. "Though I recognize zero tolerance would be impossible, I don't think it would be unfair at all. I think in terms of life and the ability to be forgiven by God and by your fellow man, I think there's unlimited opportunities for that to happen. But in terms of a person's opportunity to stay in the league and continually give the league and the game and the team or franchise a bad name and a black eye, I think there should be a limited number."

"A lot of contracts today have character clauses in them," added thirteen-year veteran Rich Caster, who retired from the NFL after winning the 1983 Super Bowl with the Washington Redskins. "I'd like to make them enforceable and let's make our expectations clear. They will have to sacrifice some people along the lines somewhere to actually make it clear. It's a shame it has to go that way, but that's a sacrifice that has to be made for the good of the league. Somewhere along the line they have to pick out some guy who has stepped out of the line one, two, three, four times too many and then step on him and say that's it and ban him, and I think with that people's jaws are going to drop for a minute, but I think they will soon get over it because I think the game will be better and better for it."

"There is always room for discretion because there are facts and circumstances," pointed out William Bennett. "But people who commit serious felonies should not be playing on professional sports teams. Period. They should not be there. I don't think that is a hard one. You can't go around beating up people, busting into places, kidnapping people, or raping women."

What, in the opinion of the authors, should the policy read like? Bright-line rules are hard to come by, but here are two:

1. Any player whose pre-NFL criminal history details a pattern of *arrests* for serious crimes should not be draft-eligible. Convictions aside, when an individual has demonstrated a pattern of run-ins with the law related to violence or drugs, he should not be permitted to earn hundreds of

thousands of dollars, carry the mantle of a role model, and have license to further disregard the law.

Examples of players in the book who would fall under this category include Corey Dillon, Ryan Tucker, Christian Peter, Charles Jordan, and Wayne Simmons.

2. Any player convicted of a "serious" crime (as defined in Chapter 1) involving violence or drugs *after* joining the NFL should be banned indefinitely.

Examples of players from the book who fall under this category include Lamar Thomas, Tim Barnett, Patrick Bates, and Cornelius Bennett.

While those two situations are straightforward, there clearly are many cases which call for discretion. The focus in such situations requires a sincere look beyond the singular incident in question in order to eliminate the gray areas. For those situations, the greater the extent of the prior record, the more likely the league should lean toward sanctions.

The answer can't be found in numbers. One DUI or two disorderly conducts can't be weighed against a rape, a domestic violence conviction, or kidnapping. It comes down to integrity. A pattern. A history of problems. The player who has been arrested seven times—even if never convicted—should not be playing. The player with no history who gets arrested—and perhaps convicted one time—deserves a second chance after substantive punishment.

Even NFL Players Association chief Gene Upshaw agrees that the commissioner must draw a line and stick to it. "We feel that as long as what is suggested protects the due process rights of players, that some kind of message would be a good thing," Upshaw said. "There are hundreds of players who are not criminals. They don't like being painted with the same brush."

"They want it to be a family game, but if you're going to employ criminals to get it done, I think it sends just a terrible message about your interest in the family," Rich Caster, now vice president of community relations for Bovis Construction Corporation, said. "It sends a terrible message to the guys back in college, the guys coming through high school, that it doesn't matter that you have a clean rap sheet, or that you stay out of trouble."

Caster, once the New York Jets' selection for participation in the NFL's feel-good United Way campaign, has one last concern: "If the league doesn't do something," he said, "they're going to run out of guys to do those United Way commercials. There won't be enough good guys left."

So now the stage is set. Opinion rests solidly in the corner of increased discipline. The commissioner now has a policy on which to lean. The research in this book lays bare the extent of the NFL's problem.

If the NFL wants more pros and fewer cons on the field, the commissioner can—and should—make it happen.

Epilogue

8:00 A.M., October 21, 1998
New York City

It was cold and blustery when twenty-three-year-old Rosie Gaynor, a publicity assistant at Warner Books, approached the revolving door leading inside the Time-Life Building on the corner of 50th and 6th Avenue in Manhattan. Her short, wind-blown blond hair barely reached the collar of her blue and white plaid blazer as she got on the elevator and took it to the eighth floor. Gaynor typically worked nine to five answering phones in the eight-foot by eight-foot cubicle she had been assigned to in the publicity department. But on this day she showed up an hour early. For the first time since being hired fresh out of Boston University a year earlier, she had been given a chance to handle the publicity on a major national book. Given her pick of titles to choose from, Gaynor—a big sports fan who grew up in Cincinnati—chose *Pros and Cons: The Criminals Who Play in the NFL.*

White boxes filled with copies of the book were stacked on the floor next to her desk. Across the top of each box was a bright orange strip carrying instructions to bookstores: "Strict on-sale date: October 21, 1998." Thousands of boxes of books had been shipped to stores weeks earlier and would simultaneously go on sale across the country over the next twenty-four hours. To coincide with the book's release in stores, Gaynor had scheduled more than twenty television and radio interviews for the authors during the day. A full-page color advertisement about *Pros and Cons* was in the current issue of *Sports Illustrated* and another ad was slated to run in *USA Today.* It was all part of Gaynor's plan for drumming up media interest in the book.

But the reporters whose attention Gaynor was courting the most, namely sports journalists, were the same ones the NFL wanted to discourage from paying attention to the book. And the league had a public relations plan of its own. The first hints of it had surfaced months earlier at the NFL's spring meetings in Orlando, Florida. Commissioner Tagliabue surprised reporters covering the meetings when he announced that the league had a new anti-crime policy that authorized him to punish players who commit violent crimes. While insisting for years that its players did not have a particular problem with off-the-field violence, the NFL suddenly unveils a new "get tough" policy to crack down on criminal players? The NFL beat writers who heard the announcement were unaware that just seven days earlier the authors had asked to meet with the commissioner in New York to discuss the research gathered for *Pros and Cons.*

The commissioner never sat down with the authors and a simple strategy emerged. First, reserve comment until after the book's release. Then admit there were a few bad apples in the league but point to the league's anti-crime policy as proof the NFL is taking a proactive stance on the issue.

But the league was unaware that the authors had checked the criminal histories of over five hundred randomly selected players and found that over 21 percent of them had been arrested or convicted of a serious crime. The statistic was not made known to the league until *USA Today*'s Larry Weisman revealed it in a book preview that ran the day before books went on sale. In the days following the book's release, media forums that rarely discuss sports—from the *New York Times* op-ed page to the Howard Stern show— began debating the statistic, which begged for a response from the commissioner's office. After nearly two weeks of stonewalling, the NFL finally dispatched its vice president of public relations, Greg Aiello, to respond on national television. But before Aiello went on the air, he placed a phone call to Alfred Blumstein at the School of Public Policy and Management at Carnegie Mellon University in Pittsburgh. Blumstein had written an appendix for the authors and endorsed the statistic. However, Aiello hoped to use something else Blumstein had written—namely that when it came to the specific crime of assault, NFL players are arrested at a lower rate than other adult males—to discredit the authors' claim that one in five NFL players had been arrested or convicted for a host of serious crimes.

"Mr. Aiello called," Blumstein told the authors, "and said, 'Doesn't this undercut the point of their book?' I said, 'Not necessarily. It depends on what your expectation is of these players and the context of their role model status.'"

The 21 percent arrest rate statistic was solid. Blumstein, the nation's leading engineer of statistical studies on crime, had said so in the book and was unwilling to waver when the NFL called. Without an expert to refute the statistic, the NFL and the players union had to say what Blumstein would not. "This research in this book is based on arrests, which is a dubious thing," Aiello told Court TV on November 6. "The professor at Carnegie Mellon . . . said the arrest rate for NFL players for assault is half of the rate compared to their counterparts in the general population. That right there tells you that football players are generally more well behaved than their counterparts in the population."

The NFL Players Association went even further. "The book is essentially claptrap," Players Association assistant executive director Doug Allen told CNN within days of Aiello's statement. "It is based on research that is stacked to a predetermined conclusion."

Allen went on to insist, "There is nothing wrong with a responsible and informed discussion on this issue. We're not defensive about it."

The real "claptrap," of course, was that the NFL was not defensive and looked forward to an informed discussion on its criminal players. When Ken Kalthoff, an investigative reporter from ABC affiliate WFTS in Tampa, Florida, called to talk to the Buccaneers about the book, he was turned away. "A spokesperson for the Buccaneers told me that he was not permitted to comment because NFL teams had been directed by the NFL not to discuss the book," Kalthoff told the authors.

Whether the NFL also influenced the major television networks that broadcast NFL games to ignore the book is not as clear. What is clear is that the 1998 season marked the first year of the NFL's record $18 billion television package with the networks. And ABC, Fox, and CBS never mentioned *Pros and Cons* on their many pregame football programs the entire season. The only program that came close was CBS's *NFL Today*. The show's producer Eric Mann and correspondent Armen Keteyian spoke to the authors numerous times about doing a piece on the book, before the show finally declined to go forward. "Journalistically, I thought it was the perfect opportunity to test the CBS-NFL partnership," Keteyian told the authors. "First, the book was certainly in the mainstream print media. Second, the NFL had taken what could be described as a proactive stance on the issue. They had an anti-violence program they could point to as trying to correct or deal with the problem. There was perfect balance between questions posed by the book and answers provided by the NFL. But for reasons which were never explained to me—and need not be—we did not do the story."

But it was ESPN's decision to avoid the book that was most curious. It offers twenty-four-hour sports coverage and *SportsCenter* is dedicated to sports "news." Lawrence Phillips's recurring off-the-field problems, which hardly qualify as a news bulletin, are a favorite news item on *SportsCenter.* Yet *SportsCenter* never mentioned *Pros and Cons* and its index of NFL criminals whose crimes had never before been detailed. An executive at ESPN dismissed the book as "old news." ESPN had 4.8 billion reasons to deem the book old news—it had paid that many dollars in cable rights from the NFL for broadcasting Sunday night games.

One sports reporter who did do the story was Mike Bruton, a columnist for the *Philadelphia Inquirer.* Bruton called the authors on October 28 and indicated he was considering doing a column about the book. Bruton, who is black, began the phone interview by suggesting the book had a racist tone to it. Since civil rights leader Reverend Jesse Jackson and African-American legal scholar Randall Kennedy had contributed to the book, Bruton was asked by the authors if he had actually read the book before reaching that conclusion. He sheepishly admitted that he had only had time to read the inside flap, insisting that he had just received his complimentary copy from Rosy Gaynor earlier that day.

The phone interview with Bruton lasted approximately one half hour. The next day, page one of the *Philadelphia Inquirer* carried the headline "Book on pros, crime invites stereotyping." In the article, Bruton equates the book with "some kind of racist manifesto" and accuses the authors of purposely making the first chapter of the book about white players assaulting a black man in order to mask a racial bias in the reporting. "The first chapter," Bruton wrote, "deals with Ryan Tucker, who along with several of his white TCU teammates, beat Bryan Boyd, a young black man." Bruton went on to write, "Putting Tucker out front . . . cries out, 'See, look, this is not racist.' "

There's one small problem. Bryan Boyd is white. Race was no more a factor in his assault or why we reported it than it is when NFL players commit crimes. (The authors appreciated the *Inquirer*'s front-page coverage of the book but would have preferred that the paper's columnist read even the first chapter carefully before levying a charge as serious as racism.)

Bruton's column appeared at the end of October, marking the end of a month that illustrated that crime by NFL players was not old news. In the month of October alone, the following events took place.

On October 1, Baltimore Ravens linebacker Cornell Brown was charged with driving under the influence near the Virginia Tech campus where he had attended college. Just five months earlier he had been convicted of assault and battery for his role in a brawl on the campus that left a man injured. He served a short jail term before beginning his rookie year with Baltimore.

On October 6, San Francisco 49ers owner Edward De-Bartolo, Jr., pleaded guilty in federal court to concealing an extortion plot connected with organized gambling.

On October 10, Lawrence Phillips was charged with striking a woman at a nightclub in Plantation, Florida.

On October 13, Cincinnati Bengals free safety and kick-off return man Tremain Mack was charged with drunken driving, resisting arrest, and driving without a license. He had to be subdued with chemical spray after he pushed the arresting officer. The arrest landed Mack in jail for a year for violating his parole—just one year earlier he had been arrested and pleaded no contest to drunken driving just outside Cincinnati. It was his sixth arrest and his third involving alcohol.

On October 20, federal authorities in Miami announced that Atlanta Falcons All-Pro wide receiver Tony Martin was under investigation for allegedly laundering money for a convicted drug dealer who had spent seven years in prison.

The same day, former NFL great Lawrence Taylor was arrested in Florida and charged with buying crack cocaine from an undercover cop.

The following day, California authorities charged Oakland Raiders head coach John Gruden with driving under the influence. A highway patrolman reported that he stopped Gruden's car after witnessing him speeding and weaving across lanes. According to the officer, Gruden, who was on his way home from a party celebrating the Raiders' victory over the Chargers and could not remember his own zip code, said, "Hey, you know, I'm the coach of the Oakland Raiders and I'm just in a hurry to get home."

Within hours of Gruden being charged, St. Louis authorities filed charges against Rams rookie linebacker Leonard

Little. Police accused Little of getting drunk at a party before plowing his sport-utility vehicle into the side of another vehicle and killing the driver, a forty-seven-year-old mother. Facing charges of drunken driving and vehicular manslaughter, Little was encouraged to get back to football. "The best way for him to continue the healing process is by going back to work," his attorney, Scott Rosenbloom, told the Associated Press.

Amid this stream of alcohol-related arrests, the NFL proudly announced on its web site NFL.com that NFL International had signed a two-year agreement with Coors, making the beer company one of the largest sponsors of NFL activities in the United Kingdom. Under the terms of the agreement, Coors will sponsor broadcasts of NFL games in the UK and be the official shirt sponsor of the Scottish Claymores.

On October 23, a jury ordered Kansas City Chiefs defensive end Leslie O'Neal to pay damages for sexual battery against a topless dancer. Also on October 23, New Orleans Saints rookie Julian Pittman was jailed in Tallahassee, Florida, for violating his probation on a 1997 burglary charge to which he pleaded no contest. Shortly after the Saints drafted Pittman in '98, a woman accused him of rape—a charge that was later dismissed when she declined to go forward in the case. Authorities did, however, charge Pittman with buying alcohol for a minor, visiting a bar, and drinking. "What'd he do? He violated his probation," Saints coach Mike Ditka complained in defense of his player. "We have a lot of people in our society do a lot of worse things. Is it fair? I don't think so, I'm sorry. Especially when the person [alleged rape victim] said she didn't want to press any charges. But then you've got someone else there, a female district attorney, who is a crusader so she crusades."

Within hours of Pittman being escorted out of a Florida court and off to jail, Tampa Bay Buccaneers defensive end Tyoka Jackson was escorted into a Florida court to be arraigned following his arrest in Tampa on a charge of soliciting sex from an undercover cop.

In the face of this onslaught of court activity, Greg Aiello appropriately appeared on Court TV and insisted that the league's new crime policy was the answer to these sorts of problems. "The disciplinary part of the policy began July 1 of this season," Aiello said. "Any convictions or guilty pleas beginning July 1 will result in disciplinary action."

"If someone now is convicted of a violent crime, what is supposed to happen?" the interviewer asked Aiello, seeking clarification.

"If they are *convicted* of a crime, the policy will call for punishment from the NFL," Aiello insisted.

To hear Aiello explain it, all the players who had been arrested in October would be punished if they pleaded guilty or were convicted at trial. But three days before Aiello made this statement, the NFL's policy got its first true test. On November 3, New Orleans Saints receiver Keith Poole was sentenced to two years' probation after pleading guilty to assaulting a man with a golf club in LaCrosse, Wisconsin. The case fit the scenario described by Aiello perfectly: it involved a guilty plea to a violent crime committed after July 1.

So was Poole suspended? No. He saw no interruption in his on-field play. So much for the new policy. The more things change, the more they stay the same.

"I don't think that the NFL should be so arrogant as to deny somebody the opportunity to [work]," Doug Allen told HBO's *Real Sports* when questioned about the NFL's unwillingness to punish players for violent crimes. "We leave it up to a body of law and a system of judges and juries to decide those issues."

If the NFL should not punish players who commit crimes, then why was it touting a policy that authorized it to do just that?

Although the NFL was not taking action against criminal players, individual teams started quietly dismissing some of the key players whose criminal exploits had been featured in *Pros and Cons*.

Patrick Bates (Chapter 2) was the first to go. The Oakland Raiders released him at the outset of the season.

On November 14, the Miami Dolphins unceremoniously released wide receiver Charles Jordan (Chapter 8), the former gang leader for the Bloods. The night before Jordan was released, he was arrested for beating a police officer in south Florida. "We'll let the judicial system run its course, but he has no future with this team," Jimmy Johnson told reporters.

On November 17, the Kansas City Chiefs released starting linebacker Wayne Simmons (Chapter 3) after his part in a flurry of unnecessary roughness penalties that plagued the end of the Chiefs-Broncos *Monday Night Football* game on November 16. No other Chiefs players—including Derrick Thomas, who was flagged for two personal fouls on consecutive plays—were released. "I think my past had a significant part in using me as a scapegoat," Simmons admitted, making reference to his lengthy arrest record detailed for the first time in *Pros and Cons*. "I heard something about the book. There's been some accusations out there and I know they are false." (Simmons was signed briefly by the Buffalo Bills, who released him at the end of the regular season.)

Then on February 17, after Cornelius Bennett (Chapter 2) led the Atlanta Falcons to its first Super Bowl, the team dismissed the five-time All-Pro. The Associated Press deemed Bennett's release a "stunning move." Then on February 26 the Falcons terminated the contract of their top receiver, All-Pro Tony Martin. He had been charged two weeks earlier by federal authorities with five counts of laundering money for a convicted drug dealer.

What prompted a Super Bowl team to cut two of its most high-profile players?

On the eve of the Super Bowl, Falcons star defensive back Eugene Robinson—known by his temmates as "the Prophet" for his prediction that the Falcons would go all the way to the Super Bowl—was arrested in Miami for offering an undercover officer $40 for oral sex. By the time he was released from the Dade County Police Department it was nearly midnight. He barely slept the remainder of the night, instead staying up to consult with coaches, teammates, and family members. Then the reliable veteran was badly beaten on numerous key plays during the team's defeat to Denver.

The shock of Robinson's arrest was unavoidably on the minds of the Falcons. Just hours before his arrest, Robinson received the Bart Starr Award from the religious group Athletes in Action. The award is given to the player who displays "high moral character." Few NFL players were touted as a bigger role model than Eugene Robinson, who returned his Bart Starr award after the Super Bowl. On March 2, the Dade County prosecutor offered Robinson a pretrial diversion program that would remove the arrest from his record if he complied with the terms of probation.

" 'Role model' is a devalued term in our society," Doug Allen told HBO just six days before the Robinson arrest. Call Doug Allen a prophet.

Jeff Benedict and Don Yaeger, March 1999

Acknowledgments

The amount of time required to research this book called for tremendous sacrifice and patience on the part of our families. First and foremost, we thank them for their support.

Nor could the research have been as thorough without the hard work and efficiency of a core of young research assistants J.R. Mastrioanni, an able and efficient researcher, tracked down hundreds of pages of background information on players. And Ron Cochran, a graduating senior at Northeastern University, worked with the authors to design and maintain the computerized index of all the NFL players and their crimes. Craig Ball and Charity and Rachel Benedict spent hours visiting courthouses and retrieving court documents.

Our agent, Basil Kane, was a source of inspiration from the outset.

Editor Rick Wolff was absolutely great to work alongside. His associates at Warner Books were likewise a pleasure to collaborate with: Rob McMahon, Emi Battaglia, Madeleine Schachter, and Julie Saltman. And a special thanks to Elizabeth McNamara.

One of the authors is particularly grateful to his classmates at the New England School of Law who helped him get through his second year of law school while writing this book. Bill Byrne, Ray Woeffler, and Detective John Whiting of the Pawtucket Police Department, thank you. And most notably, Jeff Tomlinson, a true friend who will make a far better lawyer than the author.

Countless law enforcement agencies provided the authors access to their facilities and granted exceptional amounts of time for questioning. Not all are mentioned here, but a few are: the Drug Interdiction Task Force in Rockwall, Texas; the Drug Enforcement Agency in East St. Louis; the U.S. Justice Department; the Sex Crimes Unit at the Buffalo Police Department; the University of Florida Police Department; the Seattle Police Department; the Alachua County Sheriff's Office in Gainesville, Florida; the Lincoln, Nebraska, Police Department; the Rockwall County District Attorney's Office; the Dade County Police Department; the Fulton County Sheriff's Department; the Seminole County Prosecutor's Office; the Chatham County District Attorney's Office in Savannah, Georgia; the King County Prosecuting Attorney's Office in Seattle; the Office of the State Attorney in Fort Lauderdale, Florida; the Tarrant County [Texas] District Attorney's Office; the North Royalton Police Department, the Eden Prairie Police Department, the Bloomington Police Department, and the Minneapolis Police Department, all in Minnesota; the University of Arkansas Police Department; the Washington County Prosecutor's Office in Fayetteville, Arkansas.

Records clerks from across the country were most helpful to us. There are too many to name individually, but a few who donated a particular amount of their time on our behalf include: Marti Maxwell at the Municipal Court of Seattle, three police records clerks at the Minneapolis, Eden Prairie, and Bloomington, Minnesota police departments, Vallerie at the Fulton County Superior Court, Lieutenant Mann at the Sex Crimes Unit in the Buffalo Police Department, and the folks at the University of Florida Police Department.

We are appreciative of the time given to us by members of the President's Domestic Violence Council. Also, the NFL Players Association, Empower America, the Rainbow PUSH Coalition, and members of the United States House and Senate.

Jack McDevitt and Donald Cochran, professors at the Northeastern University College of Criminal Justice, were instrumental in helping design the methodology for our research. And Professor Alfred Blumstein at Carnegie Mellon was a source of guidance.

Appendix I

Below is a partial list of the players who were discovered by the authors to have a criminal history.

Player	Team	Charge	Disposition
Adams, Mike (WR)	Pittsburgh	assault	charge dismissed
Alexander, Elijah (LB)	Indianapolis	theft	charge dismissed
Armstrong, Tyji (TE)	Dallas	aggravated battery	acquitted
Bates, Patrick (DB)	Atlanta	assault	charge dismissed
		criminal trespass	charge dismissed
		kidnapping	pled to reduced charge
		aggravated assault	pled to assault
		false imprisonment	pled to reduced charge
		reckless conduct	pled to damage to property
Beamon, Willie (DB)	NY Giants	assault	convicted
Bennett, Cornelius (LB)	Atlanta	rape	pled to reduced charge
		sodomy	pled to reduced charge
		unlawful imprisonment	pled to reduced charge
		sexual abuse	pled to reduced charge

Player	Team	Charge	Disposition
Bieniemy, Eric (RB)	Cincinnati	disorderly conduct	convicted
Blades, Bennie (DB)	Seattle	DUI	acquitted
Blades, Brian (WR)	Seattle	homicide	acquitted
		DUI	pled to reduced charge
Bradley, Freddie (RB)	San Diego	statutory rape	acquitted
Brandon, Michael (DE)	San Francisco	robbery	charge dropped
Brown, Derek (RB)	New Orleans	violating restraining order	charge dropped
		trespassing	charge dropped
		domestic violence	charge dropped
Brown, Gary (OT)	Green Bay	concealed weapon	pled no contest
		DUI	pled no contest
Brown, Gilbert (DT)	Green Bay	domestic violence	pled guilty
Cain, Joseph (LB)	Seattle	carrying concealed gun	charge dismissed with prejudice
Carter, Dale (DB)	Kansas City	assault	convicted
		possession of a gun	convicted
		weapons probation violation	convicted
		assault	charge dismissed
Carter, Dexter (RB)	San Francisco	trespassing after warning	pled no contest
		assault	convicted
		assault	convicted
Chamberlain, Byron (TE)	Denver	domestic violence	pled to reduced charge
Christy, Jeff (OL)	Minnesota	boating while intoxicated	pled guilty
Clavelle, Shannon (DE)	Green Bay	domestic violence	charge dismissed
Cobb, Reginald (RB)	NY Jets	resisting arrest	charge dropped
Copeland, Russell (WR)	Philadelphia	domestic violence	pled guilty
Cothran, Jeff (RB)	Cincinnati	DUI	convicted
		DUI	pled guilty
		felony theft	charge dropped

Player	Team	Charge	Disposition
Craver, Aaron (RB)	San Diego	grand theft property	convicted
		making false statements	convicted
Darling, James (LB)	Philadelphia	assault	pled guilty
		burglary	pled guilty
		theft	convicted
		DUI	pled to reduced charge
		vandalism	convicted
DeLong, Greg (TE)	Minnesota	boating while intoxicated	pled guilty
Dillon, Corey (RB)	Cincinnati	DUI	pled to reduced charge
		possession stolen property	pled guilty
		theft	charge dismissed
		intent to sell cocaine	convicted
		reckless endangerment	pled guilty
		obstructing public servant	pled guilty
		resisting arrest	pled guilty
		obstructing public servant	pled guilty
		assault	convicted
		criminal trespass	convicted
		assault	acquitted
		malicious mischief	convicted
Dowden, Corey (DB)	San Francisco	prostitution solicitation	pled no contest
Everitt, Steven (OL)	Philadelphia	possessing drug paraphernalia	charge dropped
Fenner, Derrick (RB)	Oakland	resisting arrest	charge dismissed
		disorderly conduct	pled to reduced charge
		murder	charge dropped
		attempted murder	charge dropped
		unlawful use of gun	charge dropped
		possession of a gun	pled to reduced charge
		possession of cocaine	pled to reduced charge

Player	Team	Charge	Disposition
Fields, Mark (LB)	New Orleans	DUI/drugs in vehicle	pled to reduced charges
Floyd, William (RB)	San Francisco	fraud	charge dismissed
		resisting arrest	charge dismissed
		DUI	acquitted
		gun possession	convicted
Footman, Dan (DE)	Baltimore	dealing in stolen property	charge dismissed
Fuller, Corey (DB)	Minnesota	domestic violence	pled no contest
		resisting arrest w/ violence	charge dropped
		petty theft	entered pretrial diversion program
		larceny	entered pretrial diversion program
Garner, Charlie (RB)	Philadelphia	cocaine possession	juvenile record unavailable
Gaskins, Percell (LB)	St. Louis	assault	charge dropped
Grasmanis, Paul (DT)	Chicago	battery	charge dismissed
Harris, James (DE)	St. Louis	domestic violence	pled guilty
		domestic violence	pled guilty
		conspiracy to sell cocaine	charge dismissed
Heyward, Craig (RB)	St. Louis	disorderly conduct	pled guilty
		public drunkenness	pled guilty
		assault	convicted
Irvin, Michael (WR)	Dallas	marijuana possession	charge dismissed
		cocaine possession	pled guilty
Jennings, Keith (TE)	Chicago	domestic violence	convicted
Jervey, Travis (RB)	Green Bay	marijuana possession	charge dropped
Johnson, Bill (DL)	Pittsburgh	DUI	convicted
		DUI	convicted
Johnson, Leon (RB)	NY Jets	DUI	convicted
		DUI	convicted

Player	Team	Charge	Disposition
Johnson, Melvin (DB)	Tampa Bay	DUI	convicted
Jones, Damon (TE)	Jacksonville	manufacturing and placing a bomb	pled guilty
		vandalism	convicted
Jordan, Charles (WR)	Miami	murder	charge dismissed
		robbery	exonerated
		auto theft	pled no contest to reduced charge
		threatening a witness	pled guilty
Kennedy, Cortez (DT)	Seattle	domestic violence	charge dropped
Lewis, Ray (LB)	Baltimore	domestic violence	charge dropped
Lynch, Lorenzo (DB)	Oakland	assault	convicted
Mack, Tremain (DB)	Cincinnati	battery on police officer	pled guilty
		resisting arrest w/violence	pled to reduced charge
		DUI	convicted of reduced charge
		DUI	pled to reduced charge
		DUI	convicted
Malamala, Siupeli (OL)	NY Jets	property destruction	deferred sentence
		trespassing	deferred sentence
		reckless endangerment	deferred sentence
Malone, Van (DB)	Detroit	burglary	completed deferred adjudication
Martin, Kelvin (WR)	Dallas	carrying a weapon	completed pretrial diversion
McCoy, Tony (DE)	Indianapolis	sexual assault	charge dismissed
		aggravated assault	charge dismissed
		sexual battery	charge dismissed
		kidnapping	charge dismissed
		aggravated battery	charge dismissed
McGinest, Willie (LB)	New England	false imprisonment	acquitted by jury
		battery	acquitted by jury

Player	Team	Charge	Disposition
Meggett, David (KR)	New England	sexual assault	charge dropped
		prostitution solicitation	acquitted
		domestic violence	acquitted
Mickell, Darren (DT)	New Orleans	grand larceny	convicted
Mims, Chris (DE)	San Diego	DUI	acquitted
Moon, Warren (QB)	Seattle	domestic violence	acquitted
Morris, Byron (RB)	Baltimore	marijuana possession	pled guilty
Moulds, Eric (WR)	Buffalo	domestic violence	pled guilty to harassment
		assault	pled guilty
Neal, Lorenzo (RB)	NY Jets	DUI	pled no contest
Newton, Nate (OL)	Dallas	sexual assault	acquitted
Nunn, Freddie Joe (LB)	Phoenix	domestic violence	charge dismissed
Perry, Gerald (OL)	St. Louis	aggravated rape	acquitted
		prostitution solicitation	pled guilty
		prostitution solicitation	convicted
		assault and battery	acquitted
		false imprisonment	acquitted
		impersonating police	acquitted
		assault	acquitted
		sexual assault	pled guilty
Peter, Christian (DL)	NY Giants	sexual assault	pled no contest
		assault	pled guilty
Phillips, Lawrence (RB)	St. Louis	DUI	pled no contest
		domestic violence	convicted
		assault	entered pretrial diversion program
		disorderly conduct	pled no contest
		assault	pled no contest
		trespassing	pled no contest
Plummer, Jake (QB)	Phoenix	sexual abuse	pled no contest
		sexual abuse	pled no contest
		sexual abuse	pled no contest
		sexual abuse	pled no contest

Player	Team	Charge	Disposition
Pritchard, Mike (WR)	Seattle	vehicular assault	pled guilty to reduced charge
		DUI	pled guilty
Randle, John (DT)	Minnesota	domestic violence	charge dropped
		domestic violence	charge dropped
Rison, Andre (WR)	Green Bay	disorderly conduct	paid a fine
		aggravated assault	charge dismissed
		gun possession	charge dismissed
		discharging a firearm	charge dismissed
Rucker, Keith (DT)	Washington	domestic violence	charge dropped
Ryans, Larry (WR)	New England	disorderly conduct	pled no contest
		resisting arrest	pled no contest
Sanders, Deion (DB)	Dallas	aggravated assault	pled to reduced charge
		disorderly conduct	pled no contest to reduced charge
		battery	pled no contest
		trespassing	convicted
		resisting arrest	acquitted
		leaving accident scene	acquitted
Sapp, Warren (DL)	Tampa Bay	marijuana possession	charge dropped
Sawyer, Corey (DB)	Cincinnati	fraud	entered pretrial diversion program
		perjury	pled no contest
Shelling, Chris (DB)	Cincinnati	marijuana possession	convicted
Shepherd, Leslie (WR)	Washington	assault	pled guilty
		assault	acquitted
Silvan, Nilo (WR)	Tampa Bay	statutory rape	charges dropped
Simmons, Wayne (LB)	Green Bay	DUI	convicted
		assault and battery	charge dropped
Smith, Bruce (DE)	Buffalo	DUI	convicted/overturned
		refusing blood alcohol test	convicted
Smith, Fernando (DE)	Minnesota	concealed weapon	convicted
Smith, Lamar (RB)	Seattle	vehicular assault	pled guilty
		sexual assault	charge dropped

Player	Team	Charge	Disposition
Spellman, Alonzo (DL)	Chicago	gun possession	charge dismissed
Spikes, Irving (RB)	Miami	domestic violence	pled no contest
Strong, Mack (RB)	Seattle	DUI	convicted of reduced charge
Stubblefield, Dana (DT)	San Francisco	assaulting police officer	charge dropped
		resisting arrest	charge dropped
Stubbs, Daniel (DE)	Miami	evading detention	convicted
Thomas, Broderick (LB)	Dallas	gun possession	charge dropped
Thomas, Lamar (WR)	Miami	aggravated battery	pled guilty
		aggravated battery	pled guilty
		battery	charge dropped
Thompson, Bennie (DB)	Baltimore	DUI	convicted
Tuaolo, Esera (DT)	Minnesota	DUI	charge dismissed
Tucker, Ryan (OL)	St. Louis	aggravated assault	pled no contest
		assault	paid a fine
Tuinei, Mark (OT)	Dallas	assault	convicted
Walsh, Christopher (WR)	Minnesota	DUI	pled to reduced charge
Warren, Chris (RB)	Seattle	assault	charge dropped
Watkins, Kendell (TE)	Dallas	carrying a gun	nonadjudication of guilt
Wheeler, Mark (DT)	New England	aggravated assault	entered pretrial diversion program
		battery	entered pretrial diversion program
Wilkinson, Dan (DT)	Cincinnati	domestic violence	pled no contest
Williams, Dan (DE)	Denver	threatening a woman	charge dropped
Williams, Erik (OL)	Dallas	sexual assault	charge dropped
		DUI	pled no contest
Williams, Harvey (RB)	Oakland	aggravated assault	pled to reduced charge
		domestic violence	convicted
		assault	acquitted
		domestic violence	charge dropped

Player	Team	Charge	Disposition
Williams, Moe (RB)	Minnesota	rape	charge dropped
		battery	charge dropped
Williams, Tyrone (DB)	Green Bay	assault	pled guilty
		unlawful use of a gun	pled guilty
Woodson, Rod (DB)	Pittsburgh	battery	acquitted
		aiding battery	acquitted
Wooten, Tito (DB)	NY Giants	domestic violence	charge dropped
		larceny	pled to reduced charge
		domestic violence	paid a fine
		theft	charge dropped
		battery of police officer	pled guilty
		disorderly conduct	charge dropped

The second column notes each player's team affiliation as of the 1996-1997 season, the season that formed the basis for the authors' statistical study.

Convictions are reflected as of August 1998; further developments may have occurred in specific cases.

It should be noted that dropped or dismissed charges can mean many different things. Sometimes charges are dropped for lack of evidence. Some dismissals were on condition that a player participate in some type of counseling program or anger-management course. And many of the cases that were dropped—particularly those involving domestic violence and sexual assault—were on account of the victims' wishes.

Please note in addition that there are several dozen players with arrest records who are not listed above.

In the hardcover edition of this book, we inadvertently referred in this Appendix to a former Buffalo Bill tight-end who has the identical name, Pat Fitzgerald, as a former Dallas Cowboy linebacker. The reference was *not* intended to allude to the former Buffalo Bill.

Appendix II

Summary of Alfred Blumstein's Report

After the authors completed their research for this book, the statistical data were turned over to Carnegie Mellon University Professor Alfred Blumstein for analysis. In return, he provided the authors a seven-page report. "This selection criterion [used by the authors]," he wrote, "should be independent of whether any individual had an arrest history, and so the sample can be seen as reasonably representative of the players in the NFL." In sum, the statistics generated by the authors are both valid and representative of the NFL population.

In light of the challenges posed by trying to find a similarly situated group of adult males to compare NFL players to for the purpose of statistical analysis (see Authors' Note), Professor Blumstein compared the arrest rates of blacks and whites in the general population to the arrest rates of blacks and whites in the NFL. It is important to understand that this comparison does not take into account other socioeconomic factors such as income or education level attained. The only factor that Professor Blumstein controlled for was race.

Also, it is important to understand that the arrest rates comparisons between blacks and whites in the general population to blacks and whites in the NFL are based only on the crime of assault. Due to arrests for assault being the most commonly reported crime involving NFL players, this crime was selected for comparison with arrests for assault in the general population.

A Summary of Alfred Blumstein's Report

Jeff Benedict and Don Yaeger have collected an intriguing array of information about the adult criminal arrest records of the men who populate the NFL. They drew a reasonably representative sample of the players, and found that 21 percent of them had experienced an arrest for something more serious than a minor brush with the law. This number sounds very high, and so raised for them the question of how unusual this arrest experience may be. They were interested in having some assessment of this level of arrest experience, and they contacted me to explore that issue.

I started the inquiry by harking back to some estimates Elizabeth Graddy and I had made in 1981. We calculated that the chance that a male in a U.S. city of 250,000 population or more (reasonably representative of NFL cities) would be arrested some time in his life for one of the seven "index" crimes (homicide, forcible rape, robbery, aggravated assault, burglary, larceny/theft, or motor vehicle theft) was rather high—23 percent—with the likelihood varying considerably between the races, 51 percent for blacks and 14 percent for whites. That estimate includes arrests as a juvenile, where most people experience their first arrests. The NFL data does *not* include juvenile arrests.

ESTIMATION OF RATES FOR VIOLENT CRIMES

Benedict and Yaeger reported that they had data on 509 NFL players and that 109 of those players had accumulated one or more serious arrests, for a total of 264 arrests.

Perhaps the most interesting crimes attributed to the NFL players are the "violent assaults," those designated as assaults (both domestic violence and other assaults). Here we have a population of men who earn outstanding incomes based on their skill and readiness to engage in vigorous albeit regulated assault with opponents on the football field, and so it is of some interest to see to what extent they exploit those particular skills in other situations where the ground rules are quite different.

The numbers for these two kinds of offenses are quite close: 31 players were arrested for each of those offenses, with a total of 42 arrests for assault and 45 for domestic violence. Using these numbers, I calculated the rates at which those events occur. The rate of arrest for assault in the U.S. population varies across racial groups considerably, with the rate for blacks being about three times that for whites, and so it is important to examine the arrest rates for assault by NFL players separately by racial groups. This is particularly important because the race mix in the NFL sample is very different from that in the general population: blacks comprised 78 percent of those identified as black or white. Thus, of the 399 black players in the sample, 96 of them (24 percent) had an arrest for something; of the 93 whites in the sample, 8 of them (8 percent) had an arrest.

There was an additional group of 17 players (3 percent) who were not analyzed further because they were either of another race (usually Pacific Islander) or whose race was unknown.

Information was unavailable on the race of the particular players arrested for assault, and so we assume that the race of players charged with assault is similar to the total arrest distribution, yielding an estimated 77.43 total assault arrests for blacks and 5.5 for whites. Dividing these total estimated arrests by the number of players in each group provides an estimate of the total assault rate of 19,406 per 100,000 population (the population base normally used for arrest-rate calculation) for the black players and 5,729 per 100,000 population for the white players. But these NFL players accumulated these rates over several years, approximately four years of college and three years in the NFL, so that we can calculate an average *annual* rate by dividing by 7. Thus, the average annual rate of arrest for assault per 100,000 population is 3,006 for black players (just over 3 percent) and 951 for white players (1 percent).

COMPARISON WITH U.S. POPULATION RATES

These estimates of assault arrest rates for the NFL population provide a basis for comparison with the arrest rates for assault in the U.S. population. To do that, we use the data in the Uniform Crime Reports (UCR), published annually by the FBI. The UCR reports do not categorize arrest rates by domestic violence or nondomestic assault, but rather as "aggravated assault" (the more serious kind) and "simple (or other) assault." In 1996, the FBI estimates that there were a total of 521,570 arrests for aggravated assault and 1,329,000 arrests for other assaults, for a total of 1,850,570 assaults. These numbers are not partitioned by age, race, or sex, but the UCR does report number of arrests recorded for each of these aspects by reporting police departments (representing about 70 percent of the U.S. population in 1996). By scaling up these reports to represent the full U.S. population, and by taking account of the gender (80.4 percent male) and race (36.8 percent black and 63.2 percent white among the whites and blacks) distribution for all assaults, we estimate that in 1996, there were 18,816 assaults by twenty-year-old black males and 32,314 by twenty-year-old white males. Dividing these by the Census Bureau estimates that the U.S. population in 1996 had 269,199 black twenty-year-old males and 1,463,139 white twenty-year-old males, we estimate that the arrest rate for assault in the general population of twenty-year-old males is 6,990 per 100,000 for black males and 2,209 (just over 2 percent) for white males. The rates will be very similar for the other ages in the NFL sample.

Thus when we compare these rates with those calculated in the previous section for the NFL sample we find that the arrest rates for assaults for blacks and whites in the NFL sample are just below half the rates of their counterparts in the general U.S. population.

DISCUSSION

The previous analysis compared the assault arrest rate for NFL players with that of young males in the U.S., controlling only for race. There must be questions about gaps in the data about very visible football players, both in their college days as well as in their professional careers. Do they attract an undue amount of taunting, leading to violent response? Do they attract greater police attention, leading to arrest? Or does their local hero status insulate them from arrest compared to the general population?

There are also questions about the appropriate comparison group. Some suggest that individuals of a similar age earning comparable income (say, an average of at least $200,000 per year) are the appropriate comparison group. But folks in this income bracket who have completed four years of college would tend to be corporate executives or professionals, undoubtedly of a very different socioeconomic status, and much more likely to be exemplars of traditional antiviolence middle-class norms. Thus, even if the data were available for such a group—which it is not—comparison with them seems less than appropriate.

There are still further questions about the appropriate level of violence. Some would suggest that NFL players should carry a strong burden of being role models for young men and guys, and should display assault rates much less than half that of their racial counterparts in the general population. This book and these analyses provide some information for addressing those issues.

Source Notes

Authors' Note

Interviews with Professor Alfred Blumstein, NFL spokesperson Greg Aiello, and J.R. Mastroianni.

1

Crime Pays

(1) "an organ donor" Interview with Sara Boyd, December 6, 1997.

(1) "I know he heard me." Ibid.

(1) "Bryan Boyd was beaten" Offense/Incident Report, May 11, 1996.

(1) assaulted him the previous year Confidentiality agreement signed June 10, 1996.

(2) compensation for medical injuries Copy of personal check dated May 28, 1996.

(2) "beat up last Thanksgiving?" Offense/Incident Report, May 11, 1996.

(2) "a worse assault" Interview with Sara Boyd, January 20, 1998.

(3) run over by a car Police photographs viewed by the authors.

(3) "This kid is dying." Interview with Sara Boyd, December 6, 1997.

(3) permanent brain damage   Crist, p. 2

(3) death or serious bodily injury   Indictment No. 0623388, May 11, 1996.

(3) "run its course"   Moran, p. 1

(4) "that's a positive"   Blackistone, p. C1.

(5) "this guy does"   Ibid.

(6) "re-enter the league"   Domowitch, p. 75.

(7) "A player has rights too."   Brubaker, "Violence Follows Some," p.1.

(9) "is unusual?"   Interview with Greg Aiello, February 1998.

(12) "in the right places"   Interview with William Bennett, April 24, 1998.

2

Crimes and Punishments

(13) "Start out with a problem"   Interview with Dan Reeves, February 26, 1998.

(14) "around the apartment"   Fulton County Police Report, March 19, 1997.

(14) "not have those situations"   Interview with Dan Reeves, February 26, 1998.

(15) criminal trespass in 1989   Case No. 103,520, Galveston County, Texas, June 9, 1990.

(15) "lives have changed"   Interview with Dan Reeves, February 26, 1998.

(16) "kill them too"   Fulton County Police Report, April 16, 1997.

(17) "their home before"   Interview with Jean Nettuno, November 19, 1997.

(18) "on our football team"   Interview with Dan Reeves, February 26, 1998.

(18) "good for him too"   Ibid.

(19) "than anything else"   Interview with Ian Greengross, March 6, 1998.

(19) "unlawful imprisonment"   General Offense Report, Buffalo Police Department, May 19, 1997.

(19) "take its course"   Interview with Dan Reeves, February 26, 1998.

(20) September 9, 1997   Transcript of Record, Docket No. 97M-18574, City Court of the County of Erie, New York, March 2, 1998.

(20) "the latter's consent"   New York Penal Law, Sec. 130.20, p. 27.

(20) "take any action"   Interview with Dan Reeves, February 26, 1998.

(20) "what to do"   Associated Press, September 10, 1997.

(21) "Cornelius had told me"   Interview with Dan Reeves, February 26, 1998.

(21) "by the commissioner"   Associated Press, "Reeves," September 10, 1997.

(22) "incident was concerned"   Interview with Dan Reeves, February 26, 1998.

(23) "clothes, which I did"   Supporting Deposition, Buffalo Police Department, September 4, 1997.

(23) "deviate sexual intercourse"   New York Penal Law, Sec. 130.50, p. 57.

(23) "and the penis"   Ibid., p. 58.

(23) "asked to do so"   General Offense Report, May 19, 1997.

(23) "pain and lacerations"   Information, State of New York v. Cornelius Bennett, September 4, 1997.

(23) line drawn through them   Ibid.

(23) "following the attack"   Police Case Log, attached to General Offense Report, May 19, 1997.

(24) "that night altogether"   Associated Press, "Bennett Sentenced," February 26, 1998.

(24) "but in Atlanta"   Buffalo Daily News, March 3, 1998.

(25) "the same sentence"   Interview with Judge Robert T. Russell, March 5, 1998.

(25) "up to the league"   Interview with Dan Reeves, February 26, 1998.

(26) two-month-old daughter   *USA Today,* May 1, 1998.

(26) guilty to battery   Final Disposition, State of Georgia v. Patrick James Bates, Case No. 292765, April 2, 1998.

(26) with the Oakland Raiders   "Raiders Sign Free Agents," Raiders. com., May 18, 1998.

3

Risky Business

(27) battery against his wife   Complaint, State of Kansas v. Timothy A. Barnett, Case No. K-70550, March 23, 1992.

(27) disorderly conduct   Journal Entry, State of Kansas v. Timothy A. Barnett, June 25, 1992.

(28) Colt Python handgun   Complaint, State of Kansas v. Timothy A. Barnett, Case No. 93CR1741, June 5, 1993.

(28) wide receiver to jail   Journal Entry, State of Kansas v. Timothy A. Barnett, January 4, 1994.

(28) "the playoffs Saturday"   Rizzo, p. D3.

(29) "comfortable with that"   Ibid.

(29) "breaking the law"   Ibid.

(29) "rest of the season"   Ibid.

(30) "the toast of the town"   Pulliam, "Barnett Makes Most," p.C10.

(30) "Do you want any service?"   Transcript from Preliminary Hearing, State of Wisconsin v. Timothy A. Barnett, Case No. F-942749, August 8, 1994.

(31) "Ain't nobody been in this?"   Criminal Complaint, State of Wisconsin v. Timothy A. Barnett, July 28, 1994.

(31) "me started hurting"   Transcript from Preliminary Hearing, August 8, 1994.

(32) "team at this time"   Pulliam, "Receiver Barnett Released," p. D7.

(32) three years in prison   Disposition and Sentencing, State of Wisconsin v. Timothy A. Barnett, August 22, 1995.

4

Born Again

(49) "going to be a criminal"   Carter, p. C1.

(49) "records as juveniles"   Interview with Linda Szymanski, February 6, 1998.

(50) "particularly inner cities"   Interview with Roger Headrick, February 16, 1996.

(51) "each case individually"   Interview with Leigh Steinberg, October 1997.

(52) Sexually molesting her   Almond, p. C10.

(53) "sparse at best"   Interview with Vicki Francies-Siedow, March 10, 1998.

(55) "for selling narcotics"   Allen, p. C1.

(55) "That is poor information."   Archer

(56) "needed to help him"   Interview with Al Roberts, February 19, 1998.

(56) the *Seattle Times* article   Archer, "First Day No Picnic," p. C1.

(56) "push it too far"   Interview with Todd Archer, February 6, 1998.

(57) "place to be"   Ibid.

(58) "drug-related stuff lately"   Interview with Al Roberts, February 19, 1998.

(58) he pleaded guilty   Statement of Defendant on Plea of Guilty, City of Seattle v. Corey James Dillon, Case No. 197842, July 11, 1994.

(58) violating the law   Criminal Complaint, City of Seattle v. Corey James Dillon, Case No. 202034, June 14, 1994.

(58) malicious mischief   First Amended Information, State of Washington v. Corey James Dillon, Case No. 92-8-05904-7.

(59) "that's what I thought"   Letter dated June 9, 1992, contained in Superior Court criminal file.

(59) owner of the car   Order of Disposition Information, State of Washington v. Corey James Dillon, Case No. 92-8-05904-7, December 8, 1992.

(60) between 1987 and 1992   Information accessed via computerized docket sheet listing at Juvenile Court in Seattle.

(61) "to wit: cocaine"   Information, State of Washington v. Corey James Dillon, Case No. S8236, February 13, 1989.

(61) a rock of cocaine   Certification for Determination of Probable Cause, contained in criminal case file on microfiche.

(61) young men's underwear   Ibid.

(61) drugs or alcohol   Abstract of Court Record, January 19, 1990.

(61) in state prison   Interview with Dan Donohoe, January 15, 1998.

(62) "serious physical injury"   Information, State of Washington v. Corey James Dillon, Case No. 90-8-00227-8.

(62) from arresting him   Information, State of Washington v. Corey James Dillon, Case No. 90-8-04982-7.

(62) "Was he around it? Yes."   Interview with Al Roberts, February 19, 1998.

(64) a police cruiser   Incident Report, Seattle Police Department, No. 94-227802, May 21, 1994.

(64) assault and obstruction   Statement of Defendant on Plea of Guilty, No. 197842, July 11, 1994.

(65) "'hood doing this"   Interview with Al Roberts, February 19, 1998.

(65) "cool with me now"   Allen, p. C1.

(66) second-story window   Interview with Al Roberts, February 19, 1998.

(67) "an office assistant"   Letter by F. James Gush contained in criminal case file located at Municipal Court in Seattle.

(68) on March 23, 1992   Information, State of Washington v. Corey James Dillon, Case No. 92-8-03379-0.

(68) graduate from college   NCAA Report, 1995.

(68) "prior to Corey Dillon"   Interview with Al Roberts, February 19, 1998.

(70) a suspended license   Birkland, p. C1.

(70) "whole nine yards"   Queenan, p. C1.

(70) "Dillon pleaded guilty"   Associated Press, "Bengals Running Back to Serve One Day in Jail," June 4, 1998.

5

Arrested Development

(71) "take care of him"   Freeman, p. 5

(72) "meeting in Texas"   Affidavit of Art Modell, October 9, 1997.

(72) "Talk about brazen."   Interview with Ray Sumrow, October 29, 1997.

(73) "are certainly different"   Interview with Ray Sumrow, September 16, 1997.

(74) with public appeal   Interview with Joyce Trent Morgan, manager of business affairs at Disney, November 12, 1997.

(74) checked in on March 17   Receipt from Radisson Resort dated March 17, 1996, obtained by the authors.

(75) four-day stay   Southwestern Bell Telephone Company records dated April 4, 1996, obtained by the authors.

(75) "of such individuals?"   Interview with Ray Sumrow, December 6, 1997.

(75) without police resistance   Fainaru, p. 12.

(76) task force in the state   Records titled "Drugs Seized by NADITF" provided to the authors by the drug task force.

(76) "the Pittsburgh Steelers"   Interview with Mark Spears, December 3, 1997.

(78) "on the highway"   Interview with John Davila, December 3, 1997.

(78) "do, quite often"   Interview with Ray Sumrow, September 16, 1997.

(78) in the Super Bowl   Arrest Report, Duane Julius Thomas, January 30, 1972.

(79) "never cashed it"   Interview with Ray Sumrow, September 16, 1997.

(79) cover of *Sports Illustrated*   "A Cowboy Stampede," *Sports Illustrated,* January 24, 1972.

(79) "felony in Texas"   Interview with Ray Sumrow, September 16, 1997.

(79) twenty-one days after his arrest   Criminal Disposition Report, Duane Julius Thomas, Case No. 10,534.

(79) "the Dallas Cowboys"   Interview with Ray Sumrow, September 16, 1997.

(80) "who they had stopped"   Interview with Jay Ethington, October 23, 1997.

(81) "in a man's body"   Interview with Ray Sumrow, December 6, 1997.

(82) "in the Super Bowl"   Interview with Jay Ethington, December 4, 1997.

(84) "they're on the inside"   Interview with Ray Sumrow, December 6, 1997.

(84) "all you found?"   Interview with Mark Spears, December 3, 1997.

(84) "the amount he had"   Interview with Ray Sumrow, September 16, 1997.

(84) immediately in jail   Ibid.

(85) "things are tough"   Interview with Dan Rooney, November 6, 1997.

(86) regular marijuana user   Interview with Mark Spears, December 3, 1997.

(87) career at Texas Tech   Pre-Sentence Investigation Report on file at Rockwall County District Attorney's Office.

(87) "overcoming a problem"   Interview with Dan Rooney, November 6, 1997.

(88) "does that send?"   Associated Press, "Morris Signs," September 26, 1996.

(88) "a mistake, he's gone"   Eisenberg, p. D1.

(89) "period of time"   Preston, p. D1.

(89) "to address it"   Ibid.

(89) "it was a shock"   Ibid.

(89) "as an individual"   Ibid.

(90) "play football here"   Ibid.

(90) substance abuse program   Hawkins, p. A30.

(91) "out its function"   Interview with Ray Sumrow, October 7, 1997.

(91) "going to do that" Interview with Jay Ethington, October 23, 1997.

(91) "matter down here" Interview with Ray Sumrow, September 16, 1997.

(92) "'about something else'" Associated Press, "Morris Reveals," September 24, 1997.

(93) "This is business." Interview with Jay Ethington, October 23, 1997.

(93) "'got Bam Morris?'" Interview with Patsy Williams, December 3, 1997.

(94) teammate Orlando Brown Groark, p. 1.

(94) "to do their job" Interview with Jay Ethington, December 4, 1997.

(94) "a big mistake" Newton, January 12, 1998.

(95) "Call it what you want." Interview with Ray Sumrow, December 6, 1997.

6

The Maverick

(96) "Thank you very much." Copy of personal letter from Bob Kraft's collection.

(96) "Only time will tell." Interview with Bob Kraft, October 1997.

(97) twice raped her Benedict, *Public Heroes, Private Felons*, p. 103.

(98) "to my wife" Interview with Bob Kraft, October 1997.

(99) "not always true" Copy of personal letter from Bob Kraft's collection.

(99) "People have different standards." Interview with Bob Kraft, October 1997.

(101) "or decreasing murders" Interview with Ralph Cindrich, February 1998.

(102) "little tougher here" Interview with Bob Kraft, October 1997.

(104) "life under control" Interview with Joel Goldberg, February 1998.

7

Wanted

(105) that was prohibited   King, p. 117.

(106) with the subpoena   Interview with Larry Fox, November 13, 1997.

(106) "person: James Harris"   Copy of subpoena in authors' possession.

(107) sentence in Nebraska   Fallik, March 11, 1997. Also, see Benedict, *Public Heroes, Private Felons,* pp. 126-48.

(107) "a good investment"   Transcript of ESPN interview, January 14, 1998.

(108) "of growing up"   Associated Press, "First Phillips," April 21, 1997.

(108) "He didn't stab anyone."   Price, p. 51.

(109) "known as 'crack'"   Indictment, United States v. James Harris, Case No. 97-M6029.

(109) "make a living"   Bosworth, p. A1.

(109) and pronounced dead   Hollingshed and Pawlaczyk, p. 1.

(109) the ambush killing   Transcript from Detention Hearing, United States v. Anthony Maurice Washington, Case No. 97-30058-01, August 1, 1997.

(110) with the case   United States v. Walter Maurice Humphrey et al., Case No. 96-CR-30102-WDS.

(110) "on the informant"   Interview with Larry Fox, November 13, 1997.

(110) "Metro East area"   Transcript from Washington's detention hearing, August 1, 1997.

(110) "son returned alive"   Ibid.

(110) shipment of cocaine   Transcript of Hearing, United States v. James Edward Harris, No. 97-CR-30058, August 21, 1997.

(111) "everybody's doing okay?"   Interview with James Harris, October 30, 1997.

(111) "made a bad decision"   Interview with Bob Shannon, October 9, 1997.

(113) "was in the car" Interview with James Harris, December 16, 1997.

(113) sell a Porsche 911 Interview with Brad Stubbs, December 15, 1997.

(114) "and my rims" Interview with James Harris, December 16, 1997.

(114) "come to me" Interview with Brad Stubbs, December 15, 1997.

(114) "in the beginning" Interview with James Harris, December 16, 1997.

(115) "it in my face" Ibid.

(115) "surprised and disappointed" Bosworth, p. A1.

(115) "before everybody else" Interview with James Harris, October 30, 1997.

(115) " 'see you through' " Ibid.

(115) Facility in Minnesota Sentence, State of Minnesota v. James Edward Harris, Case No. 95113604, October 16, 1996.

(116) and fractured collarbone Complaint, State of Minnesota v. James Edward Harris, Control No. 95029364, January 3, 1996.

(116) his first wife Petition to Enter Plea of Guilty—Misdemeanor, State of Minnesota v. James Edward Harris, Case No. 92-018124-37, December 15, 1992.

(116) domestic violence call Police Complaint, Report No. 92018124, November 30, 1992.

(116) "do it anyway" Transcript of ESPN interview, January 14, 1998.

(116) "pay it off" Interview with Patti Cohen, September 23, 1997.

(117) paid in full Ibid.

(117) were ultimately dropped Los Angeles Times, p. C9.

(118) space he wanted Pittsburgh Post-Gazette, February 9, 1995.

(118) one of the women UPI, February 24, 1992.

(118) him not guilty Brubaker, p. A25.

(118) fifteen-day jail sentence Ibid.

(118) another fifteen-day jail sentence Ibid.

(118) on May 9, 1990 Ibid.

(118) and served sixty-five   Ibid.

(118) sex with him   Ibid.

(118) "Darryl Henley's case"   Interview with James Harris, December 5, 1997.

(119) "go watch films"   Ibid.

(120) "the defendant's life"   Transcript of Detention Hearing, United States v. James Edward Harris, Case No. M-6029, July 28, 1997.

(121) "if he did that"   Ibid.

(122) "to stick with you"   Interview with James Harris, November 5, 1997.

(122) "His mind was not there."   Interview with Harold Lewis, October 30, 1997.

(123) "they called me in"   Interview with James Harris, November 5, 1997.

(123) "you wanted to see"   Thomas, p. D3.

(123) "good football player"   Ibid.

(124) " 'at 11:00 P.M.' "   Interview with Kevin Warren, September 25, 1997.

(124) Warren replied   Interview with James Harris, November 5, 1997.

(125) in federal prison   Interview with Katie Hoffman, secretary to Judge Paul E. Riley, May 28, 1998.

(125) through a workout   Interview with Harold Lewis, December 16, 1997.

(125) got the call   Oakland Raiders Press Release, "Raiders Sign Free Agent DE James Harris," March 11, 1998.

8

What to Expect When You're Expecting

(126) "spots on your roster"   Transcript of ESPN report, December 2, 1997.

(126) "in the first place"   Mell, p. C1.

(127) "highly exaggerated"   Transcript of ESPN report, December 2, 1997.

(128) "head into a wall" Lambe, p. D1.

(128) of the payoff Jackman, p. D1.

(129) Avalon Boulevard in Los Angeles Transcript of Brief in California v. Maurice Stevens, Case No. BA026324, August 28, 1991.

(129) of a rival gang Ibid.

(129) time of the murder Declaration of Matthew Kaestner in Support of Motion for Disclosure of Identity of Informant, Case No. BA026324, September 24, 1991.

(129) nothing about the murder Ibid.

(129) "victim was shot" Ibid.

(130) "did the shooting" Ibid.

(130) "committed the murder" See Transcript of Brief, August 28, 1991.

(130) in their investigation Ibid.

(130) of attempted murder Information, California v. Charles Alexander Jordan, Case No. VA011338, October 11, 1990.

(130) from going inside Reporter's Transcript, Preliminary Examination, California v. Charles Jordan, Case No. VA011338, September 27, 1990.

(131) "would leave court" Ibid.

(131) " 'that's a promise' " Ibid.

(131) "don't know where" Reporter's Transcript, California v. Terry Young and Stevie Darnell Gaines, Case No. VA011338, September 18, 1990.

(131) and received probation Guilty Plea in the Superior Court, People v. Charles A. Jordan, Case No. VA011338, March 8, 1991.

(132) "no longer involved" Reporter's Transcript of Proceedings, People of California vs. John Davis and Maurice Stevens, Case No. BA026324, April 8, 1991.

(132) "at preliminary hearing" Ibid.

(132) "in the pecking order" Ibid.

(132) three years in prison Transcript of Guilty Plea, California v. John Gentry Davis, Case No. BA026324, January 17, 1992.

(133) nearly four months   ESPN, *Outside the Lines,* December 12, 1997.

(133) thirty days in jail   Court Records on file at the Municipal Court of L.A., California v. Charles Alexander Jordan, Case No. V511333.

(133) was later dismissed   Court Records on file at the Municipal Court of L.A., California v. Charles Alexander Jordan, Case No. A973431.

(133) with illegal gambling   Court Records on file at the Municipal Court of L.A., California v. Charles Alexander Jordan, Case No. 89R11113.

(133) five days in jail   Court Records on file at the Municipal Court of L.A., California v. Charles Jordan, Case No. V518633.

(133) indicted for kidnapping   Court Records on file at the Municipal Court of L.A.

(134) "hand it to them"   ESPN, *Outside the Lines,* December 12, 1997.

(134) Mims estimated "dozens"   Ibid.

(134) "where gangs predominate"   Interview with Matt Morantz, December 19, 1997.

(135) receiver Fred Barnett   Miami Dolphins Press Release, "Miami Dolphins Release Barnett, Holmes," October 14, 1997.

(135) "team as a whole"   Associated Press, "Dolphins Release," October 13, 1997.

(135) "line is production"   Associated Press, "Barnett Out," October 6, 1997.

(136) "me to come over"   Statement of Ebony Cooksey to Plantation Police Department, Case No. 0611-96-07, July 9, 1996.

(137) "I couldn't breathe"   Ibid.

(137) "not to answer"   Ibid.

(137) "nobody was there"   Ibid.

(138) "are totally inappropriate"   Interview with Judge Ed Newman, October 28, 1997.

(138) "Sit down."   Statement of Erner Darroux to Plantation Police Department, Case No. 0611-96-07, July 9, 1996.

(138) "who she is"   Cooksey's Police Statement.

(139) Thomas and the desk   Statement of Dr. Edmund Darroux to Plantation Police Department, Case No. 0611-96-07, July 10, 1996.

(139) "was a thick window"   Cooksey's Police Statement.

(139) "into the window"   Mrs. Darroux's Police Statement.

(140) "pair of blue jeans"   Transcript of 911 call.

(140) "father this child"   Cooksey's Police Statement.

(140) a pregnant female   Warrant, No. 96-14703CF10A, April 24, 1997.

(141) "We have no comment."   Interview with Reggie Roberts, February 20, 1998.

(141) the University of Miami   Interview with Howard Weinberg, March 31, 1998.

(142) "doesn't happen again"   Mrs. Darroux's Police Statement.

(142) on February 24, 1997   Violation Report Form for Lamar Thomas, Florida Department of Corrections, April 10, 1997.

(142) LifeLine in Miami   Narrative of Violation Report Form, Case No. 96-14703CF.

(142) six weeks old   Ibid.

(142) of the police cruiser   Ibid.

(143) "law abiding citizen"   Ibid.

(143) "these things bleed through."   Interview with Howard Weinberg, March 31, 1998.

(143) "to these situations"   Interview with Liffort Hobley, October 16, 1997.

(144) knees, and right foot   Complaint Affidavit, Offense Report No. 9508-43515.

(144) "for his job"   Interview with Liffort Hobley, October 16, 1997.

(144) on May 16, 1996   Authorization for Plea in Absentia, Florida v. Irving Spikes, Case No. 95-19235MM10A, May 17, 1996.

(145) "Shula used to say"   Interview with Liffort Hobley, October 16, 1997.

(145) "Dade Circuit Court . . ."   Warrant, April 24, 1997.

(145) "situation I'm in"   Interview with Howard Weinberg, March 31, 1998.

(146) "on the perpetrator"   Interview with Judge Ed Newman, October 28, 1997.

(146) " 'I'm not a man' "   Interview with Howard Weinberg, March 31, 1998.

9

Clear and Present Danger

(149) "this is who I am!"   Supplemental Report, Eden Prairie Police Department, Case No. 97014603, July 3, 1997.

(149) "are f---in' with me"   Intoxication Report Form, Eden Prairie Police Department.

(150) "the lead officer"   Interview with Brent Griffith, November 21, 1997.

(151) and careless driving   Complaint, Minnesota v. Carl Phillip Hargrave, Case. No. 97014603.

(151) driving privileges revoked   Ibid.

(153) "those Dutcher things"   Interview with Dan Endy, November 17, 1997.

(153) "full-time guy"   Ibid.

(154) recurring police misconduct   Resignation, City of St. Paul, Rep. No. 31421, August 30, 1988.

(154) "as a Police Officer"   Letter dated December 3, 1987, in the authors' possession.

(154) ownership of a vehicle   Waiver of Resignation, Steven W. Rollins, August 30, 1988.

(154) "of my discharge"   Ibid.

(155) "force to restrain"   Interoffice Communication, City of St. Paul, July 27, 1983.

(156) never charged in the incident   Interview with Dan Endy, November 17, 1997.

(156) "we glossed it over" Ibid.

(156) reduced from DUI *Philadelphia Daily News*, p. 101.

(156) for driving drunk Powers, p. D1.

(158) "respectful relationship" Interview with Dan Endy, March 21, 1998.

(160) "for the organization" Richardson, February 6, 1993.

(161) "with the power" Interview with Dan Endy, March 21, 1998.

(161) "to the team" Letter from Dan Endy's personal collection.

(161) "He's a good one." Letter from Dan Endy's personal collection.

(163) "'you really want me'" Affidavit of Daniel G. Endy III, September 1, 1993, Hennepin County District Court.

(163) matter out of court McEnroe, p. A1.

(163) "church of some sort" Interview with Roger Headrick, February 16, 1996.

(164) to his hotel room Third-Party Defendant Amy Kellogg's Answer to Third-Party Complaint, Michelle Eaves v. Warren Moon and the Minnesota Vikings Football Club, No. 95-08382.

(164) "in leaving his room" Ibid.

(164) "player on the team" Interview with Warren Moon, April 17, 1998.

(165) settlement with Eaves McEnroe, p. A1.

(165) "needed the publicity" Interview with Warren Moon, April 8, 1998.

(165) two cheerleaders' dismissal McEnroe, Roberts, and Brown, p. A1.

(166) "they are terminated" Ibid.

(166) "a bogus firing" Interview with Vikings security personnel, March 19, 1998.

(166) bed checks are performed Interview with Roger Headrick, February 16, 1996.

(167) "a room to himself" Interview with Vikings security personnel, June 1996.

(167) "me my privacy"   Interview with Warren Moon, May 17, 1998.

(167) "to that fire"   Interview with Vikings security personnel, June 1996.

(167) "expendable, you're screwed"   Interview with James Harris, November 5, 1997.

(168) "repeated sexual advances"   McEnroe, p. A1.

(168) "woman from Stanford"   Interview with Dan Endy, March 21, 1998.

(169) 911 domestic violence call   Petition to Enter Plea of Guilty—Misdemeanor, Minnesota v. James Edward Harris, Case No. 92-018124-37.

(169) 10 years' probation   Felony Sentencing, Minnesota v. Keith Pernell Henderson, D.C. File No. 94038398, 94042935, 93106555, April 10, 1995.

(170) charges were dropped   Associated Press, October 3, 1994.

(170) were later dropped   Los Angeles Times, December 27, 1995.

(170) him in February 1995   Associated Press, "Moon Jurors," February 22, 1996.

(170) was later dismissed   Los Angeles Times, December 27, 1995.

(170) Adult Correction Facility   Sentence Felony, Minnesota v. James Edward Harris, Case No. 95113604.

(170) without a permit   USA Today, "Vikes Chief," p. C3.

(170) probation for one year   Report on file at the Florida Department of Law Enforcement, Case No. 968666.

(170) and petty theft   Report on file at the Florida Department of Law Enforcement, Case No. C9602837A.

(171) weapon in Michigan   Associated Press, "Vikings Defensive End," May 7, 1996.

(171) programs he supervised   Associated Press, "Former Vikings," September 12, 1996.

(171) contusions on her back   Associated Press, "Vikings Running Back," May 6, 1997.

(171) to kill his girlfriend Associated Press, "Prosecutors Defend," May 3, 1997.

(171) Crowley, South Carolina ESPN, *Sports Zone,* "The Year in Crime."

(171) placed by his girlfriend Incident Report, Eden Prairie Police Department, September 2, 1997.

(171) influence of alcohol Associated Press, "Two Vikings," October 14, 1997.

(172) for drunk driving *Washington Post,* May 6, 1998.

(172) f---in' up himself Interview with James Harris, November 5, 1997.

(172) " 'ruin' his career" KSTR-TV news report, September 4, 1996.

(173) "So what?" Interview with Joe Friedberg, March 24, 1998.

(173) "of the Minnesota Vikings" Text of Dennis Green's Statement, *Minneapolis Star Tribune,* September 6, 1996.

(175) for trying to sue Green Petition for Disciplinary Action Against Lori C. Peterson, State of Minnesota Supreme Court, March 18, 1998.

(176) "that kind of stuff" Ibid.

(176) crackdown on lawlessness Sansevere, p. E1.

(177) "to be around" Interview with Roger Headrick, February 16, 1996.

(177) and the Bears Complaint, Dan Metcalfe v. Steven Rollins, et al., Court File No. 97-94JMR.

(177) "wall behind him" Ibid.

(177) as the aggressor Report by Sergeant Donald Banham, Minneapolis Police Department, Case No. MP-95-332880.

(178) "to apply pressure" Ibid.

(179) "this type of behavior" O'Connor, p. C5.

(179) "Rollins is untouchable." Interview with Vikings security personnel, March 19, 1998.

(179) "to chemical testing" Sentence and Disposition, Minnesota v. Carl Hargrave.

(180) "about their character" Interview with Jennifer Inz, March 19, 1998.

(180) "high school in West Virginia"   ESPN interview, April 18, 1998.

(180) "I'm in the NFL now."   Associated Press, April 19, 1998.

(181) "offense in the NFL"   *Minneapolis Star Tribune*, April 19, 1998.

10

Dirty Little Secret

(182) "Hello. Hello?"   Transcript of 911 tape.

(183) "s—t out of me"   Interview with prosecuting attorney John Healey, October 1, 1996.

(183) "abrasions on her neck"   Associated Press, "Moon Family," October 22, 1995.

(183) "afraid for my life"   Associated Press, "Moon's Wife," October 4, 1995.

(184) "presence of the children"   Graczyk, February 15, 1996.

(185) "somebody's head off"   Interview with Warren Moon, April 8, 1998.

(185) professional football players   Copy of Bernard Sanders letter to Paul Tagliabue obtained by the authors.

(187) "it wasn't right"   Nobles, October 19, 1994.

(187) "true leader here"   Interview with Bonnie Flynn, October 27, 1997.

(188) "inside the NFL"   Interview with Liffort Hobley, October 16, 1997.

(189) "light of day"   Interview with Judge Ed Newman, October 28, 1997.

(190) "into the newspapers"   Interview with Larry Wansley, January 15, 1998.

(190) "brought to light"   Interview with Roger Headrick, February 16, 1996.

(191) "pull this crap"   Incident Report, Eden Prairie Police Department, September 26, 1991.

(192) to appear in court   Ibid.

(192) "you call the police" Offense Report, St. Paul Police Department, May 7, 1995.

(194) "I went into shock" Interview with Debbie DuBois, December 22, 1997.

(195) "and steroid abuse" Interview with Joe Janesz, February 18, 1998.

(195) " 'just have to leave him' " Interview with Debbie DuBois, December 22, 1997.

(196) "doing the same thing" Interview with Judge Ed Newman, October 28, 1997.

(196) across the room Incident Report, Complaint No. 96-1264, February 1, 1996.

(196) "out of his house" Witness Statement (attached to Incident Report).

(197) "return my calls" Interview with Debbie DuBois, December 22, 1997.

(197) "clothes into the fire" Printout of Police Log, February 14, 1998.

(198) "through with charges" Interview with Police Chief Paul Bickan, February 18, 1998.

(198) "someone by battering" Interview with Bonnie Campbell, January 15, 1998.

(200) "as discriminatory" Copy of letter written by Joe Brown obtained by the authors.

(200) "excuse this approach" Interview with Larry Wansley, January 15, 1998.

(201) "we grew up in" Interview with Liffort Hobley, October 16, 1998.

(201) no father is present Blankenhorn, *Fatherless America*.

(201) the black community Bennett, DiIulio, and Walters, *Body Count*.

(202) "it's too late" Interview with Liffort Hobley, October 16, 1998.

(202) to discipline a player National Football League Policy and Program.

(204) "spotty at best" Interview with Chief Norm Stamper, January 13, 1998.

(204) "ending domestic violence" Ibid.

(204) "Violence Against Women" Copy of letter written by Joe Brown obtained by the authors.

(205) "to deal with it" Interview with Chief Norm Stamper, January 13, 1998.

(205) "players as role models" Interview with Judge Ed Newman, October 28, 1997.

(206) "back to bite them" Interview with Bonnie Campbell, January 15, 1998.

(206) "got it and who doesn't" Ibid.

(206) "morally and legally" Ibid.

(207) "Freeze-frame on that." Interview with Chief Norm Stamper, January 13, 1998.

(207) "you're gone" Interview with Bonnie Campbell, January 15, 1998.

(207) " 'really happening here' " Ibid.

(208) "happen in the NFL" Interview with Judge Ed Newman, October 28, 1997.

(208) "in our country" Interview with Chief Norm Stamper, January 13, 1998.

(208) "cycle of violence" Interview with Judge Ed Newman, October 28, 1997.

(209) "violence is criminal" Interview with Chief Norm Stamper, January 13, 1998.

11

The Elephant in the Room

(210) "ethnic and racial groups" Copy of letter written by Joe Brown obtained by the authors.

(211) "let's face it" Interview with Greg Aiello, February 1998.

(212) "Americans as a group" Interview with Randall Kennedy, April 29, 1998.

(213) "unpleasant the answers"   Interview with William Bennett, April 24, 1998.

(214) 67 and 71 percent   *Racial Report Card,* published annually by the Center for the Study of Sport in Society.

(215) "a very positive thing"   Interview with William Bennett, April 24, 1998.

(215) "your mind-set"   Interview with Rev. Jesse Jackson, April 29, 1998.

(216) "couple of times"   Interview with Randall Kennedy, April 29, 1998.

(217) "caught selling it"   Interview with Rev. Jesse Jackson, April 29, 1998.

(218) "in unlawful activity"   Interview with Bob Shannon, October 9, 1997.

(219) "animating variable"   Interview with Randall Kennedy, April 29, 1998.

(220) "now that's racist"   Interview with Rev. Jesse Jackson, April 29, 1998.

12

Immunity

(221) assaulting a prostitute   Borges and Cafardo, p. F1.

(221) John Hall was arrested   Eskenazi, February 16, 1998.

(221) Travis Jervey was arrested   Associated Press, "Jervey Fares," February 19, 1998.

(222) Leslie Shepherd was arrested   Fernandez, p. D1.

(222) Matt Finkes was arrested   Associated Press, "Finkes," March 2, 1998.

(222) Corey Dillon was arrested   Queenan

(223) " 'need it more than me' "   Mulvihill and Ford, "Hooker," p. 1.

(224) "sexual assault claims"   Mulvihill and Ford, "Lawyer," p. 79.

(224) reached the trial stage   Benedict and Klein, p. 86.

(224) resulted in a conviction   Ibid.

(225) rooted each other on   Trial Brief, Victoria C. v. Cincinnati Bengals, Inc. et al., Case No. C92-658M, June 5, 1992.

(225) "get it from somewhere"   Benedict, *Public Heroes, Private Felons*, p. 23.

(225) earlier that evening   *Houston Post*, p. C2.

(225) "asleep during intercourse"   Ibid.

(226) declined to indict   Phillips, p. 7.

(226) "all the guys in there"   Investigation Summary, County of La Crosse, Wisconsin, Office of the District Attorney, August 1995.

(226) "players was not consensual"   Declination Report, Case No. 95-29998, County of La Crosse, Wisconsin, Office of the District Attorney, August 1995.

(227) "it's not very pleasant"   Interview with Judge Walter McGovern, September 2, 1994.

(227) "in this country"   Ibid.

(228) "endangering other women"   Interview with Lori Peterson, March 19, 1998.

(229) lobby of Yon Hall   Incident Report, University of Florida Police Department, Report No. 95047968, October 5, 1995.

(229) but did not elaborate   Narrative (attached to Incident Report), October 5, 1995.

(229) officers three times   Reports on file at the Florida Department of Law Enforcement, File No. 456558.

(229) two days in jail   Ibid.

(230) "wanted to go home"   Incident Report, October 5, 1995.

(230) one described by Nichols   Supplemental Report (attached to Incident Report filed October 5, 1995), University of Florida Police Department.

(231) "want to dignify them"   Interview with Tony McCoy, April 22, 1998.

(232) in the police reports   Interview with David Levine, April 22, 1998.

(232) "McCoy by his girlfriend"   Incident Report.

(232) felony sexual assault case   Records on file at the Florida Department of Law Enforcement, File No. 8905128CFA.

(233) the woman and Simpson   Offense Report, University of Florida Police Department, Report No. 8925314, November 20, 1989.

(233) "He's got a knife"   Ibid.

(233) "and in my chair?"   Ibid.

(234) "get some sleep"   Ibid.

(234) "mother that night"   Ibid.

(234) "been violent with her"   Ibid.

(235) "he would kill her"   Narrative (attached to Offense Report).

(235) "eyes, face and ears"   Ibid.

(235) "one half inch long"   Ibid.

(236) "side of her underpants"   Ibid.

(236) "started to choke her"   Ibid.

(236) "out the door nude"   Ibid.

(236) "stuff ever took place"   Interview with Tony McCoy, April 22, 1998.

(238) "in a domestic dispute"   Offense Report.

(239) "type cuts in it"   Ibid.

(239) "her being wounded"   Ibid.

(239) "were old tears"   Ibid.

(239) "identified as [McCoy's ex-wife]"   Ibid.

(239) were suddenly dropped   Case Action Report, Florida v. Anthony B. McCoy, Alachua County Circuit Court, No. 89-5128-CF-A, March 19, 1990.

(240) "no way to go forward"   Interview with John Carlin, March 24, 1998.

(240) " 'set up a deposition' "   Interview with Huntley Johnson, March 27, 1998.

(241) "out of the water"   Interview with John Carlin, March 24, 1998.

(241) "a hell of a lot"   Interview with Huntley Johnson, March 27, 1998.

(241) "the apartment naked"   Interview with John Carlin, March 24, 1998.

(242) "defend Tony McCoy"   Interview with Huntley Johnson, March 27, 1998.

(243) "he brought me from"   Interview with Tony McCoy, April 22, 1998.

(243) "charges will be filed"   Narrative (attached to Offense Report).

(244) "on with my life"   Interview with Tony McCoy, April 22, 1998.

(245) have sex with Bradley   Tabyanan, p. B1.

(245) "part of the law"   Interview with Chief Larry Slamons, October 30, 1995.

(245) "what they were doing"   Interview with Terry Jones, October 26, 1995.

13

Rapists Never Retire

(247) "back to the hotel"   Interview with Don McPherson, January 20, 1995.

(249) out of "politeness"   Victim Statement (Supplement to Offense Report), Eden Prairie Police Department, No. 9004903, March 4, 1994.

(249) "Just come in here"   Ibid.

(249) "This is weird"   Ibid.

(250) "have to go now"   Ibid.

(250) pulled up his pants   Ibid.

(250) "nothing had happened"   Ibid.

(252) "Take out my dick"   Supplement No. 1, Minneapolis Police Department, Case No. MP-93-335296, December 2, 1993.

(252) "Kiss it."   Ibid.

(252) penis still exposed   Ibid.

(252) "Just let me touch it"   Ibid.

(253) Sergeant Billington's summary   Supplement No. 2, Minneapolis Police Department, Case No. MP-93-335296, December 2, 1993.

(256) fifteen-year prison sentence   Complaint, Minnesota v. Keith Pernell Henderson, No. 93335296, February 9, 1994.

(256) assault on Sally Michaels   Complaint, Minnesota v. Keith Pernell Henderson, No. 94004903, May 10, 1994.

(256) call reporting a rape   Narrative, Bloomington Police Department, recorded May 19, 1994.

(256) had just been raped   Ibid.

(256) exam was performed   Supplemental Report, Bloomington Police Department, Case No. 940-07340, May 24, 1994.

(257) "smashed against the wall"   Transcript of Victim's Statement, May 20, 1994.

(257) in the third degree   Complaint, Minnesota v. Keith Pernell Henderson, No. 94007340, May 25, 1994.

(257) listed as "football player"   Booking Sheet, Hennepin County Sheriff's Department Adult Detention Center, May 26, 1994.

(257) set at $235,000   Ibid.

(257) guilty in all three cases   Felony Guilty Plea, State of Minnesota v. Keith Pernell Henderson, File No. 93106555, 94038398, 94042935.

(257) state of Minnesota   Felony Sentencing, State of Minnesota v. Keith Pernell Henderson, April 10, 1995.

(258) "average man would"   Interview with Robert Miller, March 4, 1998.

(258) "so many other ways"   Interview with Don McPherson, January 20, 1995.

(259) "forced intercourse on her"   Report on file at the Bloomington Police Department.

(259) "came in a lot"   Interview with Marilyn Scofield, November 25, 1997.

(263) "never come out"   Interview with John Billington, March 2, 1998.

(263) Medical Center hours later   Green and Villarreal, p. C1.

(264) "sexually and physically"   Interview with Tim McGee, October 10, 1994.

(264) "cut my hair off"   Transcript of ESPN, *Sports Weekly,* September 1-8, 1994.

(265) "messed with her mind"   Interview with Tim McGee, October 10, 1994.

(265) "all over again"   Transcript of ESPN, *Sports Weekly,* September 1-8, 1994.

(265) "her body, everything"   Interview with Tim McGee, October 10, 1994.

(266) "he would become violent"   Transcript of ESPN, *Sports Weekly,* September 1-8, 1994.

(266) "he wanted to control them"   Interview with Tim McGee, October 10, 1994.

(267) "and please understand"   Text of the letter published in the *Orlando Sentinel,* April 10, 1994, p. C1.

(268) "over her head"   Interview with Stewart Stone, October 26, 1994.

(268) videotaped the attack   Arrest Report, Case No. E92-4510CKA.

(268) came up with $20,000   Ibid.

(269) "who was mentally impaired"   Interview with Stewart Stone, October 26, 1994.

(269) attempted to drive away   Perez, p. A1.

(269) declined to press charges   Ibid.

(270) to physically harm her   Ibid.

(270) required police intervention   Ibid.

(270) "Williams feared Billups."   Interview with Stewart Stone, October 26, 1994.

(270) ended any other way   Transcript of ESPN, *Sports Weekly,* September 1-8, 1994.

14

The Gambler

(271) Art Schlichter said   Interviews with Art Schlichter were conducted via telephone over a period of months from the Indiana Correctional Facility.

(277) "bad apple"   Moldea, *Interference.*
(278) "the National Football League"   Ibid.
(278) riverboat gambling project   Sack, p. 1.
(279) "in infrequent situations"   Moldea, *Interference.*
(281) "intensive psychotherapy"   Interview with Valerie Lorenz, February 1998.

15

Rude Awakenings

(285) the time of his accident   Gerdes and Sylvester, p. A1.
(285) with a motor vehicle   First Amended Information, State of Michigan v. Reggie Okeith Rogers, Case No. CR88-89464-FH.
(285) Paradise Lounge in Pontiac   Gerdes, Sylvester, and George, p. A1.
(286) "but it helps"   Albom and Sylvester p. C1.
(287) "'I could have stopped him'"   Interview with Reggie Rogers, January 6, 1998.
(287) under the influence in Seattle   Basic Docket, Municipal Court of Seattle, City of Seattle v. Reggie Rogers.
(287) this time for assault   Ibid.
(287) "shouldn't draft him"   Albom, p. C1.
(287) "believe it is true"   Ibid.
(288) "bigger than football"   Interview with Reggie Rogers, January 6, 1998.
(288) two counts of drunk driving   Bell and Gerdes, p. A1.
(289) "didn't look like himself"   Gerdes, "Deputy," p. A3.
(289) "Do you know who I am?"   Bell and Gerdes, p. A1.
(289) obtained a warrant first   Gerdes, "Fontes Charge," p. A1.
(290) eighteen months' probation   Meinecke, p. D3.
(290) "for us on the field"   Ibid.
(290) "that's behind me"   Ibid.
(290) "from the hospital"   Interview with Reggie Rogers, January 6, 1998.

(290) Michigan state penitentiary   Judgment of Sentence, Michigan v. Riggie Rogers, Case No. 88-089464FH.

(291) "had a rude awakening."   Interview with Reggie Rogers, January 6, 1998.

(291) Terry Allen (charged   Incident Report, Walton County Sheriff's Department, Case No. 97-30-086.

(291) Bruce Smith (found slumped   Associated Press, "Bruce Smith," July 28, 1997.

(291) Dana Subblefield (observed speeding   Associated Press, October 16, 1997.

(291) Jeff Alm's suicide   Plaschke, p. C1.

(291) "it a little longer"   Ibid.

(292) "Hello, hello."   Transcript of 911 tape published by Associated Press on December 22, 1993.

(292) deaths in the United States   Shute, p. 58.

(293) David Overstreet   New York Times, July 5, 1990.

(293) Stacey Toran   McClain, p. 4.

(293) Brad Beckman   Atlanta Journal and Constitution, May 9, 1991.

(294) "taken away from me"   Interview with Mike Frier, December 27, 1997.

(294) twelve-ounce bottles of beer   State's Trial Memorandum, State of Washington v. Wilbur Lamar Smith, No. 95-1-00853-1.

(294) the eleven glasses of beer   Ibid.

(294) "someone else was driving"   Interview with Mike Frier, December 27, 1997.

(295) no food was ordered   Trial Memorandum.

(296) "He recognized me."   Interview with Ulysses Frier, December 27, 1997.

(296) "to keep me alive"   Interview with Mike Frier, December 27, 1997.

(297) "I'm the driver."   Information, State of Washington v. Wilbur Lamar Smith, No. 95-1-00853-1.

(297) on January 26, 1995   Ibid.

(297) "one-pound plates" Interview with Mike Frier, December 27, 1997.

(297) "didn't need to happen" Kelley, p. B1.

(297) since joining the team Order of Release, City of Seattle v. Patrick Hunter, Case No. 126974.

(297) drunk driving in Seattle Citation, City of Seattle, Incident No. 94-562591, December 13, 1994.

(297) "handle it in-house" Associated Press, "Walters," December 16, 1994.

(298) before being caught once Sullivan, p. 10.

(298) Erickson was arrested Everett District Court Docket, Case No. C00032188.

(298) avoid being hit Smith and Whitely, p. C5.

(298) "rest of the population" Interview with Douglas Cowan, January 9, 1998.

(300) "and professional football" National Football League Policy and Program for Substances of Abuse.

(301) "Sunday every year" Interview with Douglas Cowan, January 9, 1998.

(301) "out there taking chances" Interview with Mike Frier, December 27, 1997.

(301) "to stop driving drunk" Interview with Douglas Cowan, January 9, 1998.

(301) arrested six times Queenan, October 29, 1997.

(301) "try to hide problems" Interview with Mike Frier, December 27, 1997.

(302) "That's the way it works." Queenan, October 29, 1997.

(302) "to reenter the league" Interview with Douglas Cowan, January 9, 1998.

(303) "a horrible mistake" Statement of Defendant on Plea of Guilty, Washington v. Wilbur Lamar Smith, No. 95-100853-1-KNT, January 9, 1998.

(303) pulled over and arrested Citation, City of Seattle, No. 002352, April 7, 1997.

(303) charge of negligent driving Statement of Defendant on

Plea of Guilty, City of Seattle v. Mack Strong, Case No. CP22352.

(303) "makes me shake my head" Interview with Douglas Cowan, January 9, 1998.

(304) "career was cut short" Interview with Mike Frier, December 27, 1997.

(304) "Some people get caught." Katz, p. 69.

16

The Convict

(307) "myself a diehard Ram" Copy of letter obtained from Darryl Henley.

(307) first and only interview Interview with Darryl Henley, March 1998, conducted at the federal prison in Marion, Illinois.

17

Game Plan

(321) "going to make it stop?" Interview with Darryl Henley, March 1998.

(322) "got to watch out" Interview with Pat Haden, February 1998.

(322) "league will be hurting" Interview with Ralph Cindrich, February 1998.

(322) "laws of the land" Interview with Lee Roy Jordan, December 4, 1997.

(324) "and they failed" Interview with Newt Gingrich, March 1998.

(324) "much is expected" Boswell, p. B1.

(325) "how to hit and run" Interview with Steven Bucky, January 1998.

(326) "have to have standards" Interview with Bob Kraft, October 1997.

(326) "the top five picks" Interview with Jerome Stanley, January 1998.

(327) "it reacts to things" Interview with Russ Granik, February 1998.

(328) "that opens legal questions" *Seattle Post Intelligencer,* July 21, 1995.

(328) "sore point with the fans" *USA Today,* March 23, 1998.

(329) "be a limited number" Interview with Steve Largent, January 1998.

(329) "better and better for it" Interview with Richard Caster, December 1997.

(329) "or raping women" Interview with William Bennett, April 24, 1998.

(331) "with the same brush" Interview with Gene Upshaw, February 1998.

(331) "good guys left" Interview with Richard Caster, December 1997.

18

Epilogue

(333) in Orlando, Florida Covitz, *Kansas City Star.*

(334) went on sale Weisman, p. 3C.

(334) the commissioner's office *New York Times,* "Felons Don't Belong in the NFL," November 4, 1998.

(334) "role model status" Interview with Al Blumstein, March 8, 1999.

(335) "in the population" Court TV, *Prime Time Justice,* November 6, 1998.

(335) "a predetermined conclusion" CNN's *Page 1,* October 24, 1998.

(335) "defensive about it" Ibid.

(335) "discuss the book" Interview with Ken Kalthoff, November 23, 1998.

(335) with the networks Sandomir, p. 1.

(336) "not do the story"   Interview with Armen Keteyian, March 8, 1999.

(336) Sunday night games   Sandomir, p. 1.

(337) " 'is not racist' "   Bruton, p. D1.

(337) year with Baltimore   Associated Press, "Cornell Brown Arrested on DUI Charge," October 1, 1998.

(338) with organized gambling   Sack, p. 1.

(338) in Plantation, Florida   Brioso, p. 1C.

(338) the arresting officer   Associated Press, December 2, 1998.

(338) seven years in prison   Newberry, Associated Press.

(338) an undercover cop   Freeman, October 25, 1998.

(338) "to get home"   Gloster, Associated Press.

(339) "back to work"   Fallstrom, Associated Press.

(339) the United Kingdom   NFL.com, October 15, 1998.

(339) a topless dancer   *St. Louis Post-Dispatch,* October 24, 1998.

(339) Pleaded no contest   Associated Press, October 24, 1998.

(339) "so she crusades"   Foster, Associated Press.

(340) "in disciplinary action"   Court TV, *Prime Time Justice,* November 6, 1998.

(340) in LaCrosse, Wisconsin   *Boston Globe,* November 4, 1998.

(341) "decide those issues."   *HBO Real Sports,* January 25, 1999.

(341) "with this team"   Associated Press, November 16, 1998.

(341) "they are false"   Porter, Associated Press.

(342) a "stunning move"   *New York Times* "Notebook," February 18, 1999.

(342) All-pro Tony Martin   Winkeljohn, February 27, 1999.

(342) for oral sex   Freeman, D5.

(342) the Robinson arrest   *HBO Real Sports,* January 25, 1999.

Bibliography

Albom, Mitch, and Curt Sylvester. "Rogers Finally Ran Out of Green Lights." *Detroit Free Press,* October 30, 1988, p. C1.

Allen, Percy. "Steady as He Goes." *Seattle Times,* October 30, 1996, p. C1.

Almond, Elliott. "Three USC Players Are Acquitted in Assault Case." *Los Angeles Times,* June 15, 1991, p. C10.

Archer, Todd. "The Bengals' Other Draft Choices." *Cincinnati Post.*

Archer, Todd. "First Day No Picnic for Dillon." *Cincinnati Post, p.* C1.

Associated Press. "Barnett out, Lamar Thomas in at Wide Receiver." October 6, 1997.

Associated Press. "Bennett Sentenced to Two Months in Jail." February 26, 1998.

Associated Press. "Bruce Smith Arrested on DUI Charge." July 28, 1997.

Associated Press. "Cornell Brown Arrested on DUI Charge." October 1, 1998.

Associated Press. "Criminal Sexual Conduct Charge Against Former Viking Joey Browner Dropped." October 3, 1994.

Associated Press. "Dolphins Release Fred Barnett, Clayton Holmes." October 13, 1997.

Associated Press. "Ex-Giant Lawrence Taylor surrenders to face drug charges." December 18, 1998.

Associated Press. "Finkes, a Lineman, Arrested in Arizona." March 2, 1998.

Associated Press. "First Phillips, Now Tucker: Vermeil Follows Rams' Risk Pattern." April 21, 1997.

Associated Press. "Former Vikings Player Gets Stayed Jail Sentence." September 12, 1996.

Associated Press. "49er Defensive Tackle Arrested for Alleged Drunk Driving." October 16, 1997.

Associated Press. "Jervey Faces Marijuana Charge." February 19, 1998.

Associated Press. "Johnson says Jordan wasn't in Dolphins plans." November 16, 1998.

Associated Press. "Moon Family Coping with Media Scrutiny." October 22, 1995.

Associated Press. "Moon Jurors Say Some Violence in All Marriages." February 22, 1996.

Associated Press. "Moon's Wife Reveals Details of Attack." October 4, 1995.

Associated Press. "Morris Reveals He Has Attention Deficit Disorder." September 24, 1997.

Associated Press. "Morris Signs with Ravens." September 26, 1996.

Associated Press. "Prosecutors Defend Handling of Williams Case." May 3, 1997.

Associated Press. "Reeves: Falcons Will Await Judge's Sentence." September 10, 1997.

Associated Press. "Saints tackle jailed for parole violaton." October 24, 1998.

Associated Press. "Two Vikings Plead Guilty to Charges in Boating Case." October 14, 1997.

Associated Press. "Vikings Defensive End Jailed for Failing to Pay Child Support." May 7, 1996.

Associated Press. "Vikings Running Back Pleads Innocent to Rape Charge." May 6, 1997.

Associated Press. "Watters Will Play." December 16, 1994.

Associated Press. "Won't be suiting up for a while." December 2, 1998.

Atlanta Journal and Constitution, May 9, 1991.

Barr, Josh. "Moss Catching Up with Promise." *Washington Post,* December 12, 1997, p. B6.

Bell, Dawson, and Wylie Gerdes. "Cops Say Coach Blamed Crash on Phantom Driver." *Detroit Free Press,* October 29, 1987, p. A1.

Benedict, Jeff. *Athletes and Acquaintance Rape.* Thousand Oaks, California: Sage Publications, 1998.

Benedict, Jeff. "Felons Don't Belong in the NFL." *New York Times,* November 4, 1998.

Benedict, Jeff. *Public Heroes, Private Felons: Athletes and Crimes Against Women.* Boston: Northeastern University Press, 1997.

Benedict, Jeff, and Alan Klein. "Arrest and Conviction Rates for Athletes Accused of Assault." *Sociology of Sport,* Vol. 14, pp. 86-94.

Bennett, William, John DiIulio, and John Walters. *Body Count: Moral Poverty . . . and How to Win America's War Against Crime and Drugs.* New York: Simon Schuster, 1996.

Birkland, Dave. "Corey Dillon, ex-UW Football Star Arrested." *Seattle Times,* March 3, 1998.

Blackistone, Kevin B. "Rams' Vermeil Deals in Some Un-funny Business." *Fort Worth Star-Telegram.*

Blankenhorn, David. *Fatherless America: Confronting Our Most Urgent Social Problem.* New York: HarperCollins, 1996.

Borges, Ron, and Nick Cafardo. "Patriot Charged with Sexual Assault." *Boston Globe,* February 28, 1998, p. F1.

Boston Globe. "Sports Log." November 4, 1998, p. C2.

Boswell, Thomas. "Pro Sport, Drugs: Bennett Awaits 'Strong Signal.'" *Washington Post,* May 17, 1989, p. B1.

Bosworth, Charles, Jr. "Player Arrested on Drug Charges." *St. Louis Post-Dispatch,* July 29, 1997, p. A1.

Brioso, Cesar. "Dolphins release Phillips." *Fort Lauderdale Sun-Sentinel,* July 26, 1998.

Brubaker, Bill. "NFL Teams Support Perry Despite Past." *Washington Post,* November 13, 1994, p. A25.

Brubaker, Bill. "Violence Follows Some in Football Off Field." *Washington Post,* November 13, 1994, p. 1.

Bruton, Mike. "Book on pros, crime invites stereotyping." *Philadelphia Inquirer,* October 29, 1998, p. D1.

Buffalo Daily News. "Bennett Wins Week's Delay in Sentence." March 3, 1998, p. C4.

Carter, Kelly. "Johnson Eager to Hear His Name Called." *USA Today,* April 17, 1996, p. C1.

CNN's *Page 1,* October 24, 1998.

Court TV's, *Prime Time Justice,* November 6, 1998.

Covitz, Randy. "NFL policy for punishing off-field violence takes effect." *Kansas City Star,* July 1, 1998.

Crist, Gabrielle. "Initiator Victimized, Witnesses Say." *Fort Worth Star-Telegram,* March 6, 1998, p. 2.

Domowitch, Paul. "Allen Bid to Return Rejected by NFL." *Philadelphia Daily News,* August 8, 1990, p. 75.

Eisenberg, John. "Morris Fails in More Ways Than One." *Baltimore Sun,* August 6, 1997, p. D1.

Eskanazi, Gerald. "Hall Is Arrested in Florida on Marijuana Charges." *New York Times,* February 16, 1998.

ESPN *Sports Zone.* "The Year in Crime." September 1997.

Fainaru, Steve. "Trouble on the Border." *Boston Globe Magazine,* January 4, 1998, p. 12.

Fallik, Dawn. "St. Louis Rams Running Back Lawrence Phillips Is Jailed." Associated Press, March 11, 1997.

Fallstrom, R. B. "Rams expect Little to return this week." Associated Press, October 26, 1998.

Fernandez, Maria Elena. "Redskins' Shepherd Charged with Assault." *Washington Post,* February 26, 1998, p. D1.

Foster, Mary. "Saints player treated unfairly, Ditka says." Associated Press, October 26, 1998.

Freeman, Mike. "After Another Arrest, His Friends Worry for an Isolated Lawrence Taylor." *New York Times,* October 25, 1998, p. 5.

Freeman, Mike. "Disgrace and Courage on Game Day." *New York Times,* February 1, 1999, p. D5.

Freeman, Mike. "Second Chances End for Morris (for Now)." *New York Times,* February 1, 1998, p. 5.

Gerdes, Wylie. "Deputy: Lions' Fontes Was 'Hyper' in Arrest." *Detroit Free Press,* November 6, 1987, p. A3.

Gerdes, Wylie. "Fontes Charge Dismissed." *Detroit Free Press,* November 10, 1987, p. A1.

Gerdes, Wylie, and Curt Sylvester. "Reggie Rogers Investigated in Fatal Car Crash." *Detroit Free Press,* October 21, 1988, p. A1.

Gerdes, Wylie, Curt Sylvester, and Maryanne George. "Lions Player Faces 3 Manslaughter Counts." *Detroit Free Press,* October 22, 1988, p. A1.

Gloster, Rob. "Raiders coach pleads innocent to DUI." Associated Press, November 6, 1998.

Graczyk, Michael. "Felicia Moon Filed for Divorce 10 Years Ago After Beating Allegation." Associated Press, February 15, 1996.

Green, Jerry, and Luz Villarreal. "Billups, 30, Dies in the Fast Lane." *Orlando Sentinel,* April 10, 1994, p. C1.

Groark, Margaretta. "Bam Morris' Hearing Set for Jan. 12." *Rockwall Chronicle,* November 26, 1997, p. 1.

Hawkins, Christy. "NFL Player's January Drug Test Being Sought." *Dallas Morning News,* September 5, 1997, p. A30.

HBO. "The Criminal Life of Some NFL Players," *Real Sports with Bryant Gumbel,* January 25, 1999.

Hollingshed, Denise, and George Pawlaczyk. "Second Shooting Tied to Drug Trade." *Belleville News-Democrat,* February 6, 1996, p. 1.

Houston Post, "Oilers' Johnson to Face Grand Jury in Assault Case." February 20, 1992, p. C2.

Jackman, Tom. "Phillips and Ex-Girlfriend Settle Lawsuit." *Kansas City Star,* September 26, 1996, p. D1.

Katz, Michael. "Jailed Smith Gets 4-Year, $7.1M Pact from Saints." *New York Daily News,* March 2, 1998, p. 69.

Kelley, Steve. "Hawks' Alcohol Abuse Makes Everyone Sick." *Seattle Times,* April 29, 1995, p. B1.

King, Peter. "Return Man." *Sports Illustrated,* p. 114–32.

Lambe, Joe. "Phillips Sued for Assault." *Kansas City Star,* September 4, 1996, p. D1.

Los Angeles Times. "Special Report: Crime and Sports." December 27, 1995, pp. C1-C10.

McClain, John. "Jones' Life Full of Dealing with Deaths." *Houston Chronicle,* December 16, 1993, p. 4.

McEnroe, Paul. "Accusations Fly Against Moon, Then Are Dropped." *Minneapolis Star Tribune,* May 24, 1995, p. A1.

McEnroe, Paul, Salina Roberts, and Curt Brown. "Cheerleader, Moon Settle Suit Alleging Sex Misconduct Lawsuit." *Minneapolis Star Tribune,* May 25, 1996, p. A1.

Meinecke, Corky. "Fontes Says Drug Charge 'Behind Me.'" *Detroit Free Press,* November 15, 1988, p. D3.

Mell, Randall. "J.J. Close to Signing Phillips." *Sun-Sentinel,* December 2, 1997, p. C1.

Moldea, Dan E. *Interference.* New York: Morrow, 1989.

Moran, Ernie. "Grand Jury Indicts Football Players." *TCU Daily Skiff,* August 27, 1996, p. 1.

Mulvihill, Maggie, and Beverly Ford. "Hooker: Meggett 'Punched Me in the Face from Ear to Ear.'" *Boston Herald,* March 4, 1998, p. 1.

Mulvihill, Maggie, and Beverly Ford. "Lawyer: First Encounter." *Boston Herald,* March 3, 1998, p. 79.

NCAA Division I-A Graduation-Rates Reports. Kansas City, Kansas: National Collegiate Athletic Association, June 1995.

Newberry, Paul. "Falcons distracted by drug investigation, quarterback injury." Associated Press, October 22, 1998.

Newton, Chris. "NFL's Bam Morris Heads to Jail." Associated Press, January 12, 1998.

New York Times, July 5, 1984.

New York Times. "Don't Make N.F.L. Judge and Jury," Letters to the Editor, November 7, 1998.

New York Times. "Notebook." February 18, 1999.

NFL.com. "NFLI Signs Record U.K. Sponsorship Deal with Coors." October 15, 1998, No. 49.

Nobles, Charlie. "Abuse of Women: 'Not O.K.'" *New York Times,* October 19, 1994.

O'Connor, Anne. "Vikings Say Security Head Will Be Disciplined." *Minneapolis Star Tribune,* November 2, 1995, p. C5.

Perez, Robert. "More Women Say Billups Raped Them." *Orlando Sentinel,* December 18, 1992, p. A1.

Philadelphia Daily News. "Vikes' Millard Pleads Guilty." May 4, 1990, p. 101.

Phillips, Jim. "Ex-Houston Oiler Cleared in 1991 Sex Assault Case." *Houston Post,* December 22, 1992, p. 7.

Pittsburgh Post-Gazette, February 9, 1995.

Plaschke, Bill. "Oiler Tackle Alm Dies in Apparent Suicide." *Los Angeles Times,* December 15, 1993, p. C1.

Porter, Bill. "Bills welcome linebacker Simmons, waived by Chiefs." Associated Press, November 19, 1998.

Powers, Tom. "Vikings Are Playing with Others' Lives." *St. Paul Pioneer Press Dispatch,* January 24, 1990, p. D1.

Preston, Mike. "Morris Gets Ravens' Support; But 'Disappointed' Teammates Say Violation Isn't Surprise." *Baltimore Sun,* August 7, 1997, p. D1.

Price, S.L. "The Faces of Uncertainty." *Sports Illustrated,* October 7, 1996, pp. 44-51.

Pulliam, Kent. "Barnett Makes Most of Second Chance." *Kansas City Star,* January 9, 1994, p. C10.

Pulliam, Kent. "Receiver Barnett Released by Chiefs." *Kansas City Star,* July 30, 1994, p. D7.

Queenan, Bob. "Brown Defends Bengals' Pick of Mack." *Cincinnati Post,* October 29, 1997.

Queenan, Bob. "Dillon Arrested for DUI." *Cincinnati Post,* March 4, 1998.

Richardson, Ray. "Vikings Fire Swanson, Endy in Front Office." *St. Paul Pioneer Press,* February 6, 1993.

Rizzo, Tony. "Barnett Gets Jail Sentence but Is Freed on an Appeal." *Kansas City Star,* January 5, 1994, p. D3.

Sack, Kevin. "Louisiana Scandal Deepens as Chairman of 49ers Quits." *New York Times,* December 3, 1997, p. 1.

Sack, Kevin. "N.F.L. Owner Ties Ex-Governor to Extortion." *New York Times,* October 7, 1998, p. 1.

Sandomir, Richard. "CBS Guarantees Billions to Get N.F.L. Back." *New York Times,* January 13, 1998, p. 1.

Sandomir, Richard. "Monday Football Stays on ABC; NBC out of Game After 33 Years." *New York Times,* January 14, 1998, p. 1.

Sansevere, Bob. "Headrick Implores NFL to Discipline Its Scoundrels." *St. Paul Pioneer Press,* January 13, 1996, p. E1.

Shute, Nancy. "The Drinking Dilemma." *U.S. News & World Report,* September 8, 1997, pp. 55-65.

Smith, Craig, and Peyton Whitely. "Driver's Report Prompts Trooper to Follow Coach." *Seattle Times,* April 27, 1995, p. C5.

St. Louis Post-Dispatch. "Court orders O'Neal to pay topless dancer." October 24, 1998.

Sullivan, Jack. "Experts: 'First Offense' Means First Time Caught." *Boston Herald,* January 10, 1998, p. 10.

Tabayanan, Cyd. "Jury Acquits Ex-Athletes in Rape Case." *Arkansas Democrat-Gazette,* January 27, 1993, p. B1.

Thomas, Jim. "Despite Praise from Vermeil, Kirksey Misses Cut." *St. Louis Post-Dispatch,* August 18, 1997, p. D3.

UPI. "Saints' Heyward Faces June 5 Trial." February 24, 1992.

USA Today. "Behind Bars." May 1, 1998, p. C1.

USA Today. "Vikes Chief: Break Law, Lose Job." January 15, 1996, p. C3.

Washington Post. "Viking Fined." May 6, 1998.

Weisman, Larry. "NFL players vs. the law." *USA Today,* October 20, 1998, p. 3C.

Winkeljohn, Matt. "Calloway signs; Martin cut." *Atlanta Journal-Constitution,* February 27, 1999.

Index